Media, Family Interaction and the Digitalization of Childhood

Edited by

Anja Riitta Lahikainen

Professor Emerita of Social Psychology, Faculty of Social Sciences, University of Tampere, Finland

Tiina Mälkiä

Postdoctoral Researcher, Tampere Centre for Childhood, Youth and Family Research (PERLA), University of Tampere, Finland

Katja Repo

Director, Tampere Centre for Childhood, Youth and Family Research (PERLA), University of Tampere, Finland

Cheltenham, UK • Northampton, MA, USA

Chapters 2, 7, 8 and 9 © 2015 Vastapaino and the authors. Previously published in *Media lapsiperheessä*, Vastapaino, 2015

Published by
Edward Elgar Publishing Limited
The Lypiatts
15 Lansdown Road
Cheltenham
Glos GL50 2JA
UK

Edward Elgar Publishing, Inc.
William Pratt House
9 Dewey Court
Northampton
Massachusetts 01060
USA

A catalogue record for this book
is available from the British Library

Library of Congress Control Number: 2017936579

This book is available electronically in the **Elgar**online
Social and Political Science subject collection
DOI 10.4337/9781785366673

ISBN 978 1 78536 666 6 (cased)
ISBN 978 1 78536 667 3 (eBook)

Typeset by Servis Filmsetting Ltd, Stockport, Cheshire
Printed and bound in Great Britain by TJ International Ltd, Padstow

Contents

Figures and tables

FIGURES

TABLES

Pictures

Contributors

Dr **Ilkka Arminen** is Professor of Sociology at the University of Helsinki, Finland. He has investigated media in interaction in multiple contexts, including mobile media usage, Internet communities and transforming spheres of intimacy. His areas of expertise also include the development of theory and methods in the area. He has published widely both internationally and nationally.

Dr **Susan Danby** is a professor in the School of Early Childhood at Queensland University of Technology (QUT), Australia. Her research investigates children and young people's everyday social and interactional practices, with peers and teachers in preschool and school settings, and in family contexts. Recent large-scale studies investigate how young children integrate digital technologies into the flow of everyday family and school lives. She has co-edited (with Maryanne Theobald) *Disputes in Everyday Life: Social and Moral Orders of Children and Young People* (Emerald, 2012), and she is on the editorial boards of *Linguistics and Education* and *Research on Children and Social Interaction* journals.

Aku Kallio, MSSc, is a social psychologist and a researcher at the Tampere Centre for Childhood, Youth and Family Research (PERLA) at the University of Tampere, Finland. His research has focused on ordinary interaction and he has utilized conversation analysis and multimodal interaction analysis in his work. Previously, he has studied multimodal meaning-making in ordinary interaction. Currently he is doing his doctoral dissertation on emotions in family interaction.

Dr **Anja Riitta Lahikainen** is Professor Emerita of Social Psychology and former Director of the Tampere Centre for Childhood, Youth and Family Research (PERLA) between 2001 and 2009 at the University of Tampere, Finland. She was the leader of the 'Media, Family Interaction and Children's Well-Being' project. Her main areas of expertise include children's well-being, children's media use, their socialization and comparative childhood studies. Her previous projects include 'Children's Well-being and Media in Cultural and Societal Context' and 'Children's Insecurity: Its Causes and Coping'. She is the writer/co-writer/editor/co-editor of 13 books.

Dr **Tiina Mälkiä** is a postdoctoral researcher at the Tampere Centre for Childhood, Youth and Family Research (PERLA) at the University of Tampere, Finland. Her current research focuses on everyday family interaction in Finland and USA, specifically media use, directives and negotiations during lunch time. Previously, she has studied institutional interaction, such as genetic counselling and management board meetings. She has also worked as a social worker with children and families.

Eerik Mantere, MSSc, is a social psychologist whose research interests are focused on media and parent–child interaction. He is currently a PhD student in Sociology at the University of Bordeaux, France and a PhD student in Social Psychology at the University of Tampere, Finland.

Dr **Jackie Marsh** is Professor of Education at the University of Sheffield, UK. She undertakes research on young children's literacy practices in the digital age and has led and participated in research projects in this area funded by the Arts and Humanities Research Council, British Academy, Economic and Social Research Council and the EU Commission, along with projects funded by various charities and government bodies that have involved schools and children's media industry partners. Jackie is Chair of the COST Action IS1410, 'The Digital Literacy and Multimodal Practices of Young Children' (www.digilitey.eu). Her latest book, co-authored with Julia Bishop, is *Changing Play: Play, Media and Commercial Culture from the 1950s to the Present Day* (Open University Press, 2014).

Dr **Peter Nikken** is Professor of Children, Media, and Parental Mediation at the Erasmus School of History, Culture and Communication, Erasmus University, Rotterdam, the Netherlands. His chair at Erasmus University was established to improve knowledge about the role of parents in their children's use of media. Dr Nikken has written many scientific and popular articles and books on children and media on various topics, such as how parents can stimulate their children's media literacy; age and content rating systems for films, television and games; and the effects of ads, sex and violence in the media.

Dr **Sanna Raudaskoski** is Lecturer of Social Psychology at the University of Tampere, Finland. She has a strong expertise on ethnomethodology and the theory of affordances, and analysing technologically mediated interactions. Her doctoral dissertation considered the affordances of mobile phones. She has also studied augmentative and alternative communication (AAC) methods in interactions with aphasic speakers. Recently Raudaskoski has studied live remote concerts and the use of smartphones in families with children.

Dr **Katja Repo** is Director of the Tampere Centre for Childhood, Youth and Family Research (PERLA) at the University of Tampere, Finland. Her main research interests include the reconciliation of work and family, family policy, social services, cash-for-care schemes, intra-household finances, poverty and time use of families. She is one of the editors of the following books: *Cash-for-Childcare: The Consequences for Caring Mothers* (Edward Elgar Publishing, 2010) and *Women, Men and Children in Families: Private Troubles and Public Issues* (University of Tampere Press, 2013).

Dr **Eero Suoninen** is Professor of Social Psychology at the University of Tampere, Finland. His research has focused on family life and professional helping work, especially from the point of view interactional processes, variability of meaning-making and identity construction. He has specialized in discourse analytical research and co-authored several textbooks in the area.

Sanna Tiilikainen, MSSc (Sociology) and PhD candidate (Information Systems Science), is a researcher at Aalto University School of Business, Department of Information and Service Management, Finland. Her research interest is the social use of ICT, combining elements from the physical and digital worlds. In her research, Tiilikainen applies a wide variety of qualitative, quantitative and Big Data-related research methods, combined with human-centred design and social theory.

Dr **Satu Valkonen** is a postdoctoral researcher at the University of Helsinki, Finland. Her current research addresses digital learning and multiliteracies as well as participation, agency and identities. Her research interests are developmental psychology, social interaction, and media psychology concerning various forms of mediated communication, interaction and experience. She is also interested in childhood methodological questions.

Acknowledgements

We, the editors, are deeply indebted to the authors who devoted their time to making this volume come alive. We also want to express our gratitude to Edward Elgar Publishing who accepted the volume into their publishing schedule. In addition, we thank the Academy of Finland, Kone Foundation, Mannerheim League for Child Welfare and Tampere University's Faculty of Social Sciences for financial support. Our thanks belong also to families who participated in the 'Media, Family Interaction and Children's Well-Being' project and to Matthew James for his excellent copy-editing.

Anja Riitta Lahikainen, Tiina Mälkiä and Katja Repo

1. Introduction: media and family interaction

Anja Riitta Lahikainen, Tiina Mälkiä and Katja Repo

This book is a repository of new knowledge on how media and family activities intertwine with each other in daily family interaction and child socialization. In addition, it outlines the challenges and opportunities new media bring to family life and children's well-being. It addresses the question of how the digitalization of society and the changes in families' media environment influence family practices, such as family time, intergenerational interaction, and the participation of children and their time use.

The book discusses very timely and largely unexplored phenomena that are internationally identifiable. As a result of globalization, the digitalization of the living environments of children – such as the home – has become an increasingly international and universal phenomenon. The digital revolution has also complicated family life, and family interaction worldwide is affected by the presence of various media devices. However, the implications and consequences of this transformation of family interaction are still largely unknown.

The research detailed in this volume shows how delicately media affect interaction between children and parents, and how profoundly they challenge everyday parenting. This kind of information is urgently needed, since the patterns of how media are encountered in the context of the family are still unstable and controversial. The book reveals the complexity and diversity of media-related family interaction by utilizing the unique data of video recordings of the family life of 26 Finnish families with a five- or a 12-year-old child. Video cameras were placed in their homes for one weekday to document the interaction around the kitchen table and in front of the child's main television and computer. Using the video data, we have been able to analyse what really happens in family homes instead of what parents think happened, or wished had happened.

The analyses in the book are based on the Finnish research project

'Media, Family Interaction and Children's Well-being' funded by the Academy of Finland. This book will show that although the analysed data were collected in Finland, the situations and issues are universally recognizable. We are all aware of the interactional complexities of situations where parents want to catch the attention of a child who is playing a computer game, or when a child wants to get her or his parent's attention while the parent is focused on a smartphone. The case analyses demonstrate how profoundly new media changes interaction between children and parents. This change is applicable and identifiable universally.

In all, this book offers a novel and comprehensive picture of the complexity of the daily lives of contemporary families equipped with modern information and communication technologies. The issues are discussed from multiple perspectives. The first part of the book maps contemporary family life by providing methodological, theoretical and time-use reflections on media use and media-related family interaction. In addition, it discusses conversation analysis as a method for depicting the complexity of family interaction. This part utilizes time-use surveys as well as recent theoretical and methodological discussions.

In Chapter 2, Anja Riitta Lahikainen discusses theoretically how new media, family interaction and the socialization of children are intertwined and connected to each other. Lahikainen investigates what kind of challenges media present for the socialization of the child at home. Chapter 3 by Susan Danby focuses on family practices and media use. Danby's chapter is also theoretical, but instead of focusing on the aspects of socialization, her emphasis is on questions of social interaction and media use. In Chapter 4, Tiina Mälkiä introduces a new perspective, performativity, to family interaction studies. She demonstrates how the family members used the research cameras for their own amusement by creating expressive performances, and how the parents modified the image being recorded by producing moral performances. In the final chapter of the first part of the book, Chapter 5, Katja Repo and Satu Valkonen assess children's media use in relation to general time use. They focus on issues of access to media devices and the amount of time children spend with new media.

The second part of the book reaches into the private zone of family interaction, and provides the reader with detailed interactional analyses of everyday life with media devices. It contributes by offering detailed case studies of the various forms of media-related family interaction, new forms of family time, and conflict situations. This part utilizes the video recordings as data.

The second part begins with Chapter 6 by Aku Kallio on parental mediation in television viewing. Kallio explores parental mediation as an interactional phenomenon and investigates what sort of actions parental mediation can consist of and how mediation is realized in naturally occurring family interaction. In Chapter 7, Eero Suoninen focuses on the gender dimensions of interaction between parents and children in the context of watching television. His analysis includes two cases – one of father–son interaction and one of mother–daughter interaction – in which gender-related practices are prevalent. In Chapter 8, Suoninen continues by analysing the interaction that takes place in the context of playing a computer game. The analysis is based on a discussion between a parent and child in a situation where the child is strongly preoccupied with a computer game. In Chapter 9, Eerik Mantere and Sanna Raudaskoski introduce the concept of the 'sticky media device' and analyse a scenario in which a child is seeking her mother's attention when the mother is using a smartphone. In the last chapter of this section, Chapter 10, Sanna Tiilikainen and Ilkka Arminen focus on the ways families spend time together at home with and around media devices, combining individual and family time.

The concluding part of the book re-examines the themes presented in the empirical chapters. In Chapter 11, Sanna Raudaskoski, Eerik Mantere and Satu Valkonen discuss media use practices, interaction research, and theories of developmental psychology. They theorize the potential influences of parental smartphone use on child development. In the concluding chapter, Anja Riitta Lahikainen and Ilkka Arminen discuss the media-related risks, opportunities and new practices in late modern society. The final part of the book is completed by Peter Nikken's Commentary in Chapter 13 and in Chapter 14 by Jackie Marsh's Afterword.

PART I

Contemporary families and media

2. New media, family interaction and socialization*

Anja Riitta Lahikainen

> To understand the imprint of historical change on the lives of children and adolescents, we must first trace its effects to the family.
> (Elder et al., 1993, p. 13)

INTRODUCTION: FAMILY – AN ALTERED CONTEXT OF SOCIALIZATION

New media have, in the manner of a silent revolution, taken a central position in the everyday life of families and children. Whereas the first industrial revolution took place in factories, today's information revolution also takes place in the home. The emergence and evolution over the past 50 years of new communication technologies, including the proliferation and miniaturization of devices, has been evaluated by Stanford University media researchers Donald Roberts and Ulla Foehr as the most important change in the lives of children and adolescents (Buckingham, 2003; Roberts and Foehr, 2004). The implications and consequences of this transformation of childhood are largely unexplored and unexplained from the point of view of children.

Social changes at the macro level may alter both family structure and family interaction (Buckingham, 2003) and these changes have an impact on individuals. My main interest is in studying the consequences that the information and communications technology (ICT) revolution has for contemporary family life, especially for parent–child interaction and child socialization. Today's children live a very different childhood compared to earlier generations. In the current phase of history, children's lives are unique in that their childhood is best characterized as living within an accelerated process of digitalization.

NOTES ON EARLIER RESULTS

My previous project 'Media and Well-being of the Child in Societal and Cultural Context'[1] – where both children and their parents were used as informants on the children's well-being – gave me a better understanding of everyday life as it is experienced from the child's point of view. The main conclusions of the project were that even five-year-old children 'understand' their everyday life better than the adults presume. It became evident that parents are not often aware of their children's worries and fears, even though they think they are. The part of present day childhood that is lived with media remains largely unknown to the adult generations. One important reason for this is that media are already a massive factor in the everyday life of very young children; they produce flows of multiple kinds of information for children to cope with without parental presence or control (Lahikainen et al., 2006; Lahikainen, 2009).

Children are not necessarily objective in their ways of understanding the flow of the everyday events they follow in on-screen or face-to-face interaction. Instead, they are very quick to make their own interpretations – right or wrong – on the flow of the events (Valkonen et al., 2005; Lahikainen, 2009).

In the project, several distinct changes in children's media-related experiences were clearly documented in interviews with about 800 five- to six-year-old children in Finland and post-communist Estonia in the years 1993–94 and 2002–03. Over ten years, children's television-induced fears and fears of nightmares increased considerably, particularly in Estonia where the post-communist reform in 1991 had opened up access to Western television programmes at the same time as the number of televisions in homes increased (Taimalu et al., 2007).

Furthermore, only a minority of the children (one-third) reported that they turn to their parents when television programmes frighten them (Kirmanen, 2000; Taimalu, 2007; Korhonen, 2008; Lahikainen, 2009). This may indicate that already very young children want to watch virtual scenes independently and that they try to cope with their feelings without adults noticing, even though adults were present. It has also become very easy to do this with the latest mobile devices. It is possible that no significant adult is accessible for the child when the flow of events on the screen frightens them. Many small children also involuntarily watch television programmes being viewed by other family members. In such a situation, it seems that interfering with their parents' TV sessions may be too difficult (Paavonen et al., 2006). The conclusion is that it seems to be difficult for caretaking adults to know their children's television/screen-induced changes of moods and concerns.

The home is the chief site of children's media exposure, just as it is for social interaction with other family members. Children do not use media in isolation at home. Media have an impact on the child as an actor in his or her family network as 'a social being'. Other family members have expectations toward them. Simultaneously, media influence the other network partners too (Lull, 1995). In other words, the individual use of media devices also has effects on the family as a small group. These effects have remained largely unexplored, leaving room for pessimistic social comments claiming that media are destroying traditional family life and its hierarchic systems (Buckingham, 2003).

In order to acquire a better understanding of children's idiosyncratic relationship with the world of media, my colleagues and I planned a new research project in which actual everyday family social interaction is scrutinized closely by means of new technology. In this study, video cameras were brought into family homes. In such a setting, where family life is studied by using fixed video cameras in the home, researchers have the opportunity to observe all contextual factors related to media use. Furthermore, the method treats the parents and the children democratically, giving both equal positions as information sources on family social interaction for the researchers.

This book provides a new informative window, real-time observations, to/on media-related social interaction in the families with children. In comparison to the previous research, we study child–media relationships in their contextual complexity. For multiple reasons – which can be well defended – most empirical studies on children and media have been done within an implicit reductionist frame, assuming that the child is an autonomous media user. The criticism here concerns experimental studies in particular, which unfortunately suffer from deficient ecological validity despite having 'produced ample empirical evidence of that, *assuming exposure*, media messages play a significant role in the socialization of youth' (Roberts and Foehr, 2004, p. 7, original emphasis). When the context of children's media use has been taken into consideration, an enlightened adult, parent or professional has mostly been assumed to be an interactor with the child. However, it has mistakenly been assumed that the adult has limitless time for guidance of the child in front of the screen. On the whole, homes are very opaque contexts for a multiplicity of actions, many of which are not necessarily media related.

MEDIA AND FAMILY INTERACTION

At home practically all family members, irrespective of their age, have continual access to media and explosive flows of information as an alternative and an appendage to face-to-face interaction with other family members. First, interaction with significant others, with the family and peer groups has become possible without time and place dependency. Second, new contacts can be created (also anonymously) and relationships maintained without physical contact. Opportunities for self-expression on different kinds of networks and to various audiences have increased tremendously (Suominen et al., 2013).

This new situation in the lives of families has raised an array of questions. One of the most salient observations is expressed by Murdorf and Laird, who realize that the 'use of interactive media in the home is a complex phenomenon that warrants increasing attention. . .our understanding of the impact of interactivity. . .is still very limited' (Murdorf and Laird, 2002, p. 585). However, already 20 years ago Thompson emphasized the importance of answering the question: 'How does development of media and communication change traditional ways of social interaction?' (Thompson, 1995). My colleagues and I wanted to illuminate how the media invasion of our homes changes the socialization processes that occur there. Answering this question has turned out to be a complicated task, not least because of the continuous and speedy development of ICT. The popularity of different applications and the fashions of different social media, which vary by country, culture, subculture and time, also deserve to be mentioned (Suominen et al., 2013). The instability of media surroundings in homes and the diversification of media in the lives of families present challenges, but they also offer a rich field for research.

What is new today in the virtual world quickly becomes yesterday's news. We can only try to follow our children in the rapid change in their childhood's landscape. Very impressive flashes of this side of the life of children have been revealed and analysed by the media theorists Douglas Rushkoff (1997) and Sherry Turkle (2012). The family is a special and at the same time fundamental context of social interaction, especially because the child is born into the existing social network of his or her family. During the early years of growing up, children undergo a transformation from a dependent newborn towards an autonomously functioning individual in a particular social network. Families are said to be the cradle of language, the original site of everyday discourse, and the touchstone for talk in other contexts (Kendall, 2007). At the same time, for the child the family is the nest of socialization and a site for growing up as an individual personality (Berger and Luckmann, 1966). Adopting family rules and habits as well as gaining autonomy and finding individuality are basic socialization tasks for the child, and they are thought to take place in family interaction within any kind of family context (Erikson, 1950; Berger and Luckmann, 1966; Kernberg, 1980).

My colleagues and I have taken a closer look at the changes that the fast development of ICT has brought to family life over a short period of history and asked how these changes are reflected in present social interaction. Each new type of ICT device feeds different kinds of activities depending on their characteristics. They therefore have different effects on family life; they may in different ways both unite and separate family members. This is evidenced empirically in the comparison between television and computer use in families; the former feeds sociability whereas the latter tends towards solitary behaviour (Roberts and Foehr, 2004; Repo and Nätti, 2015). Adults and young people have reported different priorities in using text messages and phones: text messages are more comfortable than phone calls for young people, while the reverse is true for adults (Turkle, 2012).

Two major questions have directed this study. First, how does digitalization increase the complexity of family communication? There are many difficulties in finding a clear-cut definition of digitalization in general, and this is especially true in homes. Actually, the significance of each media device is obscure as the users themselves create and use the device's potentialities (Buckingham, 2003, p.23; Suominen et al., 2013). Each user is a potential innovator of the applications of ICT devices depending on the interests, creativity and personality of the user. In scientific evaluations of the significance of new media devices, two impact factors – the potentiality of the device and the potentiality of the user – must be differentiated. This is possible only through studying family interaction in its natural surroundings at home.

The increase in the number of the ICT devices at home and the new opportunities to participate in digital activities that their access provides to each family member complicate the family members' continually ongoing processes of decision-making and choice-making between different alternatives. Generally, choosing from an almost infinite number of possible actions/alternatives without structuring traditions that guide, limit or encourage may lead to chaotic everyday life and to the collapse of former family traditions; at the very least, it causes strain. Traditional family chores and ICT-mediated actions confront and compete with each other daily. How do families manage in this new situation (Aarsand, 2007; Rushkoff, 2013)?

Second, what kinds of challenges do media present for the socialization of the child at home? Digital devices provide new kinds of socialization agents for children. How are virtual socialization arenas, such as different kinds of websites and games, related to real-life social networks, especially to the family networks? What kind of evidence of media-induced changes in the socialization function of the parents and in the intergenerational contract can be detected on the basis of everyday family interaction? This topic has been touched upon by Postman (1982), Turkle (1995) and Rushkoff (2013).

DIGITALIZED HOMES AS THE CONTEXT FOR SOCIAL INTERACTION AND SOCIALIZATION

The development of ICT and the invasion of ICT devices into domestic space and time have unknown and unexplored consequences on family life. While being aware of the difficulties in using the concept of 'generation' in the social sciences and especially in relation to the ICT revolution, I present here a provisional sketch of media generations in families based on the shared age-related media experiences of different age cohorts. This approach deviates from the most commonly used concept of generation used in the social sciences. According to Karl Mannheim (1952), the birth of a generation is defined by the key experiences of young people when they are aged between 15 and 20 years. By choosing the concept of generation, I am taking into account the great importance of media expansion.

Although the spread of different media devices in families varies widely by country and by the income and education level, the order of acquisition of different IT devices is the same. In addition, innovations in the new devices are global, and they thus have the same kind of input for families regardless of their culture or location.

To understand the changes in families, the historical order of innovations concerning ICT devices in the media revolution must be analysed in detail. Table 2.1 provides a brief overview.

The younger the age group to which a member of the family belongs, the more numerous are the virtual experiences and number of media accessible compared with what was the case in the childhood of the older age groups in the family. Grandparents used the radio, television and the phone in their childhood. Contemporary parents' childhood was spent

Table 2.1   The waves of digitalization occurring in the home and the resultant media generations

Communication device	Media generation	Period of childhood of the media generation
Radio and telephone	Electro-magnetic generation	1880s to the 1940s
Television	Television generation	1950s to the 1970s
Home computers, games consoles and video recorders	Computer generation	1980s
Mobile phones and Internet	Internet generation	1990s
Mobile Internet	Tablet generation	2000s to the 2010s

with a computer, but without the Internet. Children today are surrounded by multiple mobile devices, phones and tablets in addition to the older devices (Rantanen, 2005). In principle, the younger the child, the greater is the probability that the child will become a more talented user of new and improved devices than his or her parents and grandparents.

The rapid and unpredictable diversification of applications is a new characteristic of ICT. The functions of old devices are combined and new functions are added. In addition, the new devices simultaneously have more power and efficiency than their predecessors. Television has replaced the radio, and digital devices have replaced the typewriter, the radio, the television and the phone. The mobile phone has made the landline phone redundant and taken over a great deal of the functions of the computer, including those of the clock, the camera and the calculator.

DIFFERENT MEDIA EXPERIENCES AND IMPACTS

One simple conclusion to be drawn is that the development of ICT devices radically differentiates the family members by their age. Following the basic idea of Karl Mannheim (1952), it can be stated that common elements in the media surroundings in childhood, both in the home and outside it, create a feeling of togetherness within age groups that are now narrower than before. Family members have different experiences from different media at different ages, and as a consequence they have different preferences concerning both devices and how they use them (Repo and Nätti, 2015). Probable preference differences between younger media generations are not yet known. High school students in the USA prefer text messages to phone calls, which they think are too intimate, whereas phone calls are more natural to the adults (Turkle, 2012).

In her analysis of the categorization of children as an individual consumer group in the late 1990s, Jyotsna Kapur (1999, pp. 128–30) maintains that 'children's consumer culture has become increasingly unfamiliar to adults'. Research on children's consumer culture reveals the growing power of markets to distance the child and adult generations from each other. This also includes a media supply with concomitant goods production for children (Partanen and Lahikainen, 2008).

The differentiation of media generations within families may be interpreted on the one hand as impoverishing shared media experiences among family members, and on the other hand as a new source of abundance, with the family members now having a larger scale of different experiences at hand. Thus, in principle, each family member – including the children – has more to offer to the others. Rapid media development in families may initiate discussion between family members and thus promote the early differentiation and individualization of the younger generations. Conversely, estrangement and feelings of separateness from other family members may increase, while connections to cyberspace and individual experiences in that space proportionally grow.

Age-differentiated or unique media-rooted fragments of human and cultural capital in the form of stories, narratives and pieces of information that the family members acquire may remain unshared and undiscussed with other family members. This particularly concerns young children's media experiences because of their as yet limited capacities to communicate their experiences to adults. According to Lull (1995, p. 75):

> Underlying all media images is cultural authority. The media routinely promote authors who capture the imagination of audiences because of their ways of thinking, and are being presented so attractively. Audience members identify with what those images can mean and put the cultural representations to work in their everyday living situations.

This means that children are immensely directly influenced by the huge supply of media in today's world.

More time together would be required for redistributing increasingly individualized experiences with others. Listening to young children is a demanding and time-consuming task, but it is at the same time essential interaction. The discrepancies of media experiences between adults and children were revealed in research interviews with five-year-olds concerning television-induced fears. The well-educated interviewers had difficulties in understanding, because the children's programmes that they dealt with and characters the children were speaking of were often unknown and strange to the interviewer (Lahikainen, 2009; Valkonen, 2012). The crucial question is this: how is a sense of togetherness and solidarity created in families, if not on the basis of shared experience?

INCREASING COMPLEXITY: MEDIA AS PART OF FAMILY SOCIAL INTERACTION

In order to understand the media-related new challenges analytically and to detect family members' joint activities, social interaction is categorized according to its media relatedness, as seen in Figure 2.1.

Media devices take part in family relationships directly and indirectly. They are used both individually and in different social compositions. They both unite and separate (Pasquier et al., 1998). In addition, family members

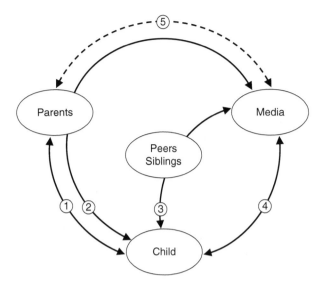

Notes:
1. Parent–child interaction independent of media.
2. Parent–child interaction related to media.
3. Child's peer-related relationship with media.
4. Children's independent relationship with media.
5. Parents' independent relationship with media.

By media, we refer to television, computers, mobile phones and video game consoles as well as their applications. All these share the ability to act as media for communication and information search (Thompson, 1995; Inkinen, 2005).

Figure 2.1   Theoretical model of the role of media in family interaction

observe other family members' media-related activities as bystanders. The indirect presence of media has not received much attention in research, although their effects are probably considerable. Already at a very young age, children are exposed to the electric information flow from screens (Wartella et al., 2005). Children receive visual and auditory impressions, which are taken in fragments of the events presented in the electric flow of television programmes, even though their parents think they are just playing in the same room or in the next room.

Passive television watching has been shown to have a more negative influence on five- to six-year-old children's sleep than active TV watching that the parents were aware of (Paavonen et al., 2006). The television may be on all day and provide a background to all kinds of activities, including the use of a computer or smartphone. More generally, other family members' media use may stimulate the bystander's attention, make his or her attention wander, and cause disintegration in actions and difficulties in concentration. The media activities of others seem more tempting to follow than the ordinary household chores that others do, and they are easier to observe than the text of the book that someone is reading.

NEW TYPES OF COMMUNICATION

There is evidence that the exposure and use of media devices in homes creates new dimensions in the family communication network. First, connections to the outside world are brought inside the home, making it possible to ignore face-to-face communication with others in the home. They enable us to take a break from ongoing face-to-face talk. This privilege concerns every user. Being online is not only a privilege of the owner of a mobile phone but also an obligation set and sanctioned by network companions. Priority is usually given to online contacts, which may continuously interrupt real-life conversations (Turkle, 2012). How is the transfer between virtual and real-life interaction regulated in families? To what extent can it be regulated?

Actually, media do not necessarily intertwine with all family interaction. Family dining is an example of the type of activity that does not need to have any connection with media. In our research, some families explicitly separated meals from media. The television was turned off and phones were not available. In some other families, the members' media uses were accepted at the dinner table as auxiliary activities. In some families again, dining was subordinated to television viewing. In our research, traditional meals without media were more common in families with five-year-old children than in families with 12-year-old children (Mälkiä and Arminen, 2015). Gathering the family together and excluding media at mealtimes seems to be easier for families with younger children.

Family meals are used for exchanging experiences outside the home. Parents ask about the children's day and the children tell stories and events from their school day. The parents exchange opinions or make plans together. Conversation is important identity work in which family members mirror other family members' outside experiences in the frame of the family's shared history. This helps in integrating experiences from different contexts into identity of family members. Sharing individual online experiences with other family members could possibly function in the same way (Blum-Kulka, 1997; Suoninen, 2015).

Second, a new level of communications is created by the necessity to relate oneself to the other members' media activities in one way or another.

Forms of relating range from evaluation and control to participation or passive adaption, with the accompanying emotional upheavals they bring to bear. The parents are challenged to control and help their offspring in the new virtual arenas. At the same time, children get a new area in which to make observations of their parents, namely as users of media. (It has become more difficult than before to reconcile the interests of the family members.)

Third, media activities cannot be incompatible with other basic activities in the home. They must be managed to function together somehow. Gradually, new media devices have eroded the old traditions of scheduling family life. We do not know to what extent families nowadays suffer from chaos or how they cope with it. To what extent have they succeeded in establishing new traditions in media use despite the fact that their media surroundings change continuously? New problems emerge related to agreeing on common timetables and negotiating shared family norms, particularly between the young and the adults in the family.

New media change the economics of time and the sharing of time. Because available time is an absolutely limited resource for all individuals concerned, its allocation to any activity in principle diminishes time allocated to other activities. The accessibility of the vast array of media at home calls for a change in this kind of linear thinking and makes it necessary to problematize it.

Media devices may provide new and quicker ways of doing traditional chores, such as shopping or the exchange of information across the traditional social network, and thus save time. They also provide an infinite number of virtual activities, which can be time demanding, like some games, time wasting, such as pointless net surfing, and tempting, such as blogging or participating in popular networks.

The development of ICT devices invites multitasking in varying ways. Virtual gaming, texting and Skyping can be combined with watching TV, listening to a face-to-face discussion and doing needlework, and so on. In one of our cases, a young boy played a game with his mobile phone during a small pause in his ongoing computer game. New media devices enable people to be alone and together at the same time (Turkle, 2012).

Many media researchers believe that the availability of media devices has eroded the distinctions between work and leisure time (Buckingham, 2003). When we now speak of the power and the potentiality of media devices, we need to remember that there are huge differences in families with regard to the number of media devices and the intensity of their use, and consequently with regard to the need to control the use of such devices.

SEARCHING FOR A NEW BALANCE IN THE CHILD–PARENT RELATIONSHIP

Mobile devices enable us to use our own logic flexibly when we schedule the use of media, and also when we combine it with other activities, like household chores or homework. The most reasonable ways to organize one's own activities and to allocate time between real and virtual life have become very individual, because the criteria for decisions are more personal than before. Decisions depend on a person's motivation, interests and obligations, temperament and other personal psychic capabilities/ qualities. This is true of children too, in principle.

Consequently, nobody can actually be sure of what is best for young children and young people with regard to media use, because most consequences of living online in its different versions and in different phases of the child's growth cannot be seen until later in life. At present, we notice only the immediate consequences. From the parents' point of view, the situation can be characterized as a state of indecision, insecurity and the rupture/breakdown of the generational contract. We do not know how to define the position of media between the parent and child.

Margaret Mead (1970) noted an emergence of a new prefigurative culture, where adults are no longer in the position to forecast the future because of the fast development of societies around the world. This makes older generations indecisive in guiding and socializing the younger generation. Mead (1970) was far-sighted, for today the notion of prefigurative culture is even more valid than 50 years ago. In addition, children's new and early learned capacities with media make them more equal than before to the older generations as citizens of the media world.

The fact remains, however, that in many ways children are not like adults. Relatively speaking, compared to adults they are more impulsive, have a lower capacity to control their pleasure impulses and have less ability to evaluate the consequences of their actions from both a short- and a long-term perspective (Freud, 1973). Differentiating reality and its virtual representations is often too difficult for young children before the age of eight years (Rich and Bar-on, 2001). In our previous research project, my colleagues and I noticed the same phenomenon in child interviews as that mentioned by Rich and Bar-on. A five-year-old boy reported that he was afraid of an elephant running directly towards him on the screen. In order to escape the approaching danger, he said he had run off to hide behind the sofa (Kirmanen, 2000). Similar reactions are not uncommon among five- to six-year-old children. A five-year-old girl saw a 'killer dog' on television, and she reported she was afraid that such a dog could appear in her own village. Similarly, the fear of war is often transferred from the screen to everyday reality. One reason for this is that children lack the capability to think in probabilities (Kirmanen, 2000; Lahikainen, 2009). All this makes an adult's guidance necessary, especially when the child faces new situations.

It seems that media have made it very problematic in research to even list the kinds of activities family members pursue in their everyday life. Media are said to be ubiquitous, but in order to be more exact, a new concept that would tag all kinds of uses of accessible media devices during the day would be useful. It could be something like 'use session', which can be defined by the duration, type of ICT device and the content. This would help us in noting and analysing how media-related actions and other actions are structured and intertwined in both families and their members' minds. We need to be able to analyse what kind of changes this type of new dual socialization context contributes to the individual capacities of the growing child.

One of the biggest questions from the point of view of socialization is, therefore, what kind of social interaction and discussions between family members do media promote or prevent, and what do media do for family talk as a rule?

THE CHANGING SOCIALIZATION FUNCTIONS OF PARENTS: SOCIALIZATION IN THE VIRTUAL AND REAL SOCIAL CONTEXTS

Although families are changing at a time characterized by the electronic media revolution, globalization, increasing networking and the lowering of boundaries (Rushkoff, 1997), they simultaneously try to keep their basic nature constant. In general, stability is not a prerequisite of continuity for family relationships; rather, continuity is enforced by the family's capacity to change and simultaneously maintain its cohesion (Erikson, 1950). Family relations are maintained and strengthened in daily family interaction, which creates and maintains both individuality and solidarity, securing the continuity of relationships.

There are long theoretical traditions that assume the family is the basic institution for social interaction between generations and that the child simply grows up to become a social being with his or her own identity (Erikson, 1950). Berger and Luckmann (1966) call this process primary socialization. In order to be able to understand the role of new media in the development of the child from the point of view of his or her identity development, I must offer a brief overview of some of the essential findings concerning the formation of identity.

The coherence of the self is based on early family interaction. In good-enough care, a young child acknowledges the other to be the person she or he needs. The first three years of life are essential for developing a secure basis for a sound identity later in life. This does not mean that family interaction loses its significance after the child's first three years; its role is continuous (Kernberg, 1980; Mannoni, 1987; Stern, 1998).

In mutual interaction, the image and value of the self to others – as well as value of others to the self – are continually processed. Reflections of other family members function like a mirror contributing images of the self and others. The coherence of the relationships is mainly the result of mutual attraction. Identity processes have their basis in history. In this sense, family life is unique. The underlying basic streams of family life stem from the mutual attractions between the parents (Klein, 1950; Kernberg, 1980).

The intersubjective is continually in a process of the transforming internal/subjective and contributing new elements to individual identities through mechanisms of internalization and identification (by interaction partners, especially by the child) (Kernberg, 1980). The value of others generates itself in the form of expectations of others in new interactions outside family. Sociability develops through learning with others in new contexts. The development of a general awareness about belonging to institutions and cultures and about citizenship results from the mainly positive experiences a person has with others (Mannoni, 1987; Stern, 1998)

Family life and the upbringing of the offspring are constructed and supported by outer and inner moral demands. The latter refer to the necessity of regulating the emotional difficulties, crises, conflicts and upheavals that arise from the desires of family members. Families create and build up their own standards, values, rules and obligations in the frames of their culture and subcultures (Laing, 1971).

Society delegates the responsibility for upbringing primarily to the parents, and secondarily to daycare institutions and schools. The authority of the parents is based on the one hand on the position delegated to them by society. On the other hand, it is based on the fact that the parents are more experienced than their offspring and thus have authority over their children in everyday life (Mayall, 2002). In processes of social interaction taking place in the family, children learn to conform to the parents' authority. They learn the significance of values and rules, and they learn to understand the inescapable necessity of limitations in social life. Furthermore, they learn to learn in the new contexts of their life.

Underlining the child–parent relationship and giving preference to it over the child's other relationships with siblings, peers and professional caretakers has been criticized by several researchers of childhood (James et al., 1998; Moss and Petrie, 2002, pp. 102–4; Dunn, 2004). Although we now have a great deal of knowledge about childhood lived with age mates and outside the family, it has not led to the neglect/ignorance of the value of parenthood. Australian media researchers, Professors Bob Hodge and David Tripp (1986, pp. 213–18) state in the conclusions of their study covering 600 children, and dealing with the role of television as a meaning-maker, 'the family remains as a powerful agent of socialization in contemporary society'. However, the parents have to compete with school and peers. The authors encourage parents to actively participate in their children's life by constructively discussing television-rooted meaning-making, instead of exercising one-sided control (ibid.).

MEDIA AND DIGITAL SYSTEMS AS SOCIALIZATION ARENAS FOR CHILDREN

Everyone is influenced by media. How do media change the interaction processes of socialization in the family? The aspects worth considering are numerous. ICT devices change the variety, duration, contents and qualities of the daily meetings of family members, both face-to-face and online. They help both parents and children to distance themselves from each other as well as to deepen and intensify relationships.

The continuous accessibility of a person who is trusted creates a feeling of security. In families where the parents and the child have a habit of communicating by mobile phone while not being physically in the same place, the children do not necessarily need to experience either a full absence of parents or the accompanying feelings of separation/longing. The development of a relatively independent, autonomous person is thought to also require experiences of the absence of significant others. The quality of fruitful absences depends on the age of the child (Mannoni, 1987; Winnicott, 1989). What happens if longing and other feelings related to the absence of the significant other, which are thought to help in the development of inner representations of significant others, remain inexperienced? Does the constant – even though virtual – presence of family members inhibit the development of relative autonomy by the young? Are we going back to overall dependence, interconnectedness, something that media make widely possible in new ways?

A child–parent relationship is not an isolated relationship. It is only one among the other dyads and wider networks that are also important. In the family, a child also has to learn to share each parent with siblings and also with the other parent. Media bring forth new kinds of competitors. How does the baby/child react and what kind of emotions arise when the caring adult speaks on the phone with somebody and/or looks somewhere else, for example, meaning the child must share her or him with the unseen and unheard virtual other? How does the parent actually manage this kind of situation? Phones are not inherently good or bad, but their use varies with different social consequences.

Has exposure to media at home changed parents' attitudes, interests and values towards their child? Media have tremendous power in their capacity to connect people almost everywhere. The baby/toddler/child needs the attention and care of his or her caretakers according to the rhythm of their bodily needs/states and in situations where he or she has difficulties coping. How common is it that the child has to compete with media for the attention of the parents and loses in that competition? Sherry Turkle (2012) gives numerous examples of the disappointments of children whose parents are not looking at them while they are online and/or using mobile phones. Surprisingly, her observations concern young people who are no longer children!

Certainly, there are also innumerable positive instances where a mobile phone helps in both care-taking and parenting as well as in peer relationships. For instance, ten-year-old Matilda bakes a cake when visiting her aunt. Then she takes a photo of the cake with her mobile phone and sends it to her mother at work, who immediately replies with a text message and shares her delight with her daughter by admiring the cake in the picture. All are satisfied.

Media also offer online interaction partners for children, such as in games, discussion forums and different kinds of networks. In many games, the child must passively adopt the profile(s) written into the game's story. Playing takes place in the ideological frame of the game, thus presenting a hidden curriculum to the child.

Games may be taken as a break or as an escape from one's everyday identity in real life and as an arena for unique success. They are programmed to reward and give prizes to the player. Usually, prizes are earned much quicker than in real life. Games are not planned to offer role models – or are they? How do they simulate everyday life? The criterion of success for the game's producers is its popularity, not its significance for the players.

Douglas Rushkoff (1997) suggests that the popularity of media lies in their ability to react/give responses to any kind of input at an unbelievable speed much superior to feedback in real life. In games, systems of reward and sanctioning are 100 per cent reliable, which they are not in real life with real people. Rewards and sanctions can be anticipated and mastered. In this respect, playing games is more satisfactory than everyday life.

But what happens to these role players' experiences of time, and what kind of psychic processes do the games trigger? Is playing just fun – tiny fragments in the memory of the past? Or are they moments of empowerment that are destined to become forgotten? What about spillover? Do children adopt ways of acting and thinking from games and apply the virtually learned practices to their real life? Spillover from television to everyday life has been documented, for example, by Tovares (2007), where family members borrow texts from the actors of a TV film. Children adopt phrases and stories from the screen and activate/imitate events in their games with their peers. The flows of events on the screen merge and are mixed into lived life (Kalliala, 1999; Valkonen, 2012). Does playing make offline life seem boring, or does success in playing help them to cope with what looks dull and gloomy in everyday life?

With all these questions without answers, I am trying to point out the wide range of media's new possibilities. Presupposing a child's immense capacity to learn, these possibilities have great significance for children. We cannot, however, know what kind of effects the different kinds of virtual connections will have.

THE COMPLICATED FACES OF MEDIA INTERACTION

Interaction in social media is different compared to face-to-face interaction, but not necessarily in a negative way. Many features of social media make participation tempting. It can be more adventurous, and it contains more surprises than ordinary, everyday life. Social media serve as many-sided arenas for self-presentation through pictures and photographs, voice and words, blogs, discussion forums and groups. They allow for big audiences and networks. The size of audiences guarantees a richness of feedback. One can have new interaction partners that one has never met, as well as anonymous, imaginary partners. Feedback and the consequences of self-expression and presentation vary from worldwide success to becoming an object of mass hatred.

Besides the positive side, such as creative self-presentation and finding new peers/age mates/people, social media have a questionable side too. It is very easy to deceive and lie in some social media. In a way, all virtual participation can become a game without common rules, because the limits of reality do not apply. The rules of good and moral behaviour need not be followed because of the lack of a means of control (Turkle, 2012; Rushkoff, 2013). Seeking intimacy and proximity, including non-verbal communication, talking, conversation, information exchange, evaluation, guidance, listening and caring easily take place in face-to-face meetings; online meetings can only weakly substitute for them with their shortage of non-verbal cues (emoticons).

Good self-esteem and coherence of the self are based on the feeling that you know who you are. Are you different in different contexts? Who are you really in reality, virtually, to yourself and to others? Online, you are an indefinite, mixed composition of different presentations with varying success or failure evaluated by an indefinite composition of different people. According to Sherry Turkle (2012), online self-presentations such as profiles are simulations of the self, and are always narrow and pale in comparison to the real-life self that has developed in peer or family relationships where others and their acceptance have become important to us.

Online presentations consist of three components: text, picture and voice. What is always lacking is the living body (the analogical self) (Turkle, 1995; Parviainen, 2006; Rushkoff, 2013). Therefore, virtual/digital selves are always less than the real embodied self, in principle. Besides the exchange of messages, communication always contains the interpretation of the messages of both the sender and the receiver. Interpretation, where both old knowledge and non-verbal cues are utilized, always makes interaction somehow limitless and obscure. In face-to-face interaction, which usually lasts longer than short online messages, it is easier to get a feeling of understanding the other and of having been understood correctly. The brevity of online messages and shortage of non-verbal cues (emoticons) in them makes them easily misunderstood.

This does not, however, mean that you experience yourself through/ in your body vitally only in face-to-face interaction. As images of online exchange, our online selves also become vitalized in our body. Expressing hate online, for example, is not only a cognition, but also an embodied emotion. When we become irritated online, others we are in face-to-face contact with can see and hear it (Parviainen, 2006; Rushkoff, 2013).

It has been suggested that as we now live with media, the self has become divided into two parts: the bodily and virtual. Alternatively, the self is thought to have entirely split into fragmented pieces without organization and an inner instance of control or evaluation. The change of selves is assumed to take place unproblematically. If we believe in a fragmentation of the self, this would mean that our life would become randomized and directed randomly by different compositions of people that we happen to meet in real life or online. This is hardly the case. It is possible that a coherent and relatively autonomous adult personality can be developed in environments where social media are omnipresent and established, provided that as a child they have enough opportunities to find a secure position within the early family interaction network (see, Turkle, 1995, 2012; Rushkoff, 2013).

CONCLUDING COMMENTS

I concur with Rushkoff (2013) in his thinking that the current era of media is best characterized by a present with a shrinking past and future, because media provide infinite alternatives for continuous decision-making, enabling us to create connections to everywhere at any time. What this means for the youngest age groups should be studied and analysed, because they do not have the same kind of context in which to grow up that their predecessors had.

Many of the questions presented here are difficult – if not impossible – to answer at the moment. However, they need to be formulated, because they help us to differentiate between the essential and the less important subjects in the discussion about media. The analyses of episodes of media-related everyday interaction between children and their parents that are presented in the following chapters give us new knowledge for continuing the discussion on the role of media in child socialization at home. They also offer multidisciplinary approaches that are needed in discussions on scientific forums and will hopefully help in finding some uniting definitions of the central concepts that deal with media and their connections to individuals and groups.

In this chapter, I have tried to describe how media have changed socialization at home. The media invasion has brought new elements into families: (1) the opportunity for early diversification of family members with the help of media devices and (2) an increase of the complexity of family communication, because (a) the borders between in-group and out-group membership have been blurred; (b) media devices increase the number of alternatives of being together with family members in different ways; (c) the relationship between children and parents has become more complicated because both are experienced and inexperienced in different ways than before; and (d) the relevance of the family relationships have become more age dependent than earlier.

NOTES

*   This chapter is based on Lahikainen, A.R. (2015), 'Media lapsiperheen sosiaalisessa vuorovaikutuksessa', in A.R. Lahikainen, T. Mälkiä and K. Repo (eds), *Media lapsiperheessä*, Tampere: Vastapaino.
1.   'Media and Children's Well-Being in Cultural and Societal Context' (2003–09), funded by the Finnish Academy, the University of Tampere and Nokia. The project leader was Anja Riitta Lahikainen, and the co-researchers were Juulia Paavonen, Satu Valkonen, Inger Kraav and Merle Taimalu.

REFERENCES

Aarsand, P. (2007), 'Around the screen. Computer activities of children's everyday lives', *Linköping Studies in Art and Science No. 388*, Linköping: Linköping University.

Berger, P.L. and T. Luckmann (1966), *The Social Construction of Reality: A Treatise in the Sociology of Knowledge*, London: Penguin Books.

Blum-Kulka, S. (1997), *Dinner Talk: Cultural Patterns of Sociability and Socialization in Family Discourse*, Mahwah, NJ: Lawrence Erlbaum Associates.

Buckingham, D. (2003), *Media Education: Literacy, Learning and Contemporary Culture*, Cambridge, UK: Polity Press.

Dunn, J. (2004), *Children's Friendships: The Beginnings of Intimacy*, Oxford: Blackwell Publishing.

Elder, G.H. Jr., J. Modell and R.D. Parke (eds) (1993), 'Studying children in a changing world', in *Children in Time and Place. Developmental and Historical Insights*, Cambridge, UK: Cambridge University Press, pp. 3–22.

Erikson, E.H. (1950), *Child and Society*, New York: Norton.

Freud, A. (1973), *Normality and Pathology in Childhood. Assessments of Development*, Harmondsworth, UK: Penguin Books.

Hodge, R. and D. Tripp (1986), *Children and Television: A Semiotic Approach*, Cambridge, UK: Polity Press.

Inkinen, O. (2005), 'The introduction to children's information society', in A.R. Lahikainen, P. Hietala and T. Inkinen et al. (eds), *Childhood in the Media Worlds*, Helsinki: Gaudeamus.

James, A., C. Jenks and A. Prout (1998), *Theorizing Childhood*, Cambridge, UK: Polity Press.

Kalliala, M. (1999), *Enkeliprinsessa ja itsari liukumäessä. Leikkikulttuuri ja yhteiskunnan muutos* [The Angel Princess and 'Suicide' Racing Down the Playground Slide. On Play Culture and Social Change], Helsinki: Gaudeamus.

Kapur, J. (1999), 'Out of control: Television and the transformation of childhood in late capitalism', in M. Kinder (ed.), *Kids' Media Culture*, Durham, NC and London: Duke University Press, pp. 122–39.

Kendall, S. (2007), 'Introduction: Family talk', in D. Tannen, S. Kendall and C. Gordon (eds), *Family Talk: Discourse and Identity in Four American Families*, Oxford: Oxford University Press, pp. 3–23.

Kernberg, O.F. (1980), *Internal World and External Reality: Object Relations Theory Applied*, New York: Jason Aronson.

Kirmanen, T. (2000), 'Lapsi ja pelko. Sosiaalipsykologinen tutkimus 5–6-vuotiaiden lasten peloista ja pelon hallinnasta' [Children and fear. Social psychology research on the fears of 5–6-year-olds], dissertation, *Kuopion yliopiston julkaisuja E. Yhteiskuntatieteet No. 78*, Kuopio: Kuopion yliopisto.

Klein, M. (1950), *Psychoanalysis of Children*, London: Hogarth.

Korhonen, P. (2008), 'Lasten TV-ohjelmiin liittyvät pelot, painajaisunet ja pelonhallinta' [Fear, nightmares and fear management associated with children's TV programs], dissertation, *Acta Universitatis Tamperensis Series No. 1332*, Tampere: Tampere University Press.

Lahikainen, A.R. (2009), 'Assessing social change from the perspective of child well-being and development', *ISSBD-Bulletin*, **55** (1), 5–10.

Lahikainen, A.R., I. Kraav, T. Kirmanen and M. Taimalu (2006), 'Child–parent agreement in the assessment of young children's fears: A comparative perspective', *Journal of Cross-Cultural Psychology*, **37** (1), 100–119.

Laing, R.D. (1971), *The Politics of the Family and Other Essays*, London: Tavistock Publications.

Lull, J. (1995), *Media, Communication, Culture. A Global Approach*, Cambridge, UK: Polity Press.

Mälkiä, T. and I. Arminen (2015), 'Perheruokailu, media ja sosialisaatio' [Family dining, media and socialization], in A.R. Lahikainen, T. Mälkiä and K. Repo (eds), *Media lapsiperheessä*, Helsinki: Vastapaino, pp. 132–57.

Mannheim, K. (1952), *Essays on Sociology of Knowledge*, in P. Kecskemeti (ed.), Oxford: Oxford University Press.

Mannoni, M. (1987), *Separation och utveckling. Om brist, begär och skapande* [Separation and Development. On Deprivation, Desire and Creativity], Stockholm: Norstedt.

Mayall, B. (2002), *Towards a Sociology for Childhood: Thinking from Children's Lives*, Buckingham, UK: Open University Press.

Mead, M. (1970), *Culture and Commitment: A Study of the Generation Gap*, London: Bodley Head.

Moss, P. and P. Petrie (2002), *From Children's Services to Children's Spaces: Public Policy, Children and Childhood*, London: Routledge Falmer.

Murdorf, N. and K. Laird (2002), 'Social psychological effects of information technologies and other interactive media', in J. Bryant and D. Zillmann (eds), *Media Effects. Advances in Theory and Research*, London: Lawrence Erlbaum Associates, pp. 583–602.

Paavonen, J.E., M. Pennonen, M. Roine, S. Valkonen and A.J. Lahikainen (2006), 'TV-exposure associated with sleep disturbances in 5- to 6-year-old children', *Journal of Sleep Research*, **15** (2), 154–61.

Partanen, J. and A.R. Lahikainen (2008), 'Lasten markkinat' [Child-targeted marketing], in A.R. Lahikainen, R.-L. Punamäki and T. Tamminen (eds), *Kulttuuri lasten kasvattajana*, Porvoo: WSOY, p. 6.

Parviainen, J. (2006), *Meduusan liike: Mobiiliajan tiedonmuodostuksen filosofiaa* [The Movement of the Medusa. On the Philosophy of Knowledge in the Age of Mobile Media], Helsinki: Gaudeamus.

Pasquier, D., C. Puzzi, L. d'Haenens and U. Sjöberg (1998), 'Family lifestyles and media use patterns. An analysis of domestic media among Flemish, French, Italian and Swedish children and teenagers', *European Journal of Communication*, **13** (4), 503–19.

Postman, N. (1982), *Disappearance of Childhood*, London: W.H. Allen.

Rantanen, T. (2005), *The Media and Globalization*, London: Sage.

Repo, K. and J. Nätti (2015), 'Lapset ja nuoret yksin ja yhdessä median parissa' [Children and young people alone and together with media], in A.R. Lahikainen, T. Mälkiä and K. Repo (eds), *Media lapsiperheessä*, Helsinki: Vastapaino.

Rich, M. and M. Bar-on (2001), 'Child health in the information age: Media education of pediatricians', *Pediatrics*, **107** (1), 156–62.

Roberts, D.F. and U.G. Foehr (2004), *Kids and Media in America*, Cambridge, UK: Cambridge University Press.

Rushkoff, D. (1997), *Children of Chaos: Surviving the End of the World as We Know It*, London: Flamingo.

Rushkoff, D. (2013), *Present Shock. When Everything Happens Now*, New York: Penguin Group.

Stern, D.N. (1998), *The Interpersonal World of the Infant*, London: Karnac Books.
Suominen, J., S. Östman, P. Saarikoski and R. Turtiainen (2013), *Sosiaalisen median lyhyt historia* [A Brief History of Social Media], Helsinki: Gaudeamus.
Suoninen, E. (2015), 'Lapsen aseman rakentuminen perheen ruokapöytäkeskustelussa' [The construction status of the child's family dining table discussion], in A.R. Lahikainen, T. Mälkiä and K. Repo (eds), *Media lapsiperheessä*, Tampere: Vastapaino, pp. 157–82.
Taimalu, M. (2007), *Children's Fears and Coping Strategies: A Comparative Perspective*, Tartu, Estonia: Tartu University Press.
Taimalu, M., A. Riitta Lahikainen, P. Korhonen and I. Kraav (2007), 'Self-reported fears as indicators of young children's well-being in societal change: A cross-cultural perspective', *Social Indicators Research*, **80** (1), 51–78.
Thompson, J. (1995), *The Media and Modernity: A Social Theory of the Media*, Oxford: Blackwell.
Tovares, A. (2007), 'Family members interacting while watching TV', in D. Tannen, S. Kendall and C. Gordon (eds), *Family Talk: Discourse and Identity in Four American Families*, Oxford: Oxford University Press, pp. 283–309.
Turkle, S. (1995), *Life on the Screen. Identity in the Age of the Internet*, New York: Simon and Schuster.
Turkle, S. (2012), *Alone Together. Why We Expect More from Technology and Less from Each Other*, New York: Basic Books.
Valkonen, S. (2012), 'Television merkitys lasten arjessa' [Television's importance in children's everyday lives], dissertation, *Acta Electronica Universitatis Tamperensis: 1213*, Tampere: Tampere University Press.
Valkonen, S., M. Pennonen and A.R. Lahikainen (2005), 'Televisio pienten lasten arjessa' [Television in the everyday life of small children], in A.R. Lahikainen, P. Hietala and T. Inkinen et al. (eds), *Lapsuus mediamaailmassa: Näkökulmia lasten tietoyhteiskuntaan*, Helsinki: Gaudeamus, pp. 54–109.
Wartella, E., E. Vandewater and V. Rideout (2005), 'Electronic media use in the lives of infants, toddlers and preschoolers', *American Behavioral Scientist*, **48** (5), 501–4.
Winnicott, D.W. (1989), *Holding and Interpretation. Fragment of an Analysis*, London: Karnac Books and the Institute of Psychoanalysis.

3. Social interactional understandings in investigating family practices of digital media use*

Susan Danby

INTRODUCTION

Children, from the earliest ages, are engaging with a range of multimedia, multimodal digital experiences with family members. From birth, young children are immersed in a digital world where parents and other family members undertake a broad array of digital practices, including knowledge and information seeking and social gaming. Despite common sense assumptions that digital activities are solitary activities, there is overwhelming evidence to show that these activities tend to be social, involving others, and happening in shared family spaces and with family members (Marsh et al., 2005; Marsh et al., 2015). Fifteen years ago, Livingstone (2002, p. 1) pointed out that 'the home is being transformed into the site of a multimedia culture' and, since then, multimedia usage has rapidly grown. It is now virtually impossible to record everyday practices of children and young people where digital technologies do not feature in some way (Ayaß, 2012).

Given the high uptake of digital media in the home, understanding everyday practices of family life also means a focus on the digital media practices of children and young people within the contexts of childhoods and family life, including leisure time. Digital media include 'material technologies (a TV set, a computer) and means through which signs – text, images, sound and numbers – are used to shape, share and store meaning' (Drotner, 2013, p. 45). Studies of family life in the digital era, then, are concerned with investigations of the interactions of family members with each other as they go about their everyday practices that increasingly include digital media. This approach goes beyond investigating the materiality of the technology as an object or artefact (Hutchby, 2001; Hutchby & Moran-Ellis, 2001). Rather, the meaning of the technology lies not in what it '"is", nor in what it specifically does, but in what it enables or affords as it mediates the relationship between its user and other individuals' (Hutchby & Moran-Ellis, 2001, p. 3). From this perspective, research questions might consider the following:

> What are the shapes and the outcomes of specific, situated encounters between children and technologies: how do children interact with, and in light of, the affordances that technologies have; how do these affordances constrain such interactions; and how is the complex of relations brought about here consequential for our understanding both of children themselves and of technological forms? (Hutchby & Moran-Ellis, 2001, p. 3)

Family contexts are social sites for informal relational networks. Within these relationships, parents, grandparents and children are participating with each other through digital media (Carrington & Robinson, 2011; Hernwall, Aarsand, & Tingstad, 2010; Marsh et al., 2005; Plowman, Stephen, & McPake, 2010a). Often, parents are unaware of their role in supporting children's use of digital technologies, attributing the children's expertise as being self-taught (Plowman, McPake, & Stephen, 2008; Stephen, McPake, & Plowman 2010). For older children and teenagers, digital contexts such as social gaming extend the physical boundaries of the home to include virtual contexts and peers (Mondada, 2012; Sjöblom, 2011). When studying family life, it is no longer possible to discount the family's digital media practices.

While digital technologies feature strongly in many children's everyday experiences, not so much is known about the influences of digital technologies on family interactions and contemporary family life (Lahikainen, Chapter 2, this volume). In her study of children's well-being within Finnish families, Lahikainen (ibid.) asks: How have the practices of digital technologies changed family interactions? What kinds of challenges are there for children's socialization and family interactions? How might family time be redistributed with the inclusion of digital (and increasingly mobile) technologies? These important questions point to new and complex ways to consider family relationships and family interactions.

In this chapter, specific attention is directed to research that investigates the everyday practices of children's engagement with family members and digital media, as these interactions unfold. These studies predominantly draw on the methodological approaches of ethnomethodology and conversation analysis. Analytic attention is drawn to the methods that members use when orienting to, and collaboratively producing, the social order underway (Francis & Hester, 2004; Heritage, 1984). The focus concerns 'what is observably-the-case about some talk, activity or setting' (Francis & Hester, 2004, p. 25) and the sequential aspects of the interactions as they unfold, moment by moment. Attention, thus, is directed to the *in situ* everyday practices of family members around digital technologies. This focus precludes considering research that addresses or explores idealized practices, or methods of data collection that predominantly rely upon accounts of practices, as found within survey, interview and focus group data.

In addition to examining theoretical understandings that inform analyses of family members' multimodal talk and actions, the chapter explores methodological considerations when engaging in research of family interactions in digital media contexts. Discussion includes considerations of video recording as a digital method of data collection. This method slows down analytic procedures to be able to review and consider in close-up detail what is happening in the video data. Undertaking social interaction research involving family practices around digital media presents both challenges and opportunities, and the chapter concludes by highlighting some of these aspects.

INVESTIGATIONS OF FAMILY PRACTICES OF MEDIA USE

Studying children's everyday social worlds is not a new phenomenon. Over 30 years ago, Cicourel (1970), Mackay (1974) and Speier (1974) introduced an ethnomethodological lens to investigate how children participate in, and organize, their everyday life experiences. These social organizations are described variously as social orders and social structures (Cicourel, 1970) and children's culture (Mackay, 1974). Children's participation in social structures constitute, and are constituted by, their social worlds (Cromdal, 2009; Danby, 2009). Children's everyday practices, increasingly, involve new media technologies.

Digital media have changed significantly in the past few years. Ayaß describes how media practices have undergone 'everydayification' as well as 'boundary dissolution' (Ayaß, 2012, p. 3). By this, Ayaß means that media are now well integrated into everyday experiences, and supported with accompanying taken-for-granted routines. Within this pervasiveness of digital media in many forms, people have appropriated media for use within the flow of their already existing practices. Media access is available all the time and across multiple contexts, and it affects everyday social activities. Given its commonness, studies of everyday social interactions increasingly show digital media-in-practice.

The first social interactional studies of families interacting with different digital media practices began with studies of family viewing and family activities related to television. Several studies explored family and child practices to highlight the complexity of family practices (Ayaß, 2012; Emmison & Goldman, 1997; Marsh & Bishop, 2012). More recent studies of family life have studied family practices involving computers, laptops and Internet-connected (smart) phones and tablets. Much of this body of work investigating digital media and family life has been informed through discourse analytic and socio-cultural frameworks, with an emphasis on children's digital participation in family contexts (Marsh et al., 2015; Plowman et al., 2010a, 2010b; Stephen et al., 2010). Understandings of family digital practices from ethnomethodological and conversation analysis explorations show children's social interactions mediated by parents and the affordances of the technology. Many of these studies rely on multimodal analysis (Mondada, 2008) to capture both the talk and embodied actions of the participants with each other and with digital media. This chapter mostly addresses these studies.

Relational Encounters with Family Members and Digital Technologies

There is scant research investigating the relationships between co-present participants when using digital media (Mondada, 2012). Even very young children, though, are engaging with digital media shaped by relational encounters where the parent or sibling may be a mediator of the digital activities and thus a co-participant of the social activity. As a collection, these studies show the situated achievements of the family members mutually attending to each other as well as to digital activities and physical artefacts.

Davidson's (2012) study explored two preschool-aged siblings and their playing of a computer game, and focused on what happened when a dispute arose, and how the players resolved it. The mother had asked the older sister to show the younger sister how to play the game, and the conflict became centred on claims about knowledge of how to play the game. What became evident was, as well as knowledge claims, the owner of the mouse had control of the actions of physically playing the game. Another Australian study investigated a father's video recording of him and his two young children using digital apps on an iPad and iPhone (Danby et al., 2013). The two young children (aged 18 months and three years) engaged in and disengaged from collaboratively produced talk with their father, which displayed their knowledge of the content of the apps they were using, while also managing their individual activity. These two siblings are shown in a later episode using an iPhone app, where the older sister shares her knowledge of alphabetic literacy with her younger brother (Scriven, 2016). These studies primarily focus on the social and the relational, but of course digital media as a resource is an integral component of the social order being built and sustained.

There is even less research that investigates intergenerational interactions among family members during the use of digital technologies. One early study that investigated intergenerational family life involving digital activities was Aarsand's (2007) study of grandparents, parents and children engaged in video and computer game activities. He showed how child and adult players alike invoked the idea of a digital divide, with children constructed as having mastery over the game whereas parents and grandparents did not, creating a generation gap. He concluded that this construction was one that achieved positive social outcomes for all parties, as the children controlled the game and the grandparents gained access to shared interaction time with their grandchildren.

The advances in digital telecommunication technologies are producing new digital contexts for understanding families' social interactions that involve intergenerational members, although there are few studies to date. The participants' task is to make sense of how the local and virtual actions and activities are assembled and accomplished to produce shared social orders 'bound to the moment of action in and through which it occurs' (Heath & Hindmarsh, 2000, p. 102). Busch (in press, 2016) explored the role of video communication technology to maintain and facilitate intergenerational family relationships. She examined the talk of young children, their mother and grandparents during a Skype session to show the complex work undertaken by the adults as they facilitated the children's interactions through prosody and gesture. This study revealed how the intergenerational participants oriented to what was happening in their immediate local environment, including the participants' local conduct, and what was happening on the digital screen, involving images of participants at a distance.

It would be unrealistic to think that the digital activities in family and home contexts are isolated events divorced from other everyday activities outside of the home. Aarsand (2010) found that young boys' shared experiences of playing computer games at home carried over into the playground talk. The findings of this study show how popular digital media flow into multiple aspects of everyday life, with boundary shifts made from the gaming console at home to the interactions in the playground.

The Seamless Integration of Shared Spontaneous Activity and Digital Technologies

A regular occurrence in young children's interactions is that they often initiate and participate in pretend or fantasy play (Butler, 2008; Danby et al., 2017; Garvey, 1990; Sheldon, 1996). This type of spontaneous activity involves young children understanding and using objects as resources for pretence (Kidwell & Zimmerman, 2007; Sidnell, 2011). While little is known about children's use of objects in digital activities, there is an emerging body of research that shows how young children seamlessly integrate the use of digital resources into their pretend play. The digital resources become a prop, like other props.

In one study of young siblings' interactions, the two participants used a desktop computer, the keyboard, the sounds projected from the computer audio speakers and a toy truck (Danby et al., 2017). The children collaboratively drew on these objects, in conjunction with their own collaborative interactions, to sustain their spontaneous pretend play of making pretend guns for the toy truck. In this game of pretence, the digital resources were critical in organizing and accomplishing their collaborative spontaneous activity.

Another study of spontaneous play showed how a young child oriented simultaneously to one technology to inform the use of another technology (Scriven, Edwards-Groves, & Davidson, in press, 2017). The young child viewed a Barbie® YouTube video as a prop for engaging in a pretend telephone conversation with Barbie® (a doll held in her hand) on a toy mobile phone. Multimodal analysis showed the interplay of action and orientation to the different devices through her gaze, gestures, and talk. Even though a family member, the mother, was present only during this sequence of activity for some of the time, she had a significant role to play as she had set up the laptop, and clicked on the YouTube video that had been requested by the child, and hence was potentially available for talk. Parents' presence, thus, may be significant as the parents can be the facilitators and enablers of the digital activity.

Web Searching and Knowledge Formation

With the intensification of digital media opportunities and Internet access, knowledge realization is happening increasingly outside of school contexts in family and informal learning and social contexts (Drotner, 2013). Indeed, home contexts may offer children more flexible environments and greater social interaction, and a broader exposure to digital technologies and greater access to scaffolding and social and technical support than do school contexts (Davidson et al., in press, 2017; Marsh, 2010; Plowman et al., 2010a).

Young children are accessing Internet-based activities at home before they even attend preschool or other early educational contexts. Davidson (2009) showed two young siblings in the home context as they searched online for information about lizards. They drew on a range of literacy resources, including Google, Wikipedia and a reference book about reptiles. Their mutual attention accomplished knowledge creation about lizards, and about how to undertake a web search, as they shifted seamlessly across the different digital and paper texts. In a related study, Davidson (2011) also showed an adult–child interaction that involved a search for lizards where the young child engaged in a web search that required reading information texts related to the search.

A study by Davidson and her colleagues (in press, 2017) showed a father and child undertaking a child-initiated exploration on Google on the topic of what makes paper white. This topic had been self-selected by the child. Even though the child sought his father's input as to how to undertake the online search, the father displayed his confidence in his son's competence to undertake the search. The father asked strategic questions while also insisting that the son undertake the physical work of keying in the questions, and considering and selecting the correct information on the screen. The competence of the child in the family context was not so visible in the preschool context. In a web search activity at preschool, the child was directed to press specific keys and was not afforded the same opportunity to draw on his considerable knowledge of spelling, as shown by the educator pointing to each letter of the words that he needed to key in to undertake the web search.

The findings of such studies of web searching, knowledge formation and parental involvement pose questions about what constitutes literacy and information-seeking practices in family contexts, and what this means for digital activities in the early years of schooling (Davidson, 2009).

Family Interactions Involving Digital Gaming

There is a long tradition of conversation analytic work in the area of children's games. From Sacks's (1995) very earliest lectures, ethnomethodological and conversation analysis approaches have investigated children's game playing. Children's game playing is concerned with how games are constituted and understood in children's social worlds (Sacks, 1980). For example, Goodwin's studies of children's games, such as jump rope (1985) and hopscotch (1995), showed the complexity of the participants' embodied actions as they negotiated and played the game. These studies of children's gaming make visible the situated and shared negotiated accomplishment of the activity that typically involves invoking rules oriented to by the players. The players' orientation to rules and local practices are present also when game playing involves digital worlds.

Digital game playing involves children producing and negotiating the social order, both locally and virtually. A relatively emerging research area, studies of children's game playing have focused on how the games are played and the accompanying negotiations, the embodied actions of the players, and the shared interactions. The social interactional approach brings analytic attention to 'identifying and describing the sets of resources and detailed practices through which activities are organized and made sense of' (Piirainen-Marsh & Tainio, 2009, p. 168). The focus, then, is on how members collaborate and engage with each other while simultaneously attending to the digital media at hand. To date, however, few studies have investigated children's gaming activities through a social interaction approach (Piirainen-Marsh, 2010). While some investigate the gaming experiences of adolescents in informal sites outside the home context, such as Internet cafés (Sjöblom & Aronsson, 2013), there are even fewer studies within the home context.

Even young children participate in computer gaming at home. Davidson's (2010a, 2012) Australian study stands out as one of the few studies that has undertaken detailed sequential analysis of young children's interactions while playing digital games. Davidson (2010a) provides an analysis of the interactions of two young children as they played a Wiggles computer game. The players had to attend to the sequence of activity predetermined within the game, but this rigidity of the game sequence afforded the opportunity for the father to introduce some actions of game playing, such as reading the symbols (the arrows), and introducing knowledge that might be helpful for the player to know in order to select the correct arrow. Davidson's findings point to the complexity of game playing, and how the children's social worlds are mediated through their use of digital media and the scaffolding of the father.

Aarsand's (2010) multisite ethnography of Swedish boys aged six to seven years old at school and at home has made possible a number of understandings about gaming in everyday family life. An aspect of this study investigated the family politics of gaming in family life, and the role of parents as they negotiated aspects of digital game play with their children (Aarsand & Aronsson, 2009a). The findings showed that the family or home space is not a single place but a series of spaces whose use is negotiated through family interactions and the gaming technology being used. In investigating the interactional resources employed by the participants when computer game playing (Aarsand & Aronsson, 2009b), family members participated in an interactional pattern where the players typically used response cries when there was a 'relatively high tempo' within the game, which worked as a device to build and maintain joint attention.

More recent investigations of everyday family life involving parent–child interactions involving digital gaming show the complexity of negotiations over computer use in family time. Child and adult members are finding new ways to engage with other family members and with digital media when present. An ongoing interactional orientation for family members is how they negotiate 'social contracts' with each other about being together as a family, and the extent to which digital media practices may be involved (Tiilikainen and Arminen, Chapter 10, this volume). Tiilikainen and Arminen (ibid.) explore how family members engage in being 'together individually'. By this description, they refer to new family interactional spaces that involve negotiating digital media practices alongside their expectations and behaviours of each other.

Family interactions are made even more challenging when there is parent–child conflict or disputes over digital media use. Suoninen (Chapter 8, this volume) explores the strategies of a 12-year-old son who resists his mother's attempts to pause a computer game in order to attend to a task requested by his mother. The son directs his attention to the computer game he is playing, and the mother has to find a range of strategies in order to successfully gain his attention. The son also draws on a number of interactional strategies that, collaboratively, produce a parent–child social context that becomes increasingly confrontational and difficult, that work to challenge the mother's positioning as empathic and reasonable, and her son as being responsible by attending to his obligations. The extended analysis of this episode shows the parent–child asynchrony as negotiations escalate, with both parent and child producing a range of interactional strategies to further their stances. Suoninen's findings highlight the work of families as they negotiate new rules of everyday family practices that take into account new forms of participation that involve digital devices.

Outside the family social order, peer social orders become increasingly sites for language learning through computer game playing. Piirainen-Marsh and Tainio (2012) and Piirainen-Marsh (2012) explored the role of knowledge when managing the peer social order of video gaming sessions. In their study of two teenage Finns playing video games at home over a two-year period, Piirainen-Marsh and Tainio sought to understand how the players managed their differing knowledge asymmetries when game playing and when solving problems or tasks related to the game. Their findings showed that the players' local social organization and their epistemic positions were not static, but dynamic and changing over time. Piirainen-Marsh and Tainio (2014) and Piirainen-Marsh (2012) showed how the players jointly constructed the narrative around the video game they were playing. The players particularly attended to, and used, the dialogue of the game's characters, and took up the gaming terms and language. The players collaboratively produced a bilingual order as they drew on their native language (Finnish) as well as the language of the game (English). In this way, the players used these locally available resources afforded by the gaming activity to build their shared social order, which displayed how they 'orient[ed] to the language of the game as a locally available and flexible resource that they attend to and use in building their own actions in the course of managing and experiencing the game' (Piirainen-Marsh & Tainio, 2009, p. 180). The focus of these studies of digital gaming was located within the family home and with family members.

THEORETICAL AND METHODOLOGICAL APPROACHES TO SOCIAL INTERACTION RESEARCH ENCOMPASSING DIGITAL MEDIA

The discussion of children's everyday family interactions and use of digital media in this chapter has an overriding analytic focus on the social orders of everyday action from ethnomethodological and conversation analysis perspectives.

Ethnomethodology's programme begins with observing everyday social practices to investigate how participants make sense of their everyday worlds (Garfinkel, 1967) and the analytic tools of conversation analysis explicate how members produce their social worlds through talk and embodied action such as gesture and gaze (Mondada, 2008; Sacks, 1995).

Ethnomethodological and conversation analysis investigations always begin with the question 'What is going on here and how is it being accomplished?' The analytic approach is undertaken through a series of procedural steps that make visible the situated actions of members, and their use of social structures of language, such as turn taking, to produce their social worlds (Francis & Hester, 2004; Pomerantz & Fehr, 1997; Sacks, Schegloff, & Jefferson, 1974). With a focus on describing members' resources for accomplishing activities, analytic attention is directed towards their situated perspectives and their practical reasoning as they go about their everyday activities. The analyst does not interpret the intentions of the members, but rather works with the visible and audible structures of the members' talk and interaction.

Naturalistic observations are the preferred approaches for studies of social interaction. This method is described as a 'natural experiment' that shows a 'situated rather than a unidimensional view' of social interaction (Goodwin, 1990, p. 284). Capturing how participants engage *in situ* affords insights into their media appropriation as it happens in real time. These approaches do not assume being able to understand digital practices in everyday social life by asking participants through interview or focus group methods. In asking participants about their interpretations of their previous actions, 'these interviews produce. . .interpretations of past events which are cast into the medium of language. . .[that is] below conscious perception [or where] memory is selective' (Ayaß, 2012, p. 8). Everyday practices, then, by their very nature of being everyday, 'lie below the retrievable and conscious, and can, as such, not be communicated' (Ayaß, 2012, p. 13).

In observational data, talk and behaviours (e.g., a gaze or overlapping talk) can be so fleeting that it is not possible to capture in detail. For this reason, video recordings of naturalistic data make the phenomenon under investigation visible, such as how children accomplish digital and social activities simultaneously, for instance online knowledge searching, gaming activities, or dispute management. Visual and auditory documentation of everyday practices provide the analytic material to explicate what members say and do with others, what is being oriented to, and how they are accomplishing their everyday social orders. Examining moment-by-moment talk and action makes an understanding of the complexity of the social interactions unfolding possible.

Video-based methods based on recordings are used increasingly across a range of methodological and theoretical approaches. As Sacks (1984), an early pioneer of conversation analysis, points out:

> We will be using observation as a basis for theorizing. Thus we can start with things that are not currently imaginable, by showing that they happened. We can then come to see that a base for using close looking at the world for theorizing about it is that from close looking at the world we can find things that we could not, by imagination, assert were there. We would not know that they were 'typical'. . . Indeed, we might not have noticed that they happen. (Sacks, 1984, p. 25)

Socially organized activities can be explored predominantly through detailed transcriptions of audio-visual recordings, and sometimes involving photos or sketches that produce a visual snapshot (for example, see Mondada, 2012; Piirainen-Marsh, 2012). Increasingly, video recordings are being used in family research to understand family practices as they go about their everyday interactions and activities. The emergence of digital activities has produced opportunities to study family life and how families orient to, and participate with, digital media. Not only are digital media the topic of investigation, digital media are also the method for production of recordings of family life for detailed analytic attention.

DIGITAL TECHNOLOGIES AS A METHOD OF DATA COLLECTION

Video data provide access to the details of everyday social activities. Data can be reviewed many times, by multiple viewers, analysed through multiple analytic lenses, and made available to the analyst, to members of the research team, to audience members, and to wider communities (Mehan, 1993). The permanence and accessibility of the data adds to the reliability and rigour of the study (Peräkylä, 1997, 2016). Video data, however, are only ever partial representations of what happens, and never a complete picture (Heath, Hindmarsh, & Luff, 2010). Where the camera is pointed, and what the researcher chooses to focus on, means that there is only ever partial representation of practices through the lens of the researcher's gaze and camera.

Within the conversation analysis approach, working with video-recorded data makes possible the production of a fine-grained transcript of that video recording. Digital software programs have made it possible to capture even the smallest details – the micro pauses, the direction of the gaze, inflections in the voice, crying and laughing. Transcripts using conversation analysis conventions can be difficult to make sense of when not familiar with the symbols and notations (Davidson, 2010b; Hepburn & Bolden, 2013; Jefferson, 2004; Mondada, 2008). When undertaking conversation analysis, the construction of a transcript is time-consuming, more time-consuming than a verbatim transcript, as only a minute of video data might take more than 30 hours to transcribe. In this way, even a few seconds of video data produce a huge amount of detail for the analyst's attention. Taking this approach means slowing down what we are seeing in the video data to be able to observe, and preserve, the talk and actions as they unfold, moment by moment.

Studies that investigate digital activities have additional considerations within the process of transcription. This issue has been managed by the addition of specific symbols that relate to particular features of the digital technology. Methods include (1) paying attention to the unfolding actions of game character dialogue (Piirainen-Marsh, 2012); (2) treating the specific talk of a software program narrator providing information as a participant within the talk (Danby et al., 2013); and (3) designing symbols specifically designed for capturing specific digital actions (e.g., keyboard strokes) (Scriven et al., forthcoming). In this way, complex multiparty and multiactivity can be shown to have happened, and further can show the coordination between the activities of the participants and the other activities occurring within the digital space.

A detailed transcript contributes to the reliability of the study, as readers can read what the participants said and did, which affords them the possibility of bringing their own analytic frameworks to the topic under investigation (Peräkylä, 1997). Such micro observations can say an enormous amount about what is in the visual data. A detailed transcript can provide sufficient detail to pick up the simultaneous talk and action. The transcript acts as a resource for the analyst to notice relevant aspects of the participants' talk and action, and produce a piece of empirical work that makes observable to others – the audience, the readers – how the interaction unfolds by slowing down the real-world moment sufficiently to see what is going on, making a phenomenon visible.

The digital affordances of slowing down analysis enough to see the event unfold moment by moment makes visible what was not visible to us before. Seeing the real-time production of social order, by observing the fine detail and sequences of talk as they unfold, makes seeing how participants constitute and organize everyday practices possible: Heath and his colleagues point out that video data offer '"time out" to play back in order to re-frame, re-focus and re-evaluate the analytic gaze' (Heath et al., 2010, p. 8). Audio- and video-recording everyday practices as they unfold, in real time, may resist, at least initially, reducing the data to codes (Heath et al., 2010). Sacks (1984) points out that: 'it is possible that detailed study of small phenomena may give an enormous understanding of the way that humans do things and the kinds of objects they use to construct and order their affairs' (p. 24). Of course, this is a researcher's problem – how to slow down what we are seeing and hearing to make sense of it. The members themselves, actively engaged in those moments, do not need the talk and action slowing down – and if they do, they have member resources that they draw on to do this.

Slowing down the analytic process means more time to bring multiple, or alternative, analytic resources to what we are seeing. This is significant because interactions involving children often seem quite familiar, as we were all children once and we draw upon memories of those experiences. Alternatively, complex multiparty interactions with digital media may seem so strange that it requires multiple viewings to be able to make sense of both what is happening within the digital media as well as how the participants are engaging with it and with each other. Both these contexts can be a problem. Consequently, a rigorous set of procedures is necessary to interpret the recorded data. Fine-grained analysis of family practices with digital media can show how they put together their shared social orders, produced collaboratively, turn by turn, to make visible what some practices can be like. To do this, analysts use their own membership resources of talk and action (such as sequential turns of talk), which are the same resources that members themselves use to accomplish their social orders.

The pervasiveness of digital media in family life means that studies of these interactions must start with what is going on in the data, by examining the sequence of talk as it unfolds *in situ*, and the participants' physical actions and linguistic resources afforded by the digital media. In this way, analysis starts with, and makes visible, what members orient to, rather than beginning with a theorized analyst's agenda (Hung, 2011). Attention is directed towards members' actions and their practical reasoning as they go about their everyday activities. Rather than the analyst interpreting the intentions of the members, or what is in their heads, the analyst works with the visible and audible structures of members' talk and action.

Studying the everyday digital media practices of families can show how such practices are intertwined in social, digital and material networks (Sparrman & Aarsand, 2009). Not only are there new ways of thinking about families' lives through the digital, the digital becomes a method of collecting, analysing and storing that data. Sitting alongside is a suite of practical matters and questions, such as keeping visual data as a permanent analytic resource and public access to that data. As Woolgar (1988) points out, 'we should try and recover the uncertainty which exists in the early stages of ethnography. . .we need continually to interrogate and find strange the process of representation as we engage in it' (pp. 28–9). The digital resources made available to analysts now make this process increasingly possible.

The act of 'close looking' at digital practices in family life makes possible an investigation of this particular digital 'cultural practice for closer investigation' (Marsh & Bishop, 2012, p. 281). As Marsh and Bishop (2012) found in their tracing of the impact of British television over 60 years, children continued to engage in imaginative play, with the television input a kind of stimulus, although contemporary children's play was now being informed additionally by the new cultural practice of reality television. As culture is 'an accomplishment of talk and action, not a determinant of it. . .the point is. . .to investigate the cultural methods and resources persons actually and observably employ in getting done whatever they are doing' (Francis & Hester, 2004, p. 31). Analysts ask questions such as: Who are the players? What relationships are being collaboratively produced? How are the children locating themselves? Cultural practices are both context shaping and context renewing: members orient to the context – the activity, setting and people – and they actively construct that social order through their talk and embodied actions. The analytic focus is on how these actions are accomplished, and the interactional and physical resources that members draw on to achieve this accomplishment of social order.

Matters of reliability and validity are necessary researcher considerations. Documentation might consist of detailed field notes, audio or video fragments, and detailed transcripts that capture the episode (Peräkylä, 1997; Silverman, 2013). As Goodwin (1990) points out, a primary concern for conversation analysis is to develop transcripts *'for the scrutiny of others'* (p. 287, original emphasis). As well, conversation analysis has a number of processes, such as 'proof procedure', that provide evidence to support the analyst's interpretation (Peräkylä, 2016). Deviant case analysis examines cases that appear different or do not fit within the existing pattern and structure of the social interaction being studied. Similarly, the proof procedure method is an analytic resource that enables the researcher to see how the members themselves treat the matter at hand, and in this way this approach anchors what the analyst can and cannot say credibly about the data.

The strategies of how the members themselves orient to being video recorded, and how they use the presence of the video-recording equipment and the process itself as an interactional resource, is of interest for researchers. Indeed, this interest is often displayed in the form of a question asked of ethnographers in terms of how the members orient to the presence of the video cameras and of the researchers (if they are present). Sometimes children orient to the presence of the cameras both in terms of what they do in front of the camera, or they self-monitor what they do and sometimes shift their activity to being outside the gaze of the camera lens (Danby et al., 2013; Given et al., 2016; Mälkiä, Chapter 4, this volume). Mälkiä (ibid.) outlines how members produce a performance in one of two ways. One way is to treat the video camera as a resource for a theatrical or musical performance, suggesting that the camera becomes a play resource. Children typically undertook this approach. The other way, most often undertaken by parents, was that sometimes they took their actions 'backstage'. They attempted to modify family routines to appear more normative and indicative of 'good' family experiences and interactions. This approach had the families treating the camera as one might treat a visitor to the home, to show a public face of family life. It is rare to be able to observe the intimacy of family life, and having family members afford researchers such access into the private spaces of family life requires the trust of the research participants, and ethical approaches by researchers.

Ethical principles and practices underpin all research activities, and there are additional aspects to consider in the digital era. There are particular ethical considerations in observational research documented through digital recordings of everyday practices. Family interactions are complex, as they often involve multiparty talk and they often occur in private spaces. Now, through digital means, these private spaces become potentially publically available for others to observe. In this way, participant involvement requires trust on the part of the participants, and sensitivity by researchers, to gain and maintain researcher access to family life. The researchers' task is to respectfully and ethically consider, with family members, matters such as permission for the inclusion of family images and selective use of video-recorded fragments or photo images for dissemination and publication, and in research and teaching activities.

The studies of social interaction investigate the everyday life of families and digital media engagement. These studies of the social organization of family life engaged with digital activities represent an emerging body of work that shows how digital environments contextualize and shape the embodied actions (such as gesture and gaze) of the participants (Mondada, 2012). Using a social interactional lens reveals how family members' activities within the digital arenas produce their talk and actions 'in an indexical way, incorporating specific locally available discursive resources in their talk and adjusting to the constantly changing contexts' (Piirainen-Marsh, 2012, p. 197). These areas of investigation, the everyday practices of family and digital media, are neither disjunct nor brought together unnaturally as an analyst's phenomenon. The focus on the everyday of family life shows family life as it unfolds, and family life increasingly flows with and around digital media practices.

CONCLUSION

In contrast to much of what has previously been written about digital technologies through a focus on accounts of family practices through surveys or interviews, the research discussed in this chapter considered the contributions of studies that use video recordings of family's everyday practices and applied ethnomethodological and conversation analysis procedures to understand digital families and childhoods. Even with the rapid and worldwide uptake of digital practices in families, little is still known about their everyday practices, often involving parents, siblings and, increasingly, grandparents. Missing from these studies are the digital activities of babies and toddlers, although there is sufficient anecdotal evidence to show that they do engage with digital devices.

The theoretical and methodological frameworks underpinning this work recognize children's and families' *in situ* competences. Collectively, they explicate the interactional complexities of grandparent–parent–child, parent–child, and sibling–sibling interactions, whether playing computer games or engaging in digital play activities that incorporate physical and virtual objects. Rather than examining what the digital technology devices afford, with a focus on what the hardware or software might deliver, the work discussed here centrally locates the participation practices of children and family members as they routinely go about their everyday activities that, increasingly, involve digital technologies.

NOTE

* The development of this chapter was supported by research funding from the Australian Research Council (ARC FT1210731). Thank you to Christina Davidson, for her insightful comments on earlier versions of this chapter.

REFERENCES

Aarsand, P. (2007). Computer and video games in family life: The digital divide as a resource in intergenerational interactions. *Childhood, 14*(2), 235–256.

Aarsand, P. (2010). Young boys playing digital games: From console to the playground. *Nordic Journal of Digital Literacy, 5*(1), 38–54.

Aarsand, P., & Aronsson, K. (2009a). Gaming and territorial negotiations in family life. *Childhood, 16*(4), 497–517. doi:10.1177/0907568209343879

Aarsand, P., & Aronsson, K. (2009b). Response cries and other gaming moves—Building intersubjectivity in gaming. *Journal of Pragmatics, 41*(8), 1557–1575. doi:10.1016/j.pragma.2007.05.014

Ayaß, R. (2012). Introduction: Media appropriation and everyday life. In R. Ayaß & C. Gerhardt (Eds.), *The Appropriation of Media in Everyday Life* (pp. 1–15). Amsterdam: John Benjamins Publishing Company.

Busch, G. (in press, 2017). How families use of video communication technologies during intergenerational SKYPE sessions. In S. Danby, M. Fleer, C. Davidson, & M. Hatzigianni (Eds.), *Digital Childhoods*. Singapore: Springer.

Butler, C.W. (2008). *Talk and Social Interaction in the Playground*. Aldershot: Ashgate.

Carrington, V., & Robinson, M. (2011). Introduction: Contentious technologies. In V. Carrington & M. Robinson (Eds.), *Digital Literacies: Social Learning and Classroom Practices* (pp. 1–9). Los Angeles: Sage.

Cicourel, A.V. (1970). The acquisition of social structure: Toward a developmental sociology of language and meaning. In J.D. Douglas (Ed.), *Understanding Everyday Life: Toward the reconstruction of sociological knowledge* (pp. 136–168). London: Routledge and Kegan Paul.

Cromdal, J. (2009). Childhood and social interaction in everyday life: Introduction to the special issue. *Journal of Pragmatics, 41*, 1473–1476.

Danby, S. (2009). Childhood and social interaction in everyday life: An epilogue. *Journal of Pragmatics, 41*, 1596–1599.

Danby, S., Davidson, C., Theobald, M., Houen, S., & Thorpe, K. (2017). Pretend play and technology: Young children making sense of their everyday social worlds. In D. Pike, S. Lynch, & C. A'Beckett (Eds.), *Multidisciplinary Perspectives on Play: From birth to beyond* (pp. 231–245). Singapore: Springer.

Danby, S., Davidson, C., Theobald, M., Scriven, B., Cobb-Moore, C., Houen, S., . . . Thorpe, K. (2013). Talk in activity during young children's use of digital technologies at home. *Australian Journal of Communication, 40*(2), 83–99.

Davidson, C. (2009). Young children's engagement with digital texts and literacies in the home: Pressing matters for the teaching of English in the early years of schooling. *English Teaching: Practice and Critique, 8*(3), 36–54.

Davidson, C. (2010a). "Click on the big red car": The social organization of playing a Wiggles computer game. Convergence: *The International Journal of Research into New Media Technologies, 16*(4), 375–394.

Davidson, C. (2010b). Transcription matters: Transcribing talk and interaction to facilitate Conversation Analysis of the taken-for-granted in young children's interaction. *Journal of Early Childhood Research, 8*(2), 115–131.

Davidson, C. (2011). Seeking the green basilisk lizard: Acquiring digital literacy practices in the home. *Journal of Early Childhood Literacy, 12*(1), 24–45. doi:10.1177/1468798411416788

Davidson, C. (2012). When 'yes' turns to 'no': Young children's disputes during computer game playing at home. In S. Danby & M. Theobald (Eds.), *Disputes in Everyday Life: The social and moral orders of children and young people* (Vol. 15, pp. 355–376). Bingley, UK: Emerald.

Davidson, C., Danby, S., Given, L.M., & Thorpe, K. (in press, 2017). Producing contexts for young children's digital technology use: Web searching during adult-child interactions at home and preschool. In S. Danby, M. Fleer, C. Davidson, & M. Hatzigianni (Eds.), *Digital Childhoods*. Dordrecht: Springer.

Drotner, K. (2013). Processual methodologies and digital forns of learning. In O. Erstad & J. Sefton-Green (Eds.), *Identity, community, and Learning Lives in the Digital Age* (pp. 39–56). Cambridge: Cambridge University Press.

Emmison, M., & Goldman, L. (1997). The Sooty Show Laid Bear: Children, Puppets and Make-Believe. *Childhood, 4*(3), 325–342. doi:10.1177/0907568297004003005

Francis, D., & Hester, S. (2004). *An Invitation to Ethnomethodology: Language, Society and Interaction*. London: Sage.

Garfinkel, H. (1967). *Studies in Ethnomethodology*. Englewood Cliffs, NJ: Prentice Hall.

Garvey, C. (1990). *Play*. Cambridge, MA: Harvard University Press.

Given, L.M., Winkler, D.C., Willson, R., Davidson, C., Danby, S., & Thorpe, K. (2016). Parents as co-researchers at home: Using an observational method to document young children's use of technology. *International Journal of Qualitative Methods*, 1–9.

Goodwin, M.H. (1985). The serious side of jump rope: Conversational practices and social organization in the frame of play. *Journal of American Folklore, 98*(389), 315–330.

Goodwin, M.H. (1990). *He-Said-She-Said: Talk as social organization among black children*. Bloomington: Indiana University Press.

Goodwin, M.H. (1995). Co-construction in girls' hopscotch. *Research on Language and Social Interaction, 28*(3), 261–281.

Heath, C., & Hindmarsh, J. (2000). Configuring action in objects: From mutual space to media space. *Mind, Culture and Activity, 7*(1–2), 81–104.

Heath, C., Hindmarsh, J., & Luff, P. (2010). *Video in Qualitative Research: Analysing Social Interaction in Everyday Life*. Los Angeles: Sage.

Hepburn, A., & Bolden, G.B. (2013). The conversation analytic approach to transcription. In J. Sidnell & T. Stivers (Eds.), *The Handbook of Conversation Analysis* (pp. 57–76). Chichester, West Sussex, UK: Wiley-Blackwell.

Heritage, J. (1984). *Garfinkel and Ethnomethodology*. Oxford: Polity Press.

Hernwall, P., Aarsand, P., & Tingstad, V. (2010). Introduction. *Nordic Journal of Digital Literacy, 5*(1), 2–6.

Hung, A.C.Y. (2011). *The Work of Play: Meaning-making in videogames*. New York, NY: Peter Lang.

Hutchby, I. (2001). *Conversation and Technology: From the Telephone to the Internet.* Malden, MA: Polity Press.

Hutchby, I., & Moran-Ellis, J. (2001). Relating children, technology and cutlure. In I. Hutchby & J. Moran-Ellis (Eds.), *Children, Technology and Culture: The impacts of technologies in children's everyday lives* (pp. 1–10). London: Routledge.

Jefferson, G. (2004). Glossary of transcript symbols with an introduction. In G.H. Lerner (Ed.), *Conversation Analysis: Studies from the first generation* (pp. 13–31). Amsterdam: John Benjamins.

Kidwell, M., & Zimmerman, D.H. (2007). Joint attention as action. *Journal of Pragmatics, 39*, 592–611.

Livingstone, S. (2002). *Young People and New Media: Childhood and the Changing Media Environment.* London: Sage.

Mackay, R.W. (1974). Conceptions of children and models of socialization. In R. Turner (Ed.), *Ethnomethodology: Selected readings* (pp. 180–193). Harmondsworth: Penguin Education.

Marsh, J. (2010). The relationship between home and school literacy practices. In R. Andrews & J. Hoffman (Eds.), *The International Handbook of English, Language and Literacy Teaching* (pp. 305–316). London: Routledge.

Marsh, J., & Bishop, J. (2012). Rewind and replay? Television and play in the 1950s/1960s and 2010s. *International Journal of Play, 1*(3), 279–291. doi:10.1080/21594937.2012.74 1431

Marsh, J., Brooks, G., Hughes, J., Ritchie, L., Roberts, S., & Wright, K. (2005). Digital beginnings: Young children's use of popular culture, media and new technologies. Sheffield, UK: Literacy Research Centre, University of Sheffield.

Marsh, J., Hannon, P., Lewis, M., & Ritchie, L. (2015). Young children's initiation into family literacy practices in the digital age. *Journal of Early Childhood Research*, 1–14. doi:10.1177/1476718X15582095

Mehan, H. (1993). Why I like to look: On the use of videotape as an instrument in educational research. In M. Schratz (Ed.), *Qualitative Voices in Educational Research* (pp. 93–105). London: Falmer Press.

Mondada, L. (2008). Using video for a sequential and multimodal analysis of social interaction: Videotaping institutional telephone calls. *Forum: Qualitative Social Research, 9*(3), Art. 39.

Mondada, L. (2012). Coordinating action and talk-in-interaction in and out of video games. In R. Ayaß & C. Gerhardt (Eds.), *The Appropriation of Media in Everyday Life* (pp. 231–270). Amsterdam: John Benjamins Publishing Company.

Peräkylä, A. (1997). Reliability and validity in research based on transcripts. In D. Silverman (Ed.), *Qualitative Research: Theory, method and practice* (pp. 201–220). London: Sage.

Peräkylä, A. (2016). Validity in qualitative research. In D. Silverman (Ed.), *Qualitative Research* (pp. 413–427). Los Angeles: Sage.

Piirainen-Marsh, A. (2010). Bilingual practices and the social organisation of video gaming activities. *Journal of Pragmatics, 42*(11), 3012–3030.

Piirainen-Marsh, A. (2012). Organising participation in video gaming activities. In R. Ayaß & C. Gerhardt (Eds.), *The Appropriation of Media in Everyday Life* (pp. 197–230). Amsterdam: John Benjamins Publishing Company.

Piirainen-Marsh, A., & Tainio, L. (2009). Collaborative game-play as a site for participation and situated learning of a second language. *Scandinavian Journal of Educational Research, 53*(2), 167–183.

Piirainen-Marsh, A., & Tainio, L. (2014). Asymmetries of knowledge and epistemic change in social gaming interaction. *The Modern Language Journal, 98*(4), 1022–1038.

Plowman, L., McPake, J., & Stephen, C. (2008). Just picking it up? Young children learning with technology at home. *Cambridge Journal of Education, 38*(3), 303–319.

Plowman, L., Stephen, C., & McPake, J. (2010a). *Growing Up With Technology: Young children learning in a digital world.* London: Routledge.

Plowman, L., Stephen, C., & McPake, J. (2010b). Supporting young children's learning with technology at home and in preschool. *Research Papers in Education, 25*(1), 93–113.

Pomerantz, A., & Fehr, B.J. (1997). Conversation analysis: An approach to the study of social action as sense making practices. In T.A. van Dijk (Ed.), *Discourse as Social Action: Discourse studies: A multidisciplinary introduction Volume 2* (Vol. 2, pp. 64–91). London: Sage.

Sacks, H. (1980). Button button who's got the button. *Sociological Inquiry, 50*(3–4), 318–327.

Sacks, H. (1984). Notes on methodology. In J.M. Atkinson & J. Heritage (Eds.), *Structures of Social Action: Studies in conversation analysis* (pp. 21–27). Cambridge: Cambridge University Press.

Sacks, H. (1995). *Lectures on Conversation* (G. Jefferson, Trans. Vol. I and II). Oxford, UK: Blackwell.

Sacks, H., Schegloff, E.A., & Jefferson, G. (1974). A simplest systematics for the organization of turn-taking for conversation. *Language, 50*, 696–735.

Scriven, B. (2016). Producing knowledge with digital 2 technologies in sibling interaction. In A. Bateman & A. Church (Eds.), *Children and Knowledge: Studies in Conversation Analysis.* Dordrecht: Springer.

Scriven, B., Edwards-Groves, C., & Davidson, C. (in press, 2017). A young child's use of multiple technologies in the social organisation of a pretend telephone conversation. In S. Danby, M. Fleer, C. Davidson, & M. Hatzigianni (Eds.), *Digital Childhoods.* Singapore: Springer.

Sheldon, A. (1996). You can be the baby brother, but you aren't born yet: Preschool girls' negotiation for power and access in pretend play. *Research on Language and Social Interaction, 29*(1), 57–80.

Sidnell, J. (2011). The epistemics of make-believe. In T. Stivers, L. Mondada, & J. Steensig (Eds.), *The Morality of Knowledge in Conversation* (pp. 131–155). Cambridge: Cambridge University Press.

Silverman, D. (2013). *Doing Qualitative Research* (4th ed.). London: Sage.

Sjöblom, B. (2011). *Gaming Interaction: Conversations and competences in internet cafes.* (PhD), University of Linköping, Linköping, Sweden. (No. 545.)

Sjöblom, B., & Aronsson, K. (2013). Participant categorisations of gaming competence: Noob and Imba as learner identities. In O. Erstad & J. Sefton-Green (Eds.), *Identity, Community, and Learning Lives in the Digital Age* (pp. 181–197). Cambridge: Cambridge University Press/

Sparrman, A., & Aarsand, P. (2009). Review and Commentary: Towards a critical approach on children and media. *Journal of Children and Media, 3*(3), 303–307.

Speier, M. (1974). The everyday world of the child. In B. Berger (ed.), *Readings in Sociology: A biographical approach* (pp. 55–60). New York: Basic Books.

Stephen, C., McPake, J., & Plowman, L. (2010). Digital technologies at home: The experiences of 3- and 4-year-olds in Scotland. In M. Clark & S. Tucker (Eds.), *Early Childhoods in a Changing World* (pp. 45–54). Stoke on Trent, England: Trentham Books.

Woolgar, S. (1988). Reflexivity is the ethnographer of the text. In S. Woolgar (Ed.), *Knowledge and Reflexivity: New frontiers in the sociology of knowledge* (pp. 14–34). London: Sage.

4. Performative family life

Tiina Mälkiä

INTRODUCTION

Over the last few decades, video recording has become one of the most illuminating ways of researching family life. By analysing video-recorded home life, researchers are able to access aspects of family interaction that are usually hidden from outsiders and sometimes also from the family members themselves (such as children's actions during their parents' absence). Family life is traditionally considered a private domain that has a hidden side or 'backstage' quality, with the family members as possessors of secret knowledge (Gubrium and Holstein, 1990). Therefore, researchers – including myself as a team member of the project 'Media, Family Interaction and Children's Well-Being' – feel privileged to gain access to family homes (e.g., MacLean, 2011; Ochs and Kremer-Sadlik, 2013).

Although using video recordings as data in family research has increased recently, family interaction research has concentrated on family practices such as shared meals (Ochs et al., 1996; Paugh and Izquierdo, 2009), cleaning practices (Fasulo et al., 2007) and homework (Wingard, 2006), or on aspects of interaction such as directives (Craven and Potter, 2010). There is a demand for research into how research subjects respond to the presence of cameras, and what kind of possibilities the video cameras create with their presence. In this chapter, I will meet this challenge and analyse how family members create expressive and moral performances for the cameras and researchers (see also Mälkiä, 2015).

The video data in our study were recorded with four stationary cameras located at strategic points in the home in order to get as comprehensive a picture as possible about the family interaction with and without media (there is more information about the data collection in Appendix 1). I will reflect on the benefits and constrains of our specific data at the end of this chapter. Next, I will review some basic concepts of performativity and the objectives in using these concepts in family interaction research.

PERFORMATIVE FAMILY

Erving Goffman (1959) introduced the theory of how performativity is a part of basically every interaction and performances are created in order to manage the impression that other people get from us. Goffman did not see performances as lies or deceptions, but as an inevitable social game with roles and settings. There may be differences in how much the performers themselves believe that the impression of reality he or she plays is true and in how much the audience believes the performance. However, people avoid open conflicts concerning the definitions of situations and agree with the 'working consensus' (Goffman, 1959, p. 10). A performance can be seen as a ceremony, 'as an expressive rejuvenation and reaffirmation of the moral values of the community', or at an individual level, as presenting an idealized view of the situation (Goffman, 1959, p. 35).

'Family' can be understood as a particular type of performance that is created for certain purposes. Gubrium and Holstein (1990) call family a 'practical accomplishment' construed from concrete challenges and responses to the challenges (ibid., p. 58). Families and their features, qualities and history are often illustrated in the descriptive practices of narratives. In narrative performance theory (Langellier and Peterson, 2006), storytelling is seen as one way of 'doing family', that is, constituting family identity in a performative way. Performativity is seen as a collection of strategic discursive practices through which certain interests are mobilized and served (ibid.).

In addition to narratives, another way of 'doing family' can be understood through family practices. By viewing families from the perspective of family practices, we can avoid thinking of families as merely biological, economic or legal entities. Instead, we can look at family members' regular everyday practices and analyse their own understanding of what their family is about (Morgan, 1996, 2011). Furthermore, certain practices that people perform may be looked at as 'displaying family', 'the process by which individuals, and groups of individuals, convey to each other and to relevant audiences that certain of their actions do constitute "doing family things" and thereby confirm that these relationships are "family" relationships' (Finch, 2007, p. 67). The difference between 'family practices' and 'displaying family' is that the latter is displayed more intensively and explicitly, especially in non-conventional family relationships such as non-heterosexual families or transnational kinship, and is not necessarily displayed in face-to-face interaction. The diversity and fluidity of contemporary family relationships make displaying the family necessary (Finch, 2007).

By studying these performances and displays of 'family' we can access the idealized views and moral values of the performers, as well as their cultural understandings of 'good' or 'normal' family life. Next, I will describe the data and methods used in this chapter, and then continue to the results.

DATA AND METHODS

The data for this chapter consist of interviews and the video-recorded home life of 26 Finnish families collected for the 'Media, Family Interaction and Children's Well-Being' project (more information about the data is available in Appendix 1). We chose families with either a five-year-old or a 12-year-old target child to get comparable data from two age groups. We recorded an afternoon and evening of one weekday in every research family with stationary, carefully placed video cameras. The cameras were situated to achieve maximum coverage to answer our research questions. One camera was pointed at the dinner table, usually in the kitchen. With this camera, we aimed to get media-free interaction data that could be compared with the other, media-saturated data. A second camera was pointed at the television and a third to the place where the people watching television were sitting, usually the sofa in the living room. A fourth camera recorded the computer that the target child ordinarily used. With these latter three cameras, we aimed at capturing most of the family's – and especially the target child's – media use. We collected a total of 665 hours of video data. The family members were interviewed before and after the video recording. In this chapter, I will use both the interviews and video recordings as data. I adopt a multimethod approach, combining conversation analysis, multimodal interaction analysis and discourse analysis. All personal details have been anonymized in the transcripts and all names have been changed.

EXPRESSIVE AND NORMATIVE PERFORMANCES

In the interview data are fragments of family narratives that can be analysed from the angle of performativity. However, in the video data we can see much more than narratives. Although the family members also talk about themselves and their family in the videos, the main focus of the analysis in this chapter are the *actions*. The analysis goes beyond talk, namely to the expressive performances that the family members display in front of the cameras, and to the normative performances that they produce for image control.

I separate expressive and normative performances analytically, since they appear to be quite different types of actions. By expressive performances, I mean the types of actions that children usually do in front of and for the cameras, such as flirting with the camera or performing dance, singing, or other kinds of demonstrations of skill. By normative performances, I refer to actions that are usually performed by parents in order to manage the impression of family life that is being recorded, such as telling their child to behave nicely or organizing family routines differently for the recordings. The second kinds of actions are often hidden and implicit, but with a little detective work, I was able to find examples in the data.

CHILDREN'S EXPRESSIVE PERFORMANCES FOR THE CAMERAS (AND VIEWERS)

Expressive performances were usually displayed by the children. They were performing for the cameras and/or potential audiences behind the cameras by displaying their skills or abilities, such as dancing, acting or turning off the television, as in Extract 1. These performances were usually executed individually, or in some cases with friends.

Example 1: Displaying Skills

Dinner is ready and the mother asks the children to come to eat. Six-year-old Sanna and her brother are playing with the cameras by grinning and talking at them and looking at themselves in the small viewfinder screen of the video camera. The mother asks the children to turn off the television, not addressing either of them directly. This first example (Picture 4.1), like most of the children's performances, is produced by an individual child for the camera.

Extract 1: Look at me

```
1  Mother:   no ni. (.) [telkkari kiinni ja syömään.
             okay. (.) [turn off the telly and come to eat.
2  Sanna:              [@sa fa faa faa zaana nanna nanna nanna
3            NAAA NAAAAAAA@. ((grinning for the camera))
4            ((the mother and brother are talking about the cameras))
5  Sanna:   ((talking to the camera))
             hei kato ku mä (.) kato ku (.) kato ku mä pistän ton
             hey look at how (.) look at how (.) look at me turning off that
6            teeveen kii ku mä oon HYVÄ pistään teeveetä kii.
             TV since I am GOOD at turning off the TV.
7            ((goes to turn off the TV))
```

Picture 4.1   Sanna turning off the television

8   Sanna: .hhh mä oon kuules ni̲i̲ hyvä et ku̲kaan ei usko mua (.) eiks ni̲i̲.
             .hhh listen I am s̲o̲ good that n̲o̲body believes me. (.) aren't I.
9   ((flirts at the camera and blows a kiss))

Although the mother has not specifically asked her, Sanna self-selects as
the one to turn off the TV, talking to the camera at the same time. She is
simultaneously 'doing being good' by obeying her mother, and turning
the action into an expressive performance of her skills. She is asking the
camera to look at her turning off the TV, although the TV is out of the
reach of the camera that she is talking to. After turning off the TV, she
comes back to the camera to give herself more praise and asks the camera
to acknowledge her skills at turning off the television. She flirts with the
camera by smiling and waving her hair. To complete her little performance,
she blows a kiss at the camera.

Sanna's performance is the typical way that the small children oriented
to the cameras. They often talked to them and looked at themselves on
the small viewfinder screen of the camera. Small children typically did not
orient to potential audiences behind the cameras, such as the researchers
looking at the recordings. They simply oriented to the camera as the viewer
and observed themselves while performing. Small children also acted as
if the cameras had minds of their own, as if they were sentient beings. In
Sanna's case, she asked the camera to look and listen to her and acknowledge her skills at turning off the television. Her flirting moves, facial expressions and kiss-blowing were also targeted to the camera as the audience.

Picture 4.2   Mikko's fight show

Example 2: Pretended Television Show

In the second example, eight-year-old Mikko is also orienting to the camera as an independent actor in his imaginary television show. Mikko has been expelled from the family living room after a dispute about playing a console game. Mikko wanted to play a game with his little sister, but the parents refused because Mikko 'always wins'. Mikko is very upset about this and goes to the bedroom to play with the computer. Before starting the game, he greets the camera and performs his imaginary show (Picture 4.2).

Extract 2: Fight show

1	Mikko:	AI TERVE. Täällä on Mikon (0.5) tappeluohjelma.
		OH HELLO. This is Mikko's (0.5) fight show.
2		oo. oo. hmm. hmmm. ((boxing in the air at the camera))
3		MITÄ (.) uhitteletko sä.
		WHAT (.) are you threatening me. ((looking aggressively at the camera))
4		turpa kii °kamera°.
		shut up °camera°. ((goes to play with a computer))

Mikko starts by greeting the camera (and viewers?) imitating a television show. He introduces the name of the 'show' as 'Mikko's fight show', defining the show as his own (Mikko's) and the type of the imaginary television show (fight show). He then performs the show by boxing in the air and staring aggressively at the camera. He is projecting an intentional mind onto the camera, imagining it as an antagonist, his opponent in the fight. He takes an initiative stance towards the camera's 'threatening' by challenging the imaginary behaviour and telling the camera to shut up. In this way, he becomes the winner of the fictitious fight, and this seems to calm his mood as he moves to play with the computer.

Mikko's performance seems to function as aggression alleviation, as he stages a fight situation in which he becomes the winner. After being upset by the dispute with his parents, he also gets imagined attention from the camera. By framing his shadow boxing as a show, he also indicates that the fight is not 'real', but instead fiction in a familiar format, a TV show. Like Sanna before, Mikko seems to talk and act for the camera, not addressing any potential viewers. Older children, like the 12-year-old friends in the next example, often expressed their awareness of potential viewers, especially the researchers that may watch the recordings later.

Example 3: Cheerleading Stunts for the 'Guys'

Marja is at home with her two girlfriends. They come up with the idea of performing cheerleading stunts for the camera. They do the tricks and giggle, occasionally looking at the cameras (Picture 4.3), until Marja's mother comes home. After performing the stunts, the girls comment on how they might look in the recordings.

Picture 4.3   Cheerleading stunts

Extract 3: Cheer 1

1 Marja: miettikää miltä toi oikeesti näyttää noille kameroille.
            think about what that really looks like for the cameras.
2   miettikää miltä se näyttää ku ne tyypit kattoo sitä.
            think about what it looks like when [those guys watch it.
3 Aino: [Hei Taina (.) kato mikä
                                                 [hey Taina (.) look at the
4   temppu me on keksitty.
5   stunt we've come up with.
            (the girls start showing the stunt, fall against the wall and laugh))
6 Mother: HEI (.) HEI NYT MÄ SUUTUN.
            HEY (.) HEY NOW I'M GETTING ANGRY.
7   (2.0)
8 Mother: tuuppas Marja tänne.
            come here Marja.

Marja starts to comment on what their stunts may look like in the recordings, specifying the audience as 'those guys/types'. Previously, she talked about the recordings with her mother in the context of the mother watching the recordings (the families received copies of selected moments of the recordings), but here she introduces another audience, the researchers. She uses the Finnish word *tyypit* (types), which refers to unspecified individuals with no gender reference. Therefore, the audience she talks about may be anyone at the university looking at the recordings. Here we can see an explicit reference to a potential audience that the older children orient to and perform for. Friend Aino invites Marja's mother to watch their stunt. Aino and Marja start performing the stunt, but they fail and fall against the wall with a loud bang. The mother expresses her disapproval and calls Marja to the hall to be upbraided.

Extract 4: Cheer 2

1 Mother: mitä mä oon sanonu niistä tempuista.
            what have I told you about the stunts.
2   (2.5)
3 Mother: mä oon sanonu aika monta kertaa et sä teet vaan semmosia
            I have told quite many times that you only do stunts
4   temppuja et sä oot turvassa. nyt mä en rupee ollenkaan
            in which you are safe. now I'm not having this at all.
5   toho .hhh ja sitte tota toinen juttu on se että kamerat (0.5)
            at all .hhh and then another thing is that the cameras (0.5)
6   ei oo täällä sen takia? että niihin niinku tehään jotain
            temppujah,
            are not here? for you to perform like some stuntsh,
7   vaan ne on täällä sen takia et meil on ihan normi arki ja
            they are here for us to have a normal everyday life and

8   niillä niinku katotaan et mikä on sun mediakäyttäytymine.
           they are like used to watching what your media behaviour is like.
9 Marja: okay? kokay?

Here, Marja's mother asks her to move 'backstage', away from the cameras, to lecture her about the stunts. The mother therefore constructs two areas for two different modes of action: in front of the cameras, 'the front', using Goffman's (1959) terms, for presenting 'normal everyday life' and 'backstage' for giving instructions about what kind of behaviour is appropriate to show for the cameras. The mother expresses her stance towards the cheerleading stunts by reminding Marja about the importance of safety when performing tricks, indicating that the stunt that the girls showed her was not safe. She also explicates her view of the purpose of the research and recording, namely that the cameras are there to watch Marja's 'media behaviour'. From the mother's point of view, constructing a performance for the cameras is not appropriate behaviour and not 'normal everyday life', which she indicates to be what the researchers want of the recordings. While the girls wish to play with the cameras and the images that they show the researchers, the mother seems to want to show 'authentic' and 'normal' life in the recordings. This brings us to the types of performances that the parents display, namely normative performances. In the previous extract, the mother is trying to manage the image of family life being recorded and the appropriate behaviour in front of the cameras. These kinds of normative performatives are also present in the following examples.

PARENTS' NORMATIVE PERFORMANCES FOR THE RESEARCHERS

Parents did not arrange dance performances or (usually) talk to the cameras, but they nevertheless conducted performative actions to control and modify the impression of their family and home life. According to Goffman (1959), managing the impression is the main goal of constructing performances in interaction with other people. Performances in interaction are often implicit and carefully hidden (see Goffman, 1959, p. 8 on 'calculated unintentionality'), but sometimes, with careful detective work, we may find evidence of performative actions. Although the interaction with the researchers in the context of recording home life for research purposes is limited and unilateral, the parents seemed to wish to give an impression that their children and family life were 'good', 'positive' or 'normal'.[1] The most prevalent means to achieve this goal were either modifying the children's behaviour or altering family routines.

By examining these normative performances, I glean information about what the parents consider negative ('bad', 'abnormal', 'undesirable') or positive ('good', 'normal', 'desirable') according to their impression management.

One of the most common ways of managing the recorded family life was to dictate the children's behaviour in front of the cameras. In Extract 4, I showed how the mother told her daughter not to perform stunts in front of the camera, since the cameras were there to record 'normal everyday life'. In another family, the father told his son not to display football tricks in front of the camera, since 'this is not filmmaking'. These parents tried to modify their children's behaviour from 'unnatural' acting for the cameras to 'normal' family life, ignoring the cameras. Another way of modifying children's behaviour was to tell them to behave nicely because of the cameras, when the 'normal for them' would be 'bad' behaviour like cursing, name calling or tantrum-throwing.

Example 4: Correcting Child's Behaviour

In the next extract, five-year-old Väinö has called his little brother 'a poo bum'. His mother asks him to come to another room (away from the cameras) to be corrected. Although I could not see the interaction in the cameras, I could hear what happened.

Extract 5: Think how you talk here

1	Mother:	Väinö tuus käyt täällä.
		Väinö come here.
2	Väinö:	mittä.
		where.
3		(2.0) ((Väinö goes to his mother))
4	Väinö:	mitä.
		what.
5	Mother:	nyt kun on noi kamerat täällä ni mieti vähän millä lailla puhut
		now that the cameras are here, think a little how you talk
6		täällä. et rupee niinku iskälle ja äitille ( ) kiukuttelemaan.
		here. don't like throw a tantrum for dad and mum.
7		ne kaikki kuuluu niissä kameroissa.
		they can all be heard on the cameras.
8		nyt yrität sitte olla vähän niinku siivosti.
		now you will try to be a little like polite.

The mother tells Väinö that he should consider the way he talks in front of the cameras because everything can be heard (by the researchers). We can deduce that talking nicely is perhaps not usual for Väinö, from the mother's words 'now that the cameras are here' in line 5 and 'now' in line 8. The mother directs Väinö to behave nicely for the cameras (and potential audiences), and, unlike in the above examples, to take the cameras into account and modify his actions from his normal behaviour. In other words, the mother conducts a normative performance to manage the impression of her son's behaviour and their family life.

Parents in our research families value family meals, but for practical reasons do not always manage to eat together (Mälkiä and Arminen, 2015). In the interviews, parents talked about 'trying to' and 'aimed to' eat together every day and regret not being able to do so (Mälkiä and Arminen, 2015, pp. 136–7). Sometimes we can see a discrepancy between what the parents report in the interviews and what we can see in the recordings. Children have a tendency to 'reveal' their parents' performative actions and implicitly or explicitly disclose the actual routines of their family.

Example 5: Compulsory Family Meal

In the next example, the family is about to start eating dinner. Twelve-year-old Jere is playing a computer game and, despite continuous summons from his mother, does not show any intention of stopping the game and going to the kitchen for dinner. The father takes his turn to get Jere to disengage from the game.

Extract 6: We are eating together now

1	Father:	JERE SYÖMÄÄN!
		JERE COME TO EAT! ((shouting from kitchen to living room))
2	Jere:	@MIKS.@
		@WHY.@ ((irritated tone))
3	Father:	se on pakko. nyt on yhteinen ruoka.
		it's compulsory. now we are having a shared meal.
4		(15.0) ((faint conversation in the kitchen, father comes to Jere))
5	Father:	°nyt syömään Jere.° (2.0) hei. (1.0) oikeesti.
		°come to eat now Jere.° (2.0) hey. (1.0) really.
6		(17.0) ((Jere continues playing))
7	Father:	°no ni.°
		°come on.°
8	Jere:	mh.
9	Father:	NYT!
		NOW!
10	Jere:	mul ei oo nälkä,
		I'm not hungry,
11	Father:	eiku nyt syödään yhdessä.
		No we are eating together now.

It takes several minutes after this extract before Jere finally goes to kitchen, but here we will concentrate on what Extract 6 and the mother's interview together disclose to us. In the interviews, the mother told us about their dinner routines: they are 'trying to have' dinner together but there is only one day a week when they actually all eat together. The family has four children and both parents work outside the home. In Extract 6, by asking 'why' to his father's summons, Jere is implying that the family dinner is not an obligatory routine that he should join. The father responds by telling Jere that joining dinner *is* compulsory, explicating that 'now' they are having a dinner together. Jere still does not comply with his parents' demands and continues playing the game. The father comes to Jere, stands behind him as Jere continues playing and goes on persuading Jere to come to family dinner in line 5. Jere continues playing and does not respond to his father. In line 8, Jere proffers a small, absent sound, but does not really reply to his father. The father seems to get annoyed and continues with the command 'NOW' in a loud voice. Now Jere replies, offering an excuse as to why he does not want to – or have to – come to dinner at the moment: he claims not to be hungry. The father overrides this claim ('no') and tells Jere that they are having a family meal 'now' and Jere has to participate whether he wants to or not.

There are several indications of the performative nature of the family meal. The father stresses that joining the family dinner on this occasion is compulsory, which indicates that eating together is not a self-evident, everyday routine. The father also uses word 'now' on several occasions (lines 3, 5, 9 and 11). This also indicates that this particular family meal is different from the routine. Jere also demonstrates his understanding that the family meal is not (usually) obligatory by asking 'why' (line 2) and delivering an excuse for not coming to dinner (line 10). These conversational clues together with the mother's answer in the interview lead to the impression that the family meal has been arranged especially for the cameras and researchers. Arranging a family dinner can be seen as a normative performance to give a certain impression of the family life, such as closeness, routines, and traditional values, which are usually associated with eating together.

Example 6: Rare Family Dinner

The last example shows another family that has arranged a family dinner especially for the recordings, and one of the children revealing this with an innocent comment. The family of five is about to start dinner, and they are placing food on their plates from the stove.

Extract 7: Funny

1	Sari:	tämmönen kai.
		I think something like this. ((pointing to something in the sink))
2		(0.6)
3	Jusu:	hassua kun me syödään yhdessä.
		funny that we eat together.
4		(2.5)
5	Mother:	m-hm.
6	Jusu:	no [on ku ↑ei me olla ↑ennen [syöty.
		well [it is since ↑we haven't eaten [↑↑before.
7	Sari:	[äiti. [äiti.
		[mommy. [mommy.
8	Mother:	ku ei me olla koskaan samaan aikaan kotona.
		because we are never home at the same time.
9		(0.8)
10	Sari:	äiti,
		mommy,
11	Mother:	mutta nyt syödään.
		but now we do.
12	Sari:	äiti voitsä tulla tähän näin (.) niin jos mää meen toho.
		mommy can you come here (.) if I go there.

At the beginning of Extract 7, the mother and ten-year-old Sari are talking about dirty plates. Eight-year-old Jusu starts commenting on the rarity of family dinners. He frames eating together as being 'funny', implying that it is something unusual and odd. The mother looks at Jusu, looking a little annoyed about her son's comment and responds with a conversation token (line 5) with an austere quality in her voice. Jusu seems to apprehend his mother's mood and starts to justify his comment. He claims that they haven't eaten together before, defending his comment about eating together being 'funny'. In line 8, the mother implicitly confirms Jusu's claim of never eating together by proffering an explanation for the absence of family meals: the family is never home at the same time. In line 11, the mother verifies the extraordinary nature of this family meal by stating 'but now we do' (eat together).

In the interview, the mother stated that the family 'tries to have two meals a day', implying that they eat together. Extract 7, however, shows that eating together is at least a rare – if non-existent – event in the everyday life of the family. As in the previous family, this family also seems to have arranged a special family meal for the cameras, a kind of normative performance for the researchers. I have now shown examples of children's performances for the cameras and parents' performative actions in arranging their 'normal' family life in order to manage the impression of the family for the researchers. I now move to draw conclusions and reflections on the unique data.

CONCLUSIONS AND REFLECTIONS ON THE DATA

In this chapter, I have presented two types of performative behaviour. In the first type, children produce an individual performance for the camera, either to show their abilities or to play-act being on a television show. These performances resemble artistic performances such as theatre or music performances, or some media content that the child has seen. The intended audience in these performances is at least the video camera, but older children were also able to speculate about other audiences, such as the researchers watching the recordings. For children, the video cameras seemed to function simply as a new thing that they could play with – in other words, the children used the cameras as instruments for their own purposes.

The parents, on the other hand, produced less obvious normative performative actions, which were executed 'backstage' in order to manage the impression that would be recorded. They modified either the conduct of their children or the family's routines in a more favourable direction to perform 'normal' or 'good' family life. Although executed 'backstage', the effects were intended to be visible at the 'front'; the children behaved better (at least for a moment) or the family had a rare shared meal. Usually, these types of normative performances are not accessible to outsiders, and we were lucky to capture these cracks in the facades of family life.

When discussing normative performances to manage impressions, I do not want to say that these parents are trying to lie or deceive. I consider these kinds of actions as ordinary things that people do when they receive guests into their homes. It is ordinary that people want to show a 'better side' of themselves, their family and their homes to others. Usually, when people expect guests, they clean the house a little better, prepare special food, dress better, and tell their children to behave themselves. The normative performances shown are the same kind of things; the parents treated the cameras and the researchers behind them (figuratively) as guests in their homes. Analytically, we can treat these kind of actions as rich sources of cultural understandings of what the parents consider to be 'good' or 'normal' family life, and this special, comprehensive data allows us to analyse them.

Compared to previous studies on family interaction, the data collection method is unique. Instead of researchers running around the family with their cameras (see Ochs and Kremer-Sadlik, 2013) we used stationary video cameras and the researchers were not present during recording. This allowed us to get special data in which the obtrusive nature of recording itself was minimized. Many family members told us in the interviews that they forgot that the cameras were there, and on many occasions we could see this was true. On the other hand, as shown before, the presence of the cameras allowed some specific actions to occur, such as the children's expressive performances. Just by being there, the cameras inspired the children to use them for their own purposes, to play with them, create little expressive performances, and admire themselves on the screen. On the meta-level, the parents also used the cameras to create a certain image of their family life. For both the children and the parents, the stationary video cameras allowed a wider agency concerning their ability to determine what was recorded and what kind of image they created for the recordings (and for the researchers). The family members were able to create expressive performances that they could not do without the cameras in their everyday life. On the other hand, they were able to control what was recorded simply by moving to another room with no cameras to avoid being recorded, as some teenagers did. Despite being under examination as research objects, they were able to use spatial and interactional resources to determine and manage the boundaries between private and public spheres, and remain active, self-governing subjects.

NOTE

1. We use these definitions only to describe the stance that the family members display in their interaction, not our own evaluations.

REFERENCES

Craven, A. and J. Potter (2010), 'Directives: Entitlement and contingency in action', *Discourse Studies*, **12** (4), 419–42.

Fasulo, A., H. Loyd and V. Padiglione (2007), 'Children's socialization into cleaning practices: A cross-cultural perspective', *Discourse and Society*, **18** (1), 11–33.

Finch, J. (2007), 'Displaying families', *Sociology*, **41** (1), 65–81.

Goffman, E. (1959), *The Presentation of Self in Everyday Life*, New York: Doubleday.

Gubrium, J.F. and J.A. Holstein (1990), *What Is Family?* Mountain View, CA: Mayfield Publishing Company.

Langellier, K.M. and E.E. Peterson (2006), 'Narrative performance theory: Telling stories, doing family', in D.O. Braithwaite and L.A. Baxter (eds), *Engaging Theories in Family Communication. Multiple Perspectives*, London: Sage, pp. 99–114.

MacLean, A. (2011), 'Unfamiliar places and other people's spaces: Reflections on the practical challenges of researching families in their homes', in L. Jamieson, R. Simpson and R. Lewis (eds), *Researching Families and Relationships. Reflections on Process*, London and New York: Palgrave Macmillan.

Morgan, D.H.J. (1996), *Family Connections. An Introduction to Family Studies*, Cambridge, UK: Polity Press.

Morgan, D.H.J. (2011), *Rethinking Family Practices*, Basingstoke, UK: Palgrave Macmillan.

Mälkiä, T. (2015), 'Tutkijan kamerat kodeissa' [Researchers' cameras in homes], in A.R. Lahikainen, T. Mälkiä and K. Repo (eds), *Media lapsiperheessä*, Tampere: Vastapaino, pp. 55–79.

Mälkiä, T. and I. Arminen (2015), 'Perheruokailu, media ja sosialisaatio' [Family dining, media and socialization], in A.R. Lahikainen, T. Mälkiä and K. Repo (eds), *Media lapsiperheessä*, Tampere: Vastapaino, pp. 132–56.

Ochs, E. and T. Kremer-Sadlik (eds) (2013), *Fast-Forward Family: Home, Work and Relationships in Middle-Class America*, Berkeley and Los Angeles, CA: University of California Press.

Ochs, E., C. Pontecorvo and A. Fasulo (1996), 'Socializing taste', *Ethnos*, **61** (1–2), 7–46.

Paugh, A. and C. Izquierdo (2009), 'Why is this a battle every night? Negotiating food and eating in American dinnertime interaction', *Journal of Linguistic Anthropology*, **19** (2), 185–204.

Wingard, L. (2006), 'Parents' inquiries about homework: The first mention', *Text and Talk*, **26** (4/5), 573–96.

5. Children's media use: the perspective of time use

Katja Repo and Satu Valkonen

INTRODUCTION

In this chapter, we approach children's media use from the perspective of time use. Time use resonates with and reflects the overall structures of societies, as well general attitudes and norms. Societal changes, such as technological development and digitalization, influence our social practices: they change the way we do things. For example, the phone was at first used to make and receive calls, mobile phones added texting, taking photos, and simple gameplay, and smartphones have a multitude of different features. Digitalization has changed the way we interact with each other, what we can do, with whom, when, and for how long. Technological development has thus had a vigorous impact on the time-use patterns of children and families. Therefore, in order to understand the daily life of children in the digital era, it is essential to study their time use.

The aim of this chapter is to present the main trends of media-related time use among children in Finland, the USA, and Great Britain at the beginning of the twenty-first century. In addition, we discuss what kind of media environments homes offer to children, and how the media use of children is related to time spent alone, with family members, and with friends. Much of the debate here focuses on issues of access and the amount of time children are spending with new media. We will show that many children have access to new technology at home. However, this does not necessarily mean that new media are used heavily, and, due to the availability of technology in Western welfare countries, it is not always necessary to have one's own device to access the Internet and spend time with media. As Buckingham (2006) has justly pointed out, access is not only a matter of the technology available to children; it is also a question of the digital literacy required to use new media in an appropriate manner.

The chapter begins by examining how homes as media environments have changed over the last few years. It continues by discussing parenting and childhood in the digital era. Thereafter, it provides an overview of children's time use with media. Finally, we pay attention to media use in relation to time spent alone or together with family members.

We realize that studying children's media time has become increasingly challenging due to media convergence. Questionnaires and time use surveys usually examine children's time use in relation to certain media, such as how long children spend watching television or how much they use their phones. As mentioned, using a smartphone can entail a number of things – for example, watching television or listening to music – and thus it makes more sense to explore the time-use trends of media in general. We also argue that although contextual issues have an impact on children's media use, children in Western societies are still witnessing the same trends and changes. These overwhelming trends and changes in children's lives and time use are our primary focus here.

THE HOME AS A MEDIA ENVIRONMENT

Many Western societies have faced a change in children's time use away from time spent outside the home towards time spent primarily in the home. The home has become a zone of safe play and exploration for children, and as a result there is increasing pressure on families with children to provide children with media-rich environments (Burdette and Whitaker, 2005; Karsten and van Vliet, 2006; Livingstone, 2007, 2009). Importantly, children themselves also perceive the home as an important – and sometimes even the primary – media-use environment and context (Livingstone et al., 2001, 2011; Noppari, 2014).

In effect, contemporary families with children possess divergent technical tools. Despite the increasing varieties of modern media devices, television has maintained its central role of most families' media environments (Wartella et al., 2013; Rideout, 2015). At the beginning of the 2000s, almost all children in Finland, the UK, and the USA had access to television in their home. In Finland, 93 per cent of families with children (10–14 years old) owned a TV set in 2009–10 (Repo and Nätti, 2015a). In the USA, fewer than 1 per cent of families with children under eight years old did not have a TV set in 2012 (Wartella et al., 2013, p. 12). Similarly, in the UK 100 per cent of 3–4-year-olds and 99 per cent of 5–15-year-olds had a TV set at home in 2015 (Ofcom, 2015, p. 42).

In recent years, it has also become more common for families to possess several media devices. Taking television as an example, it has become evident that families that own just one TV set are very rare. In 2009–10, almost 40 per cent of Finnish families with children (10–14-year-olds) owned two TV sets, and a third of families owned at least three TV sets

(Repo and Nätti, 2015a). In the USA, as many as half of families with children under eight years had three or more TV sets, and a quarter of families had four or more TV sets in the home in 2012 (Wartella et al., 2013, p. 12).

Thus, for families with children, the TV set is one of the most commonly owned media devices. Many children also have access to a TV set in their own bedroom. In Finland, almost half of the children aged between 10 and 12 years old have the opportunity to watch television in their own bedroom (Suoninen, 2013, p. 17). A recent British study, however, shows that the number of children with a TV set in their own bedroom has actually declined. The phenomenon can be explained by the aforementioned fact that an increasing number of children are using different portable devices to watch television in the UK (Ofcom, 2015, p. 26), Finland (Noppari, 2014), and the USA (Wartella et al., 2013; Rideout, 2015).

Computers can also be regarded as everyday media devices. An increasing number of families with children own one or more computers. In the USA, almost 80 per cent of families with 3–17-year-old children had a computer in the home in 2013 (Child Trends DataBank, 2015, p. 3). In Finland, 92 per cent of families with children (10–14 years old) owned a computer in 2009–10, with 65 per cent owning at least two (Repo and Nätti, 2015a). In the UK, 86 per cent of children aged 5–15 years live in a household with a desktop, laptop, or netbook, and 81 per cent have a tablet in the home (Ofcom, 2015, p. 33).

Just as computers have established a stable position in the home, the number of children using tablet computers has also risen dramatically. In effect, tablets have quickly penetrated the market and the home: as prices have fallen, tablets are no longer a novelty. They are extremely popular with families with small children, probably because so many teens have their own smartphones and can more easily use their phones when outside the home (Rideout, 2015, p. 57).

In fact, portable devices are becoming the preferred media choice for children because of their mobility, screen size, interactive capability, opportunities to stream content, and decreasing costs (Kabali et al., 2015, p. 1045). In the UK, more than half of 3–4-year-olds and three-quarters of 12–15-year-olds used a tablet in 2015 (Ofcom, 2015, p. 6). In the USA, 42 per cent of households with children under eight years old owned a tablet in 2012 (Wartella et al., 2013), and in 2015 as many as 80 per cent of 10–12-year-olds had a tablet in the home. Importantly, 53 per cent of these 10–12-year-olds had their own tablets (Rideout, 2015). Almost all American children under four years old use mobile devices, and most start before their first birthday (Kabali et al., 2015). Tablets are also common in Finland. According to the Children's Media Barometer 2013, over one-third of families with a child under eight years old owned a tablet (Suoninen, 2014, p. 13).

Smartphones have also widely penetrated families with young children. In the USA, seven in ten families with a child under eight years old possessed a smartphone in 2013 (Wartella et al., 2013). In 2015, eight in ten families with a child over eight years old had at least one smartphone (Rideout, 2015, pp. 57–8). However, these newer mobile devices are not commonly owned by young children themselves (Wartella et al., 2013). In the UK, only 5 per cent of children aged 5–7 years had their own mobile phone in 2015. However, the number of children possessing their own phone increases with age: 35 per cent of children aged 8–11 and 77 per cent of children aged 12–15 had one in 2015. Altogether, 58 per cent of British children aged 5–15 had access to a mobile phone at home in 2015, whether it was their own or someone else's (Ofcom, 2015, pp. 38, 48).

The Internet – along with TV sets, computers, and smartphones – can be regarded as everyday technology. The speed of Internet diffusion into the home has been distinctive (Livingstone, 2009; Repo and Nätti, 2015a). As Rice and Haythornthwaite (2006) report, the Internet reached 30 per cent of American households in just seven years – a level of penetration that took as long as 17 years for television and 38 years for the telephone. As homes acquire more digital technologies, and as those technologies become more portable and diverse, ever younger children are using the Internet at home (see Livingstone et al., 2015, p. 5). Almost all British children had Internet access at home in 2015. Whereas only six in ten (61 per cent) of 8–11-year-old children had access to the Internet at home in 2005, the corresponding figure was nine in ten (91 per cent) in 2015 (Ofcom, 2015). The same trend is also noticeable in Finland. In 2009–10, almost all Finnish families with small children aged 10–14 years old had Internet access. The penetration of Internet access has been very rapid, since in 1999–2000 only half of Finnish families with children of the same age had Internet access in the home (Repo and Nätti, 2015a).

Although many children live in homes with a range of digital tools, the digital equality gap is an unfortunate reality for many children. As such, children in lower-income families are still significantly less likely than their wealthier peers to live in homes with digital technologies. In the case of tablets, there is a big gap between higher- and lower-income families, especially in the USA (Wartella et al., 2013, pp. 13–14). In addition, in the USA lower-income teens are much less likely to have their own smartphones, and one in ten lower-income teens only has dial-up Internet at home, compared with zero in ten higher-income teens (Rideout, 2015, p. 17).

CHILDHOOD AND PARENTING IN THE DIGITAL AGE

As a social category, childhood has grown in importance (e.g., Alanen, 1992; Jenks, 1996; James and Prout, 2015). We are more aware of children's rights, their well-being, and overall status in Western societies. Nevertheless, the contemporary relationship between adults and children is still dualistic: it simultaneously comprises elements of nostalgia and futurity. Within the realm of nostalgia, parents try to hold onto a romantic conception of childhood and want to protect the purity of their children. Futurity, conversely, represents more the conception of an active and participating child (Wyness, 2006). There is thus a tendency to understand childhood in terms of risks and protection. Besides such an approach, children are increasingly regarded as participants in and active members of society (Wyness, 2006; Strandell, 2012).

This dualism in the general constructions of childhood resonates with the discussion of children's media use. Some parents may even assess the increased use of media devices as a threat to a 'proper' and 'natural' childhood. The discussion on children's media use maintains a promise of the better future, while simultaneously raising fears about change. This ambiguity particularly concerns the impact of new media on children's lives. On the one hand, new media are seen to offer children new ways to learn and participate, and on the other hand, they are seen to provide access to harmful and intimidating content. As such, children are viewed 'both as the avant-garde of the media users and as the ones who are most at risk from new media' (Buckingham, 2006, p. 75; see also Buckingham, 2000).

Children and young people are viewed, amongst other things, as 'digital natives' (Prensky, 2001), the 'digital generation' (Buckingham, 2006) or as the 'post-modern generation' (Green and Bigum, 1993); they are competent users of digital technology and their time use and identity are influenced by the digital environment in which they live. These new developments – and the contrasting perspectives involved – create complex dilemmas for parenting. Parents may feel that they should be exercising greater control and authority over media use (Buckingham, 2006, p. 77). On the other hand, parents are quite used to giving children mobile devices very early on, especially when doing the housework or trying to keep their children calm (see Kabali et al., 2015, p. 1047). Parents use media as a resource to control children's behaviour and to manage everyday family life in general.

It is therefore not surprising that the future of media devices depends on how well they are suited to daily family routines (Pasquier, 2001, p. 161). In fact, parenting styles have an essential role in what devices are used and for how long. Thus, it makes sense to say that parents establish a media environment in the home (Wartella et al., 2013, p. 26). Parents monitor young children's media use in particular and they have rules that place restrictions on how digital devices are used (Chaudron, 2015; see also Valkonen, 2012). With regard to school-aged children, most parents in the USA favour talk as a mediation strategy, and such active mediation is also the most popular strategy adopted by European parents. However, as the EU KIDS Online's analysis shows, the cross-national variations in parental mediation are considerable. The Nordic countries exercise the most active mediation, whereas in the UK and several Central and Southern European countries, restrictive mediation is preferred. Eastern European countries apply all types of parental mediation, but it can be passive as well. It has been argued that the parents' own familiarity with digital media define the type of regulation and monitoring (Livingstone et al., 2015). One can therefore say that media evoke different parenting styles: there are media-centric parents, media-moderate parents, and media-light parents (Wartella et al., 2013, pp. 7–8).

Generally, parents see digital technologies as positive but challenging; for example, in the USA parents are more likely to say technology has a positive rather than a negative effect on children's creativity and educational skills, but they still think that new mobile devices have not made parenting any easier (Rideout, 2015). In the context of the family, children's media use is often negotiated, discussed, and controlled by parents. Despite this, it has also been maintained that media use among families goes beyond regulation and mediation (Wartella et al., 2013). Livingstone et al. (2015, p. 24) have argued that the type of medium, form of engagement, and amount of time spent with any technology is related to domestic issues. Thus, the meaning of a digital device is not fixed; it depends on the availability and the location of devices in the household, as well as overall family dynamics, media use habits, and rules. Media technologies are also intertwined with parenting practices in such a way that media and technology use has become a new family affair (Wartella et al., 2013, p. 30). In all, media use can be a shared activity that produces new kinds of interaction and communication between parents and children. Thus far, little attention has been paid to the role of parenting in the use of digital technologies by children (Ólafsson et al., 2014).

MEDIA-RELATED TIME USE

The ideal of private family time continues to be salient as a cultural ideal, but a variety of forces make the realization of this goal difficult. One of these forces is technology, which plays a major role in reshaping the meanings of family time (Mesh, 2006). Media have come to occupy a central position in the time use of children; children and young people in particular are usually those who are the earliest and most active users of information and communication technologies (Livingstone, 2009). For example, in Finland, when computers began to enter private homes in the 1980s, their most common and active users were young boys. As such, in the family context, children played a pioneering role in introducing computers into the daily life practices of families (Repo and Nätti, 2015a). Nowadays, children are in daily contact with a wide range of digital tools. Children are also interested in new technologies and they use them willingly for entertainment purposes.

Children may start using media devices at a very early age. Even one-year-olds are used to watching television and visual recordings as well as playing digital games. However, parents or other adults normally supervise small children's media use (Suoninen, 2011; Valkonen, 2012). Parents may also report using new media technology with their children, but this 'joint media engagement' drops off markedly when children get older and children can engage with media independently (Wartella et al., 2013, p. 7; Noppari, 2014).

Despite all the new types of media available to children today, television continues to be one of the most popular and widely used among young children. In the USA, 75 per cent of 8–12-year-olds say they watch television (Rideout, 2015, p. 33) and in the UK, children aged 5–15 spend more time watching television than using other media (Ofcom, 2015). Likewise, in Finland, small children still watch more television than use other media devices (Repo and Nätti, 2015a). However, as children get older, they tend to spend more time online than watching television.

It clearly appears that digital media use is still trailing behind traditional media use. However, watching television can mean a variety of things. One can watch television programmes or films as they are broadcasted, or by time shifting, recording or watching them on demand or online. One can also watch videos on websites; these can range from funny cat videos to tutorials and music videos. One can watch television on a TV set, computer, tablet, or smartphone, so watching television is not what it used to be. However, audio-visual media content is still the most popular and most used media for children and teenagers (Rideout, 2015). In Finland the most popular use of the Internet among the youngest children is to watch programmes via YouTube or on-demand services. The Children's Media Barometer 2013 interestingly shows that many parents did not perceive this as Internet use (Suoninen, 2014, p. 26); perhaps parents perceive this as just a new way of watching television, and the same could also be true among children and teens.

The changes in the ways children value media can be studied by specifying what children would buy with their own money, what they would like to have as a birthday present or by analysing the activities children say they would miss the most if the activity were taken away (d'Haenens, 2001). According to an Ofcom report (2015), in 2005 both 8–11-year-old and 12–15-year-old British children reported that they would miss watching television the most. In 2015, the TV set still comes first for younger children, but the mobile phone has overtaken the TV set by a considerable margin among 12–15-year-olds (Ofcom, 2015, p. 26).

Despite these findings, children and young people are generally spending an increasing amount of time on their computers and online and respectively less watching television. The trend is especially visible among young people (15–19 years old). In Finland, the time young people spent on computers exceeded the time they spent watching television at the beginning of the 2000s (Repo and Nätti, 2015a). In the UK, the amount of time 8–11-year-old children spend online more than doubled between 2005 and 2015: from 4.4 hours a week in 2005 to 11.1 hours in 2015. In comparison, the time spent watching television has increased just slightly: from 13.2 hours in 2005 to 14.8 hours in 2015 (Ofcom, 2015, p. 5).

It is essential to highlight that time spent with media does not preclude children or parents from doing something else at the same time. For example, parents can make dinner or clean the house at the same time as browsing social media sites, children can listen to music, chat with their friends, and look up information while doing their homework. Media-related time use does not necessarily – indeed, rarely does – refer to time spent only with media, or even with one specific form of media. Due to media multitasking, it is challenging to set media-related time use in relation to the tradition understanding of time use. For example, eight hours of media use a day does not mean that children do not do anything other than sleep, eat and stare at a screen (Rideout, 2015).

It should be noted that children also enjoy non-digital activities (Chaudron, 2015). Technology plays an essential role in children's lives, but its use is balanced with many other activities, such as outdoor play, play with toys and play with friends (Livingstone et al., 2015). Already, young children's lives are increasingly played out in online as well as offline spaces (Marsh, 2005). However, Finnish studies also show that while children's media-related time use has increased, their time spent on exercising, studying, reading and socializing with friends has simultaneously decreased (Miettinen and Rotkirch, 2012; Myllyniemi, 2014; Pääkkönen, 2014).

ALONE OR TOGETHER WITH MEDIA

Many media devices begin their domestic careers first being used collectively, but, as the price of the technology decreases and the mobility of devices becomes feasible, they move to more individualized use, often in more unsupervised spaces (Livingstone, 2009). Flichy (1995) referred to the phenomenon as 'living together separately' long before online mobile technologies were so prevalent in households. Some argue that new media technology is pulling family members apart, whereas others in turn claim that digital devices are actually increasing family connectedness by providing family members unprecedented opportunities to connect with each other.

On the one hand, media seem to unite the family. Korkeamäki et al. (2015) have noted that families with young children may be engaged in digital activities together, either playing the same game or watching audio-visual programmes together. For example, watching television is one of the most common activities Finnish families with children do together, and families with small children in particular spend time together watching television (Repo and Nätti, 2015b). It has also been noticed that although access to new media is spreading rapidly, parents still rely widely on television for their family's entertainment and shared family activities (Wartella et al., 2013, p. 30). Among American parents, watching television or films together at home was the most commonly reported media-related activity that families enjoy doing together. This was followed by using a computer, tablet, or smartphone and playing video games together. More precisely, about three in ten American parents report that when their children are watching television, using the computer, or playing on a smartphone, the parent is doing so along with the child at least most of the time. By contrast, fewer parents recognize the same level of co-viewing when using a tablet or similar device (Connell et al., 2015).

As such, parents are more likely to co-use traditional media like television, whereas joint media engagement is least likely to happen with newer media (ibid.). In addition, the younger the children are, the more frequently parents use media technologies with them (Wartella et al., 2013, p. 15). Media co-use is also linked to parents' time spent with media as well as parent demographics, such as age, gender, ethnicity, and level of education, and child demographics, such as age and gender. Joint media engagement of most types of media technology is predicted by the amount of time the parent is at home with the child (Connell et al., 2015).

What we do know so far about media co-use is that television brings the family together and promotes family interaction, but it can also have hampering effects (see Morley, 1986; Lull, 1990; Spiegel, 1992; Paavonen et al., 2009). As for computer co-use, we know that mothers are more likely to engage with their children's Internet use than fathers (Nikken and Jansz, 2011). In addition, it has been established that parent–child interaction varies during computer use based on the child's competencies (Lauricella et al., 2009). However, we are still lacking information about joint media engagement with newer devices, such as smartphones and tablets (Connell et al., 2015, p. 6).

Besides media co-use, it has been argued that media use is negatively associated with family time. The main contention is that time spent on one activity cannot be spent on another. In general, children themselves also prefer using digital technology individually rather than socially (Chaudron, 2015). As the TV set can be seen to bring family members together, the autonomy of media use has also increased. There has been a shift in media use from the collective family TV set to individualized media lifestyles and, for children, to a private bedroom culture (Bovill and Livingstone, 2001; Livingstone, 2007). In addition, the methods of going online have become more private concurrently as the locations and devices of Internet access have diversified. Although the home still remains the main location of children's media use, Internet access in private bedrooms and on the move has increased.

We are thus witnessing a greater privatization of children's media use: children value the privacy and convenience of new media. Tweens are especially keen on possessing personal devices that they do not have to share with other family members (Mascheroni and Cuman, 2014, pp. 5–6). Consequently, it is reasonable to assume that smartphones are devices that children are more likely to perceive as being for private use. According to children and young people, the advantage of smartphones is, most importantly, their convenience. As media devices, they are small, portable and private (ibid., p. 13). Nevertheless, traditional desktop computers are also commonly used alone (Repo and Nätti, 2015b). As such, personalized media use and ownership of devices has constructed distinct spaces within the home that may also affect social interaction (for more, see Chapters 9 and 11 in this volume).

CONCLUSION

It has been argued that opportunities to use media and the access and availability of media in the home increases the allure of the home as a place of leisure – and also learning – and will reshape the social organization of family life (Pasquier, 2001, p. 162). Parents' own media behaviour also has an influence on their children's orientation towards screen media

(Wartella et al., 2013, p. 30). When parents' attitudes towards media in the USA were explored, it became clear that parents are assured enough that media have more positive than negative effects on children. Thus, they take a permissive stance on the time children spend on media; the children's use of media is not a top concern among parents. However, parents still worry about what the future holds in terms of their children's social skills, possible 'addiction' to mobile media, and the lack of physical activity caused by increasing media use (ibid.).

Despite the changes in children's media environment, television still has a central role in children's time use and also watching television is the most common shared activity with family members. Watching television and listening to music are among the most traditional and most accessible media activities in the sense that almost everyone has access television and music, and devices for engaging in these activities have been around for a relatively long time compared to digital media tools (Rideout, 2015, p. 85).

We can argue that television still brings families together, whereas computers – especially tablet computers – and smartphones are creating the increasing privatization of family time. These digital media devices may be a form of socialization for children and youths outside of the home, but inside the home, digital media take away time that children would spend with their families (Jennings and Wartella, 2004, p. 605). It can also be argued that privatized media use provides a means of escape from the interruptions, interference and the gaze of others (see Livingstone, 2007; see also Chapter 11 in this volume), facilitates family members' use of privatized space as opposed to collective family space (Livingstone, 2007, p. 9) and hinders interaction and involvement among family members. It may be that digital media were not necessarily designed to support shared interaction within homes, but in future we need to consider how we can encourage intergenerational interaction among family members using personally owned media devices. However, it is also good to notice that what matters for well-being is not merely the amount of time that families spend together, but rather the kind of activities they engage in when together (Offer, 2013).

REFERENCES

Alanen, L. (1992), *Modern Childhood? Exploring the 'Child Question' in Sociology*, Jyväskylä: Kasvatustieteiden tutkimuslaitos.

Bovill, M. and S. Livingstone (2001), 'Bedroom culture and the privatization of media use', in S. Livingstone and M. Bovill (eds), *Children and Their Changing Media Environment: A European Comparative Study*, LEA's Communication Series, Mahwah, NJ: Lawrence Erlbaum Associates, pp. 179–200.

Buckingham, D. (2000), *After the Death of Childhood. Growing Up in the Age of Electronic Media*, Cambridge, UK: Polity Press.

Buckingham, D. (2006), 'Children and new media', in L.A. Lievrouw and S. Livingstone (eds), *Handbook of New Media. Social Shaping and Social Consequences of ICTs*, student edition, London: Sage, pp. 75–91.

Burdette, H.L. and R.C. Whitaker (2005), 'A national study of neighborhood safety, outdoor play, television viewing, and obesity in preschool children', *Pediatrics*, **116** (3), 657–62.

Chaudron, S. (2015), *Young Children (0–8) and Digital Technology. A Qualitative Exploratory Study Across Seven Countries*, European Commission, Joint Research Centre, Institute for the Protection and Security of the Citizen, Report EUR 27052 EN.

Child Trends DataBank (2015), *Home Computer Access and Internet Use*, accessed 11 April 2017 at https://www.childtrends.org/indicators/home-computer-access/.

Connell, S.L., A.R. Lauricella and E. Wartella (2015), 'Parental co-use of media technology with their young children in the USA', *Journal of Children and Media*, **9** (1), 5–21.

d'Haenens, L. (2001), 'Old and new media: Access and ownership in the home', in S. Livingstone and M. Bovill (eds), *Children and Their Changing Media Environment. A European Comparative Study*, Mahwah, NJ: Lawrence Erlbaum Associates, pp. 53–84.

Flichy, P. (1995), *Dynamics of Modern Communication: The Shaping and Impact of New Communication Technologies*, London: Sage.

Green, B. and C. Bigum (1993), 'Aliens in the classroom', *Australian Journal of Education*, **37** (2), 119–41.

James, A. and A. Prout (2015), *Constructing and Reconstructing Childhood: Contemporary Issues in the Sociological Study of Childhood*, 3rd edition, London: Routledge.

Jenks, C. (1996), 'The post-modern child', in J. Brannen and M. O'Brien (eds), *Children in Families: Research and Policy*, London: Falmer, pp. 13–25.

Jennings, N. and E. Wartella (2004), 'Technology and the family', in A.L. Vangelisti (ed.), *Handbook of Family Communication*, Mahwah, NJ: Lawrence Erlbaum Associates, pp. 593–608.

Kabali, H.K., M.M. Irigoyen and R. Nunez-Davis et al. (2015), 'Exposure and use of mobile media devices by young children', *Pediatrics*, **136** (6), 1044–50.

Karsten, L. and W. van Vliet (2006), 'Increasing children's freedom of movement. Introduction', *Children, Youth and Environments*, **16** (1), 69–74.

Korkeamäki, R.-L., T. Myllylä-Nygård, M. Niska and A.-S. Heikkilä (2015), 'Young children (0–8) and digital technology. A qualitative exploratory study – national report – Finland', in S. Chaudron (ed.), *Young Children (0–8) and Digital Technology. A Qualitative Exploratory Study Across Seven Countries*, European Commission, Joint Research Centre, Institute for the Protection and Security of the Citizen, Report EUR 27052 EN, pp. 174–235.

Lauricella, A.R., R.F. Barr and S.R. Calvert (2009), 'Emerging computer skills', *Journal of Children and Media*, **3** (3), 217–33.

Livingstone, S. (2007), 'From family television to bedroom culture: Young people's media at home', in E. Devereux (ed.), *Media Studies: Key issues and Debates*, London: Sage, pp. 302–21.

Livingstone, S. (2009), *Children and the Internet. Great Expectations, Challenging Realities*, Cambridge, UK: Polity Press.

Livingstone, S., L. d'Haenens and U. Hasebrink (2001), 'Childhood in Europe: Contexts for comparison', in S. Livingstone and M. Bovill (eds), *Children and Their Changing Media Environment: A European Comparative Study*, Mahwah, NJ: Lawrence Erlbaum Associates, pp. 3–30.

Livingstone, S., L. Haddon, A. Görzig and K. Ólafsson (2011), *Risks and Safety on the Internet. The Perspective of European Children. Full Findings and Policy Implications from the EU Kids Online Survey of 9–16-year-olds and their Parents in 25 Countries*, London: London School of Economics.

Livingstone, S., G. Mascheroni and M. Dreier et al. (2015), *How Parents of Young Children Manage Digital Devices at Home: The Role of Income, Education and Parental Style*, London: EU Kids Online, LSE.

Lull, J. (1990), *Inside Family Viewing: Ethnographic Research on Television Audiences*, London: Routledge.

Marsh, J. (2005). *Popular Culture, New Media and Digital Literacy in Early Childhood*, London: Routledge.

Mascheroni, G. and A. Cuman (2014), *Net Children Go Mobile: Final Report: Deliverables D6.4 and D5.2*, Milan: Educatt.

Mesh, G.S. (2006), 'Family relations and the Internet: Exploring a family boundaries approach', *The Journal of Family Communication*, **6** (2), 119–38.

Miettinen, A. and A. Rotkirch (2012), *Yhteistä aikaa etsimässä: Lapsiperheiden ajankäyttö 2000-luvulla* [Looking for Time Together. Time Use of Families with Children in the 2000s], *Perhebarometri 2011. Väestöntutkimuslaitoksen katsauksia E 42/2012*, Helsinki: Väestöliitto.

Morley, D. (1986), *Family Television. Culture Power and Domestic Leisure*, London: Comedia.

Myllyniemi, S. (2014), 'Tilasto-osio' [Statistics section], in S. Myllyniemi (ed.), *Ihmisarvoinen nuoruus, Nuorisobarometri 2014*, Opetus- ja kulttuuriministeriö, Nuorisoasiain neuvottelukunta, Nuorisotutkimusverkosto, pp. 11–124.

Nikken, P. and J. Jansz (2011), 'Parental mediation of young children's internet use', Netherlands: Erasmus University Rotterdam.

Noppari, E. (2014), *Mobiilimuksut: Lasten ja nuorten mediaympäristön muutos, osa 3* [Mobile kids: The Changing Landscape of Children's and Tween's Media Environment, Part 3], Journalismin, viestinnän ja median tutkimuskeskus, Tampere: University of Tampere.

Ofcom (2015), *Children and Parent: Media Use and Attitudes Report*, London: Ofcom.

Offer, S. (2013), 'Family time activities and adolescents' emotional well-being', *Journal of Marriage and Family*, **75** (1), 26–41.

Ólaffson, K., S. Livingstone and L. Haddon (2014), *Children's Use of Online Technologies in Europe. A Review of the European Evidence Base*, revised edition, London: EU Kids Online, LSE.

Pääkkönen, H. (2014), *Uusi teknologia on vaikuttanut koululaisten elämäntapoihin, Hyvinvointikatsaus: Lasten ja lapsiperheiden elinolot 2014:1* [New Technology Has Changed Schoolers' Lifestyle, Review of Welfare: Living Conditions of Children and Families with Children 2014:1], Helsinki: Tilastokeskus, pp. 57–61.

Paavonen, J.E., M. Roine, M. Pennonen and A.R. Lahikainen (2009), 'Do parental co-viewing and discussions mitigate TV-induced fears in young children?', *Child: Care, Health, and Development*, **35** (6), 773–80.

Pasquier, D. (2001), 'Media at home: Domestic interactions and regulation', in S. Livingstone and M. Bovill (eds), *Children and Their Changing Media*

Environment. A European Comparative Study, Mahwah, NJ: Lawrence Erlbaum Associates, pp. 161–77.

Prensky, M. (2001), 'Digital natives, digital immigrants', *On the Horizon*, **9** (5), 1–6.

Repo, K. and J. Nätti (2015a), 'Lasten ja nuorten median käytön aikatrendit' [Time trends in children's and young people's use of the media], in A.R. Lahikainen, T. Mälkiä and K. Repo (eds), *Media lapsiperheessä*, Tampere: Vastapaino, pp. 80–107.

Repo, K. and J. Nätti (2015b), 'Lapset ja nuoret yksin ja yhdessä median parissa' [Children and young people alone or together with media], in A.R. Lahikainen, T. Mälkiä and K. Repo (eds), *Media lapsiperheessä*, Tampere: Vastapaino, pp. 108–31.

Rice, R.D. and C. Haythornthwaite (2006), 'Perspectives on Internet use: Access, involvement and interaction', in L.A. Lievrouw and S. Livingstone (eds), *Handbook of New Media. Social Shaping and Social Consequences of ICTs*, student edition, London: Sage, pp. 92–113.

Rideout, V. (2015), *The Common Sense Census: Media Use By Tweens and Teens*, accessed 11 April 2017 at https://www.commonsensemedia.org/research/the-common-sense-census-media-use-by-tweens-and-teens/.

Spiegel, L. (1992), *Make Room for TV*, Chicago, IL: Chicago University Press.

Strandell, H. (2012), 'Policies of early childhood education and care: Partnership, individualization', in A.-T. Kjørholt and J. Qvortrup (eds), *The Modern Child and the Flexible Labour Market: Early Childhood Education and Care*, Basingstoke, UK: Palgrave Macmillan, pp. 222–40.

Suoninen, A. (2011), 'Children's media use as described by their parents', in S. Kotilainen (ed.), *Children's Media Barometer 2010: The Use of Media Among 0–8-year-olds in Finland*, Helsinki: Finnish Society on Media Education, pp. 9–14.

Suoninen, A. (2013), *Lasten mediabarometri 2012. 10–12-vuotiaiden tyttöjen ja poikien Mediankäyttö* [Children's Media Barometer 2012. 10–12-year-old Girls' and Boys' Media Usage], *Verkkojulkaisuja No. 62*, Helsinki: Nuorisotutkimusverkosto/Nuorisotutkimusseura.

Suoninen, A. (2014), *Lasten mediabarometri 2013. 0–8-vuotiaiden mediankäyttö ja sen muutokset vuodesta 2010* [Children's Media Barometer 2013. 0–9-year-olds' Media Usage and its Change from 2010], *Verkkojulkaisuja No. 75*, Helsinki: Nuorisotutkimusverkosto/Nuorisotutkimusseura.

Valkonen, S. (2012), *Television merkitys lasten arjessa* [The Importance of Television in Children's Everyday Lives], Tampere: Tampere University Press.

Wartella, E., V. Rideout, A.R. Lauricella and S.L. Connell (2013), *Parenting in the Age of Digital Technology. A National Survey*, Report of the Center on Media and Human Development, School of Communication, Northwestern University.

Wyness, M. (2006), *Childhood and Society. An Introduction to the Sociology of Childhood*, Basingstoke, UK: Palgrave Macmillan.

PART II

Media-related practices and family interaction

6. Practices of parental mediation in television viewing

Aku Kallio

INTRODUCTION

In recent years, many studies on children's media use have focused on the notion of parental mediation. Parental mediation theory is founded on the idea that media influence children's attitudes and behaviour. These influences may be enhanced or diminished by parental actions that affect the way children receive and process media content. Parental mediation is defined as the strategies utilized by parents to manage and regulate the effects that media are believed to have on children and to help children to become more competent media users (Clark, 2011). It is considered a form of parental socialization that is realized in the daily activities and routines of contemporary families replete with media devices (Shin, 2015). Three types or strategies of parental mediation have been established: restrictive mediation, co-viewing and active mediation (Austin et al., 1999; Valkenburg et al., 1999). Restrictive mediation refers to rules and restrictions that parents set in order to control the amount and/or quality of their children's television viewing. Co-viewing refers to situations when children and parents watch television together because of a common interest in the programme, but do not engage in discussion about the programme. Active mediation refers to discussing the programme with the child in order to help the child understand the programme better. This includes a spectrum of parents' comments, explanations and evaluations on the events on the screen as well as explanations regarding production techniques (e.g., tricks and special effects) and intents (e.g., selling in advertisements) (Valkenburg et al., 1999; Warren, 2003; Buijzen and Valkenburg, 2005).

Previous research indicates that active mediation is the most effective of the three types of mediation in equipping the children with the necessary media skills, helping them to understand plots and protecting them from the negative influence of media (Nathanson, 1999; Fujioka and Austin, 2003; Buijzen et al., 2007; Lwin et al., 2008). Further, Austin et al. (1999) stress that it is important to notice how parents talk to their children about television. They distinguish between two strategies or types of active parental mediation, namely negative mediation and positive mediation. Negative mediation refers to parental judgement, rejection, critique and disapproval of television content, while positive mediation refers to agreement, approval or endorsement of television content. Negative mediation of television violence has been found to relate to less aggression, while positive mediation of violent content is related to more imitation of aggressive behaviour (Hicks, 1968; Nathanson, 1999). Negative mediation is also associated with critical viewing and protective motivations by the parents, while positive mediation may also occur as part of regular everyday interaction between family members (Austin et al., 1999). Nathanson and Botta (2003; also Nathanson, 2002) make a further distinction by adding the category of neutral mediation. Neutral mediation refers to a combination of positive and negative mediation or discussion that cannot be classified as positive or negative, such as questions like 'What do you think will happen next?' and neutral statements like 'This show is filmed in New York' (Nathanson and Botta, 2003, p. 309). Further, Nathanson (2004) distinguishes between factual mediation (e.g., stating facts about the production techniques) and evaluative mediation (evaluations on characters). She demonstrates in an experimental study that evaluative mediation is more effective in decreasing the vulnerability of five- to seven-year-olds to violent television, while factual mediation has either no effect or might even increase the negative effects of media.

While parental mediation research has largely focused on negative media effects, some researchers have also paid attention to positive media effects. It has been well established, for example, that children learn from television (e.g., Ball and Bogatz, 1970; Fisch, 2000; Piotrowski, 2014) and that parental commentary enhances both learning from television (Reiser et al., 1984) and the understanding of plots (Desmond et al., 1985).

It should also be noted that parental mediation research has primarily consisted of surveys. Relying on surveys in which people tend to report on their purposeful actions might have skewed the appraisal of active mediation towards goal-oriented action through which the parents intentionally seek to help their children. As a consequence, the ordinary everyday interaction that may also be connected to parental mediation in many ways has largely been ignored. While quantitative research has proved to be an effective method in mapping out different mediation strategies and in revealing why, to what extent, and with what consequences these strategies are used in families, it does not necessarily help us to understand how mediation is realized in parent–child interaction.

I approach the idea of parental mediation without presumptions about the possible intentions behind mediating actions or the outcomes of the mediation. This enables me to scrutinize the variety of interactional phenomena that could be linked to parental mediation. I ask: What sort of actions can parental mediation consist of? How is mediation realized in naturally occurring family interaction? Using a detailed systematic qualitative analysis of parent–child interaction in television viewing situations, this chapter seeks to explore parental mediation as an interactional phenomenon.

DATA AND METHOD

The video-recorded data collected by the 'Media, Family Interaction and Children's Well-Being' project (see Appendix 1) were used in this study. Every viewing episode in which a five-year-old child was watching a programme together with at least one of the parents was selected from the data corpus and examined. This included a total of ten programmes from six families, circa 330 minutes of video data. Eight of the programmes were television broadcasts viewed on a television screen, one was viewed on a computer, and one on a television screen from a DVD. The genres that were viewed together were varied. They included acted and animated children's shows (seven cases), reality TV (one case), a soap opera (one case) and funny home videos (one case). The duration of the viewing episodes varied from ten minutes to two hours. In some cases, conversation continued after the show had ended, and these conversations were included in the analysis as well. It should be noted that by 'watching together', we mean situations in which a parent and a child were present in the same room and oriented to the screen at least partially, even if oriented to other activities as well.

All the viewing episodes were transcribed. The sequences of talk in which the participants oriented to the ongoing media content or their own viewing were included to create a collection of sequences potentially related to parental mediation. All the sequences in the collection were categorized by their practices. Some of these practices had been introduced in previous research, while others were identified while examining the collection.

The method employed in this study is conversation analysis. A basic assumption of conversation analysis is that any turn of talk is orienting to the previous turn, and also providing the context for the following turn (Heritage, 1984b, p. 242). Thus, interaction is organized in adjacency pairs – for example, question–answer pairs – and larger sequences. The sequential organization of talk is emphasized as I demonstrate how participants orient to the ongoing media content and to each other's talk concerning the content. All names have been changed.

RESULTS

Four practices that are linked to parental mediation were identified: (1) interpreting and explaining the media content, (2) doing teaching, (3) talking about viewing experience and (4) assessing the media content. These practices serve various functions regarding parental mediation.

Interpreting and Explaining Media Content

One of the key elements of active parental mediation is the interpretation and explanation of media content to children. Extract 1 illustrates how this type of mediation occurs in interaction. Here, Peetu (six years old), Elli (eight years old) and their mother are watching the film *Howl's Moving Castle*. On the screen, the protagonists have just escaped from some monsters by using a spell that enables them to walk in the air.

Extract 1

```
1  Peetu:    miks noi kävelee tuolla, .h miks ne ei voi
             why are they walking up there, .h why can't they
2            kävellä maassa.
             walk on the ground.
3            (0.7)
4  Mother:   no ku siel ne (.) hirviöthä
             well'cos there those (.) you know the monsters
5            just jahtas niitä siellä.
             were just chasing them down there.
```

In the extract, the mother answers Peetu's question of why the protagonists are walking in the air. Despite the fact that Peetu has just seen the monsters and the narrow escape, the mother treats Peetu's question as a real question that needs to be answered. Indeed, the mother designs her answer as something that Peetu should already know by producing the suffix '-hAn' (translated 'you know', line 4) after the word 'monsters'/'hirviöt+hä(n)'. This design further emphasizes the explanatory nature of the mother's turn. Thus, with her answer, the mother is able to explain the characters' behaviour to Peetu, and thus help him to understand what is going on in the film.

In Extract 2, we find Juho (five years old) and his mother watching the Finnish children's show *Pikku Kakkonen* together. On the screen, a treasure hunt is about to reach its climax. Here, the mother utilizes a different strategy to help her child to follow the programme.

Extract 2

1	Mother:	mitähän siäl huavan alla o?
		I wonder what's under the blanket?
2		(0.4)
3	Juho:	en tiä.
		I don't know.
4		(2.6)
5	Mother:	onkohan siäl jotain- (.) hahh
		is there some- (.) hahh ((looks at Juho))
6		(2.3)
7	Mother:	keksejäkö.
		is it cookies.
8		(2.2)
9	TV:	suklaa aarre.
		a chocolate treasure ((Juho turns to mother))
10		(1.6) ((mother turns gaze towards Juho and smiles))
11	Mother:	aa:: ↑suklaa↓kolikoitah.
		o::h ↑chocolate↓ coinsh.
12		(3.8)
13	Mother:	muistaks sää ku meilläki ollu joskus noita.
		do you remember we had those once as well.
14		((Juho nods))

The mother utilizes mock questions (lines 1, 5 and 7) in following the programme. The questions are designed to build up the suspense. The first question (line 1) sets the problem and marks the blanket as the focus of interest in the scene, the second one is left unfinished so that it builds up tension, and finally the third question offers a candidate answer. With these questions, the mother is able to guide Juho to pay attention to and recognize relevant aspects of the plot. She is also making the show more interesting by emphasizing the mystery with her questions.

When the mystery is solved (in line 9), Juho disengages from the television and turns his head towards his mother. The head turn is placed right at the 'punchline' that the mother has foreshadowed. Thus, Juho is displaying that he has followed the plot and the mother's guiding talk and knows the right answer now.

The mother's response also indicates that this sequence was produced in order to help Juho follow the programme. First, the mother affiliates with Juho by turning her gaze towards Juho and smiling (line 10). Then, she continues by producing an exaggerated change of state token (prolonged 'oh' in line 11; see Heritage, 1984a, 2012) indicating she has realized something, and then explicitly stating the correct answer. With these actions, the mother is able to emphasize the solving of the mystery.

Doing Teaching

While there is evidence that actively talking with children is related to learning from television (Reiser et al., 1984; Nathanson, 2002), little is known about the practices of interaction that propel this. Next, I examine moments in parent–child interaction in which parents provide information that does not concern understanding the show but instead relates to facts about the real world. I will demonstrate how through these sequences of talk parents are 'doing teaching' and children are responding to these educational turns.

In Extract 3 the mother, Joanna (four years old) and Pepe (five years old) are watching the Finnish children's programme *Pikku Kakkonen*. When a warthog appears on the screen, the mother initiates talk.

Extract 3

```
 1    Mother:   mikä toi o.
                what's that.
 2              (7.0)
 3    Joanna:   vi::llitika.
                a wi::ld boar.
 4              (1.1)
 5    Mother:   pahkasika. (.) sil on niinku (.) .hh emmä tiä
                a warthog. (.) it's got like a (.) .hh i dunno is
 6              onks=sil on pahkan (.) pahkan näkönen nenä, (.)
                it=it has a nose (.) nose that looks like a wart,
 7              sil on tommonen <iso kuo:no> ja sit sil on
                (.) it has that kind of <big snout> and then it
 8              tora°hampaat () () (.) ()° näyttää vähä
                has °fangs () () (.) ()° looks a bit like
 9              pahkalta.
                a wart.
10              (1.1)
11    Joanna:   jaa.
                oh.
```

Here, a typical teaching sequence with a question (line 1), response (line 3), and feedback (lines 5–9) is acted. Sequences like these have been reported to take place frequently in classroom situations (Mehan, 1979; Koole, 2015). Here, it is the mother who initiates the teaching sequence with a 'known information question' (Mehan, 1979) that is answered by Joanna. Joanna's answer is incorrect, and the mother corrects it. The mother's feedback (lines 5–9) not only reveals that she knew the answer, but she also gives a lengthy educational description of the warthog, explaining how the warthog got its name. Joanna responds with a 'jaa'/'oh' (line 11) that registers the new information and closes the sequence.

In Extract 4, a mother, father and their sons Lars (eight years old) and Joni (five years old) are watching an episode of an old Swedish children's programme *Pippi Longstocking*. In the programme, Pippi is using an old, manually operated water pump.

Extract 4

```
 1   Lars:     mikä toi o.
               what's that.
 2   Mother:   se on pumppu.
               it's a pump,
 3             (0.9)
 4   Mother:   oi: joi.
               oy: oy.
 5             (2.5)
 6   Mother:   tulee vettä ku pumppaa vaan.
               water comes when you just pump it.
 7             (2.1)
 8   Mother:   kun ei o mitään hanaa mistä vaan käännettäis.
               'cos there's no tap that you could just turn.
 9             (2.0)
10   Joni:     () (toi) () oli ennen vanhaan.
               () (that) () was in the old times.
11             (0.5)
12   Mother:   mm:::?,
```

Lars asks what it is (line 1) and the mother answers by providing the requested information (line 2). However, the mother's answer does not explain what is happening in the scene, and for someone who has never seen a pump in a kitchen, the given information may not be sufficient in order to understand what Pippi is doing. Indeed, Lars does not respond to this in any way. The mother goes on to elaborate the pump's mechanical principles (line 6) and compares it to the modern technology that is more familiar to the children (line 8). Joni responds to this explanation by displaying his understanding of the differences between the modern and the old times (line 10).

Sequentially, this extract shares some characteristics with Extract 1. Here, too, we have a question by a child (line 1) and a response by a parent (line 2). However, our focus lies on the extensions of the answer that are provided by the mother in lines 6 and 8. The information provided in the extensions exceeds the original request, which has already been answered in line 2. With the first extension, the mother provides information concerning the operating mechanism of old pumps in more general way (line 6), and in the second one she compares the mechanism to the modern technology (tap/faucet) that is more familiar to the children (line 8). Thus the mother is able to familiarize the unknown apparatus to the children, and point out the difference between Pippi's world and modern times. This is indeed how Joni treats the mother's extension in his response (line 10).

This extract also demonstrates how the categories of interpreting and explaining media content and 'doing teaching' are closely related. Even if the information given by the mother leans more towards 'doing teaching', it also explains the world Pippi is living in, and her actions in it. Indeed, in some cases providing general background information might be necessary in order to successfully interpret and explain media content to children.

Extract 5 comes from the same viewing episode. In the scene, Pippi rides down a city street and passes a character travelling using a kicksled (a small sled consisting of a chair mounted on a pair of flexible metal runners). A moment later, she passes another character who is carrying a spruce. This character falls down as Pippi passes him.

Extract 5

1	Father:	potkukelkka on kai ruotsalainen keksintö
		kicksled is presumably a swedish invention
2		[°että.°
		[°so.°
3	Mother:	[@hiljaa mäessä,@
		[@slowly down the hill,@ ((reads subtitles))
4	Mother:	oho,=siel o varmaan joulu nyt tulossa
		oh,=there's probably christmas coming
5		kyllä ku' joulukuusta kanne^taan.°
		'cos someone's carrying a christmas °tree.°
6		(.)
7	Lars:	oho,=se kaatu sinne.
		oh,=he fell down there.
8		(0.5)
9	Mother:	joo,=se varmaan (1.0) puoliks liukastu ja
		yea,=he probably (1.0) half slipped and
10		puoliks pelästy.
		half got scared.

The parents are commenting on the show to the children in various ways. First, when the kicksled appears on the screen, the father opens the discussion by noting that the 'kicksled is presumably a Swedish invention so' (lines 1–2). This turn of talk is evidently evoked by the show and it offers information rather than explains or interprets the scene. The information is not relevant for following the show. Rather, it is designed to give general knowledge concerning kicksleds.

The second point of interest concerns the talk regarding the man carrying the spruce. The mother gives an interpretation for the children and explains the spruce by suggesting that it is Christmas time (lines 4–5). While this interpretation (it is Christmas time) might contextualize the plot, it is not relevant for following the show. Neither does it teach the children anything new, as bringing a spruce indoors is a typical Christmas tradition in Finland (as in many Western countries). The mother's interpretation illustrates a process of deduction: it gives an example of how people connect information they see with a possible conclusion that can be made by drawing upon it. By stating the obvious, the mother makes her own deduction process available to the children. This is observable in the details of her turn. First, she produces a change of state token ('oho'/'oh') indicating that she has acquired some new information (Heritage, 1984a) and then moves on to explicate what sort of conclusions can be made of it (line 4). Second, she uses the word 'varmaan'/'probably', which intimates that her conclusion is speculative. Third, she designs her turn in a way that explicates the deduction process (there is probably Y because of X). A design like this may be utilized in order to teach children how to read the symbols of the programme and draw conclusions from them. Thus, this kind of talk might be both helping children to understand the programme better, and teaching them media literacy and deduction skills more generally.

Talking About Viewing Experience

Another way to engage in active parental mediation is to focus on the child instead of the media content. Our findings indicate that parents also monitor their children's reactions and talk about their children's thoughts and emotions concerning the media content. Parents usually initiate this type of mediation by asking questions such as 'Is this scary?', 'Do you like this show?' or 'Have you seen this show before?' This is exemplified in Extract 6, in which the mother and Peetu (six years old) are talking about the film *Howl's Moving Castle* that they have just watched.

Extract 6

```
1    Mother:   tykkäät sä tost leffasta.
               do you like that film.
2    Peetu:    tyk↑kään.
               ↑yes I like it.
3              (0.3)
4    Peetu:    mä syän suth.
               I'm gonna eat youh.
5              (.)
```

6   Mother: mikä siin on parasta.
                what's the best part in it.
7   (1.0)
8   Peetu: tämmönen?
                this?((imitates a dog in the film))
9   Mother: .hhh @ai se pikkukoirah.@ ((haukotellen))
                .hhh @oh that little doggyh.@ ((yawning))
10   (.)
11   Peetu: nii:h?
                yea:h?

The mother initiates the sequence by asking Peetu to evaluate the film (line 1). The question is designed as a simple yes/no question with a strong preference towards 'liking the film' as the answer, which Peetu provides (line 2). The mother moves on and asks Peetu to elaborate on what is good about the film (line 6). The turn is designed as an open question that invites Peetu to reflect upon what he has just seen. Peetu provides the answer by mimicking a character in the film (line 8). Regarding parental mediation, this sequence exemplifies how talking about viewing experience both invites the child to reflect upon the programme and, as a consequence, enables the parent to get some idea about how the child is experiencing the programme.

Extract 7 shows a more complex exchange of turns through which emotional experiences are negotiated. Here, the mother, Salla (seven years old) and Samuel (six years old) are watching a Finnish soap opera (*Salatut elämät*). In the show, a baby boy has been born and the characters are talking about the baby and the mother.

Extract 7

1   Salla: t(h)oinen oli tyttö toinen   [p(h)oik(h)a.
                (h)one was a girl and the other was [a b(h)oy.
2   Mother: [hhmh n(h)ii.=
                ((turns to Salla))   [hhmh y(h)eah.=
3   Mother: =.h[hh itkeks sää.
                =.h[hh are you crying.
4   Salla: [heheh
5   Salla: e, hh.
                no, hh.
6   (0.3)
7   Mother: no ku sä oot iha sen näkö   [ne.
                well you look like you   [are.
8   Salla: [ehheh hehhehehehehe
9   .hh minä en o y- itkenyt yhtään.
                .hh I haven't a- cried at all.
10   (0.9)

```
11   Salla:     heheh
12              (.)
13   Samuel:    aina äi- .hh äiti ku @tulee joku suruohjelma? (.)
                whenever mo- .hh mom when @there's some sad show?
14              ni sitten m(h)ä rupeen melkein itkeen.@
                (.) then I(h) almost begin crying.@
15   Mother:    vo::i.
                aw[w::.
16   Samuel:       [heheh heh[heh heh
17   Mother:                  [hehheh heh
18   Salla:     hehheh
19   Mother:    .hh se on ihan hienoo,
                .hh that's pretty wonderful,
20              (1.3)
21   Mother:    pys[tyy eläytyyn.
                you [can empathize.
22   Samuel:        [hianoo vai.
                    [wonderful uh.
```

In line 2, the mother looks at Salla and asks 'are you crying?' (line 3), which Salla answers negatively. The mother's question is hearable as implying that there is something in the show that has made Salla cry. Indeed, Samuel treats the mother's question as such (lines 13–14). Though the question is not directed to him, he responds by describing how he almost cries whenever something sorrowful comes on the TV with a sad tone in his voice. The mother responds to Samuel's confession by producing a prolonged 'vo::i'/'aww::' (line 15). The 'aww' is both treating Samuel's turn as news to her (Heritage, 1984a) and affiliating with it. Samuel moves on to downplay his confession by laughing (line 16). The mother affiliates again by joining in the laughter (line 17). The mother continues by complimenting Samuel's ability to empathize (lines 19, 21). With this, she is able to display that there is nothing wrong with crying when one is feeling sad. Thus, the mother is supporting Samuel's emotional skills.

Assessing the Media Content

There is one more type of practice that parents frequently utilize while watching a programme with their children. They evaluate or, in the terms of conversation analysis, assess the programme. By assessing the programme, parents may display their understanding of the programme and also display a (moral/emotional) stance towards characters and their actions. Assessments can be used to construct shared understanding regarding the programme and togetherness between the parent and the child.

In Extract 8, the mother and Juho (five years old) are watching the children's show *Pikku Kakkonen*. In the programme, the protagonists are

engaged in imaginary play and are imitating swimming by waving their
arms around while walking on the ground. When their mother appears, the
protagonists pretend that she is a mermaid.

Extract 8

```
1   Mother:   khihihi (.) [uiko ne?
              khihihi (.) [are they swimming? ((gazes at Juho))
2   TV:                  [katsokaa kapteeni. (.) [merenneito
                         [look captain, (.)      [a mermaid.
3   Juho:                                        [°joo.°
                                                 [°yeah.°
4             (0.5)
5   Mother:   mh mh (.) hih hih [hih ((gazes at Juho))
6   Juho:                       [hih hih
7             (2.0)
8   Mother:   hehheh
9             (2.5)
```

Our focus is on line 5, where the mother displays a stance towards the
programme by laughing. As she laughs, she leans towards Juho and turns
her gaze towards him. Juho treats this as an invitation to affiliate, and joins
in the laughter (line 6). With these actions, the participants are able to
produce a shared humorous stance towards the programme. By producing
a shared stance and marking it with a mutual gaze, the participants are
making their congruent understanding of the situation visible (Goodwin
and Goodwin, 1992). They are also co-constructing an intimate moment
of closeness within the television-viewing situation. In other words, the
participants are able to construct togetherness (see Chapter 10 in this
book).

This extract also demonstrates the fine line between what has been
dubbed active mediation and co-viewing. As there is not much 'discussion'
here, the extract may be leaning more towards co-viewing. Moreover, there
is hardly any evidence that the participants are orienting to the ongoing
media content as something that requires mediation. Instead, this seems
like a regular everyday interaction. However, this sequence clearly shows
how the mother positively assesses the media content, which is a sign of
active positive mediation (Nathanson and Botta, 2003).

In Extract 9, the mother, Elli (eight years old) and Peetu (six years old)
are watching the film *Howl's Moving Castle* together. In the ongoing scene,
one of the characters, the granny, takes the magical fire out of the fireplace
of the moving castle. Due to this act, the castle loses its powers and is
about to crumble.

Extract 9

1	Mother:	toi pilas kaiken toi mummo.
		she ruined everything that granny.
2		(0.4)
3	Elli:	no ni[i:.
		yea[:h.
4	Mother:	[ku sen piti mennä ottaan se.
		[cos she had to go and take it.
5	Elli:	niin,=se on kauhee se mummo.
		yeah,=she's awful that granny.

The mother makes a negative assessment on the behaviour of a character in the programme (line 1). Elli affiliates with the mother (line 3) and the mother continues to explicate the character's disapproved action (line 4). This is also interpretable as an account of why she took such a strong stance towards the character (line 4). Again, Elli affiliates by agreeing (yeah) and upgrading the negative assessment of the character (line 5).

This exchange of turns embodies two closely intertwined functions regarding parental mediation. First, by strongly condemning the behaviour of the character in question, they are constructing a shared understanding of not only what is going on in the film, but also what is good and bad. In other words, they are co-constructing a shared moral stance. Second, with the shared stance the mother and Elli are also positioning themselves 'on the same side' regarding the assessed character (Du Bois, 2007). Thus, they are constructing togetherness. In sum, assessments can be involved in both constructing togetherness and mediating norms and morals.

In Extract 10, Pepe (five years old), Joanna (four years old) and their mother are watching an episode of *Les Dennis's Home Video Heroes*. On the screen, a man is cleaning a toilet when he suddenly falls straight into the toilet bowl.

Extract 10

	[(X) marks the man falling down in the transcription]
1	(0.9)
2 Mother:	@miten niin miehet eivät osaa tehdä monta
	@how come men can't do many
3	#asiaa kerralla.#@
	#things at the same time.#@ ((reads subtitles))
4	(1.8) (X)
5 Mother:	↑hoijoi,
	↑oy oy,
6	(1.7) ((clip ends, replay begins))
7 Pepe:	ehhheh [heh

8	Mother:	[#ai jai.#
		[#ow ow.#
9		(1.3)
10	Mother:	@kotitöiden tekemisestä saa pistei(X)tä.@
		@doing household duties gives you extra poi(X)nts.@ ((reads subtitles))
11		(1.2)
12	Joanna:	ähhähähä .hhhh
13	Mother:	.hh ai.
		.hh ouch.
14		(0.5)

Right after the man falls, the mother assesses the mishap with an empathetic 'oy oy' (line 5). Pepe's assessment (line 7) is radically different and contradicts the mother's assessment (laughter in line 7). The mother responds to Pepe's laughter by producing another empathetic assessment (line 8). Almost an identical exchange of turns can be found later on in the extract when a replay of the accident is shown. This time Joanna laughs at the mishap (line 12). Again, the mother responds by displaying sympathy for the unfortunate man (line 13).

The genre of 'funny home videos' is two-folded. It is regarded suitable entertainment for the whole family, and the idea of the genre is to laugh at people's (by definition 'funny') mishaps and accidents. The extract shows how children respond to the show exactly like this. However, people and their mishaps and accidents that are shown in the programme are real events, and it is not considered appropriate to laugh at such accidents. Unlike the children, the mother orients to these video clips as real events, and assesses them accordingly.

By displaying an appropriate stance, after the children's inappropriate assessments, the mother is setting an example. With her own actions she is telling her children how to respond to someone's mishap. Thus, she is able to show children what it is acceptable behaviour and teach them good manners. This example shows an interesting side to parental mediation as well. Here, the mother is not trying to explain any aspect of the media content to the children. Nor is she condemning the media content. Instead, she is orienting to the children's responses, and displays her 'correct' stance every time one of the children displays an inappropriate stance. With these actions the mother mediates social norms and moral codes.

Extract 11 originates from the same viewing of the episode of *Les Dennis's Home Video Heroes* as Extract 10. On the screen, two boys are playing Chinese checkers when one of the boys suddenly punches his opponent in the face.

Extract 11

[(X) marks the punch in the transcription]
```
1               (1.4)
2    Mother:    @kun tappio häämöttää on yksi tapa yllättää.@
               @when defeat is certain there's one way to surprise.@ ((reads
               subtitles))
3               (3.9) (X)
4    Mother     .mthh ai kamala,=noin #ei voi teh#°dä.°
               .mthh oh that's horrible,=#you can't do# °that.°
5               (2.4)
6    Mother:    hy::i.
               e::ww.
7    Pepe:      ehh h'h. [.hh
8    Joanna:             [hy::i.
                         [e::ww.
9    Mother:             [no ni?, (.) nyt loppu sitte
                         [okay?, that's it for the
10                       [k[ingit kotivideot.
                         [h[ome video heroes. ((changes channel))
11   Pepe:               [E[I:: ÄITI:::,
                         [N[O:::: MO::::M, ((taps the floor, kicks air))
12   Joanna:             [EEE::II:::.
                         [NO:::::::::.
```

When the punch comes, the mother displays a strong moral stance by
disapproving of the behaviour and instructing the children that this is
something one should not do (line 4). At this point, the children don't
make any assessments and the mother continues with a 'hyi'/'eww', a
Finnish expression that strongly displays both disgust and disapproval
(line 6). While Joanna affiliates with the mother (line 8), Pepe displays a
contradicting stance (line 7). At this point, the mother changes strategy
and moves on to restrictive mediation by attempting to stop the viewing
(lines 9–10).

SUMMARY AND DISCUSSION

In this chapter, I have examined different kinds of interactional practices
utilized by parents while watching television with their children. These
practices serve various functions that are connected to parental mediation
and thus to the children's socialization process. This is illustrated in Table
6.1.

One of the key elements of parental mediation is interpreting and
explaining the programme for children to help them to understand and
follow what is happening. Our findings show that the interpretations

Table 6.1   Practices of parental mediation and their functions

Practice	Function(s)
Interpreting and explaining the programme	Helping the child to follow/understand the programme better
Doing teaching	Increasing the child's general knowledge Teaching reasoning
Talking about the viewing experience	Enabling the parent to understand how the child has experienced the programme Enhancing the child's emotional skills
Assessing the programme	Producing togetherness Mediating norms and morals Helping the child to follow/understand the programme better

and explanations are made in various ways, such as answering the child's questions, talking through a scene, reading the subtitles for the child and directing the child's focus. A distinction between providing information that explains or interprets the action on the screen and information that exceeds the ongoing plot is also relevant for our analysis. Regarding parental mediation, the latter form of informing is directed towards increasing the child's general knowledge (doing teaching) rather than helping him or her to understand what is happening in the programme. However, the distinction is not clearcut, as this kind of information might also serve as background information that helps the child to understand the ongoing plot (see Extract 4).

Parents also mediate children's emotional responses to television by monitoring their responses and talking about the viewing experience. Parents invite children to evaluate the media content in order to initiate talk about the viewing experience (Extract 6). Parents might use this strategy in order to obtain some idea about how their children are experiencing the media content. This is important for parental mediation as parents may use this type of information in selecting suitable programmes for their children. Furthermore, by asking about the viewing experience, parents are able to give feedback to children and enhance their children's emotional skills (Extract 7).

The assessments made by the parents are also stressed here. By assessing the events and characters, parents are able to invite children to affiliate, and thus construct a joint understanding of the media content. In these situations, family members also construct togetherness. Assessments are also important for parental mediation because through them the participants negotiate how to evaluate the media content. Parents are able to mediate norms and morals by strongly condemning the action on the screen (Extract 11) and by setting an example of how to assess delicate situations (Extract 10).

By taking an interactional approach to parental mediation and utilizing naturally occurring interaction in family settings, this chapter has explored parental mediation as a situated practice that is manifested in parent–child interaction. Four practices that are linked in different ways to parental mediation were identified. While the identified practices were in line with earlier research, the functions that these practices served were more ambiguous and diverse than expected. Our findings suggest that parental mediation plays a significant role in the children's socialization process in contemporary families. It comprises not only parental attempts to diminish the negative effects of media, but parental mediation also has positive qualities, such as increasing children's general knowledge, teaching them reasoning, enhancing their emotional skills, passing on social norms and building togetherness among family members. These findings support Clark's (2011) suggestion that parental mediation should be understood as a larger concept, not just as the parents' responses to potentially harmful media. Our findings also gave some support to the suggestion of Austin et al. (1999) that parental mediation does not necessarily need to be goal oriented or intentional, rather, it may occur 'due to happenstance' as a part of ordinary family interaction.

It should be noted that our analysis is limited to examining interaction. The further outcomes of the practices of parental mediation I have described here – and their effectiveness – are beyond the scope of this study. These findings open up new possibilities for future research. For example, talking about one's viewing experience might be related to various positive outcomes regarding child development.

Our findings also suggest that the broad classification of positive, negative and neutral mediation may not be sufficient to adequately describe the variety of interactional phenomena that are involved in parental mediation. For example, asking (neutral) questions might be involved in interpreting the show (Extract 2), doing teaching (Extract 3) and talking about the viewing experience (Extract 7). Moreover, it is not only parental actions that count. Children also shape the interactional contexts in which parental mediation may occur with their actions, such as asking questions (Extract 1) or making their own assessments (Extracts 8–12). Indeed, one important finding that I have not discussed in detail here involves the children's position in parental mediation. The mere term 'parental mediation' emphasizes the parents' role. However, our findings indicate that children also play a crucial part in the mediation process. In

Extracts 1 and 4, the sequences were initiated by the child's question, and in Extract 6, the child's self-initiated response set the interaction on a new trajectory about emotion skills. In light of this, parental mediation seems more like a co-constructed phenomenon. More thorough research of children's input in parental mediation is therefore needed.

REFERENCES

Austin, E.W., P. Bolls, Y. Fujioka and J. Engelbertson (1999), 'How and why parents take on the Tube', *Journal of Broadcasting and Electronic Media*, **43** (2), 175–92.
Ball, S. and G.A. Bogatz (1970), *The First Year of Sesame Street: An Evaluation*, Princeton, NJ: Educational Testing Service.
Buijzen, M. and P.M. Valkenburg (2005), 'Parental mediation of undesired advertising effects', *Journal of Broadcasting and Electronic Media*, **49** (2), 153–65.
Buijzen, M., J.H.W. van der Molen and P. Sondij (2007), 'Parental mediation of children's emotional responses to a violent news event', *Communication Research*, **34** (2), 212–30.
Clark, L.S. (2011), 'Parental mediation theory for the digital age', *Communication Theory*, **21** (4), 323–43.
Desmond, R.J., J.L. Singer, D.G. Singer, R. Calam and K. Collimore (1985), 'Family mediation patterns and television viewing: Young children's use and grasp of the medium', *Human Communication Research*, **11** (4), 461–80.
Du Bois, J.W. (2007), 'The stance triangle', in R. Englebretson (ed.), *Stancetaking in Discourse: Subjectivity, Evaluation, Interaction*, Amsterdam: John Benjamins, pp. 139–82.
Fisch, S.M. (2000), 'A capacity model of children's comprehension of educational content on television', *Media Psychology*, **2** (1), 63–91.
Fujioka, Y. and E.W. Austin (2003), 'The relationship of family communication patterns to parental mediation styles', *Communication Research*, **29** (6), 642–65.
Goodwin, C. and M.H. Goodwin (1992), 'Assessments and the construction of context', in A. Duranti and C. Goodwin (eds), *Rethinking Context*, Cambridge, UK: Cambridge University Press, pp. 147–90.
Heritage, J. (1984a), 'A change-of-state token and aspects of its sequential placement', in J.M. Atkinson and J. Heritage (eds), *Structures of Social Action*, Cambridge, UK: Cambridge University Press, pp. 299–345.
Heritage, J. (1984b), *Garfinkel and Ethnomethodology*, Cambridge, UK: Polity Press.
Heritage, J. (2012), 'The epistemic engine: Sequence organization and territories of knowledge', *Research on Language and Social Interaction*, **45** (1), 30–52.
Hicks, D.J. (1968), 'Effects of co-observer's sanctions and adult presence on imitative aggression', *Child Development*, **39** (1), 303–9.
Koole, T. (2015), 'Classroom interaction', in K. Tracy (ed.), *International Encyclopedia of Language and Social Interaction*, Hoboken, NJ: Wiley-Blackwell.
Lwin, M.O., A.J.S. Stanaland and A.D. Miyazaki (2008), 'Protecting children's privacy online: How parental mediation strategies affect website safeguard effectiveness', *Journal of Retailing*, **84** (2), 205–17.

Mehan, H. (1979), *Learning Lessons: Social Organization in the Classroom*, Cambridge, MA: Harvard University Press.

Nathanson, A.I. (1999), 'Identifying and explaining the relationship between parental mediation and children's aggression', *Communication Research*, **26** (2), 124–43.

Nathanson, A.I. (2002), 'Then unintended effects of parental mediation of television on adolescents', *Media Psychology*, **4** (3), 207–30.

Nathanson, A.I. (2004), 'Factual and evaluative approaches to modifying children's responses to violent television', *Journal of Communication*, **54** (2), 321–36.

Nathanson, A.I. and R.A. Botta (2003), 'Shaping the effects of television on adolescents' body image disturbance: The role of parental mediation', *Communication Research*, **30** (3), 304–31.

Piotrowski, J.T. (2014), 'The relationship between narrative processing demands and young American children's comprehension of educational television', *Journal of Children and Media*, **8** (3), 267–85.

Reiser, R.A., M.A. Tessmer and P.C. Phelps (1984), 'Adult–child interaction in children's learning from "Sesame Street"', *Educational Communication and Technology Journal*, **36** (1), 15–21.

Shin, W. (2015), 'Parental socialization of children's Internet use: A qualitative approach', *New Media and Society*, **17** (5), 649–65.

Valkenburg, P.M., M. Krcmar, A.L. Peeters and N.M. Marseille (1999), 'Developing a scale to assess three styles of television mediation: "Instructive mediation," "restrictive mediation" and "social coviewing"', *Journal of Broadcasting and Electric Media*, **43** (1), 52–66.

Warren, R. (2003), 'Parental mediation of preschool children's television viewing', *Journal of Broadcasting and Electronic Media*, **47** (3), 394–417.

7. Masculine and feminine aspects of interaction in the context of watching TV*

Eero Suoninen

INTRODUCTION

When we 'watch TV', a lot more than just watching may occur. Watching TV may offer an important arena for interaction between family members and the socialization of children. In this chapter, I analyse two very different modes of interaction between parents and children in the context of watching TV. The focus is based on findings from videotaped data: these data indicate that in some families, the interaction in front of the TV between parents and their children clearly relates to the gender of participants.

In order to make sense of this gender dimension, I analyse two cases in detail – one of father–son interaction and one of mother–daughter interaction – in which gender-related practices are prevalent. The two cases include the most clearly masculine and feminine practices from a corpus of 26 families whose everyday life was videotaped with four cameras during one weekday afternoon (see Appendix 1). In the final section of this chapter, I compare the aspects of the masculine and feminine cases.

AN INTERACTIONAL PERSPECTIVE ON GENDER-RELATED PRACTICES

The American sociolinguist Deborah Tannen (1991) has analysed the difference between women's and men's communication, and she suggests that most women favour the language of personal relations whereas most men favour the language of independence. On the other hand, from the feminist perspective, it has been emphasized (Ridgeway, 1999) that unequal gender relationships are recreated through everyday interaction. However, the connection between gender and activity is not straightforward. It would clearly be an over-interpretation to assume that gender determines the activities of everyday family life. In many families, it is the local family culture and negotiations of culturally known ideals rather than general rules that explain what happens in everyday situations (e.g., Goodwin, 2007; Tannen et al., 2007; Tovares, 2007; Gordon, 2009). Nevertheless, the general ideals and practices may be tightly interwoven. In order to avoid the impression of the deterministic causation of the gender system, I conceptualize it in terms of the gender-related practices that family members use as masculine and feminine resources for everyday interaction. From this theoretical perspective, the aim of this chapter is to analyse in detail the masculine and feminine aspects that are found in today's Finnish families in the context of watching TV. The analysis compares the differences and similarities between masculine and feminine practices, but does not aim at generalizations of gender-specific practices.

The methodological starting point is to avoid the analyst's pre-understanding and instead conclude from the data how the participating family members themselves interpret each other's interactional turns. In addition, the analytical aim is to interpret how interactional processes become constructed in and through the participants' turns. This data-driven strategy, which applies the principles of discourse analysis (Potter and Wetherell, 1987; Gee and Handford, 2012), conversation analysis (Hutchby and Wooffitt, 1988; Sacks, 1992) and multimodal discourse analysis (Goodwin, 2007; Raudaskoski, 2011), avoids gross generalization and instead aims at a detailed interpretation of the most essential features of interaction concerning the position-taking of the participants, cooperation and atmosphere, and the rhythm of dialogue.

The interaction between the parent and child includes much more than words, such as gestures, movements, changes of gaze, different tones of voice, and changes of volume and intonation. In order to preserve this non-verbal side, the data extracts contain a collection of notation marks that are generally used in interactional analysis (see Appendix 2). The interactional processes in both father–son and mother–daughter interaction have been divided into small data extracts in a way that the next extract is always a direct continuation of the previous one.

Father–Son Interaction

The father–son interaction comes from a videotaped scenario in which a father and his two sons, 12-year-old Saku and eight-year-old Jusu (all names have been changed), watch an ice hockey match. Also present is a ten-year-old daughter, Sari, who mainly concentrates on her homework.

Picture 7.1   Father–son interaction watching an ice hockey match

The location of the family members in the room at the beginning of the episode can be seen in Picture 7.1.

The TV screen was recorded with another video camera in order to simultaneously analyse family interaction and the TV programme. Detailed transcription is difficult because of the loud TV volume that overwhelms some parts of the talk. Nevertheless, loud voices characterize the practice of watching sports. The first data extract starts as the father calls out when he notices something interesting in an ice hockey match. Barkov, Ahtola and Plihal are names of ice hockey players.

Extract 1

1	Father:	<u>Oh dear,</u>
2	Jusu:	Barkov really is a slow °skater°.
3	Father:	Ahtola surely tackles s- strongly.
4	Jusu:	Soon they'll make Plihal run again.
5	Saku:	Heh. ((laughter))
6	Father:	((Looks smiling at Jusu and utters a laugh.))
7	Jusu:	Plihal will surely be beaten'cause he is being lazy there
8		all the time. (5.0) Now Barkov.
9	Saku:	Soon Ahtola will get a penalty.

In line 1, the father cries out in surprise at a tackle in the game. Although the impulse comes outside the conversation between the father and sons, it seems to create a common focus among the participants. While the father explains the reason for the surprise ('Ahtola surely tackles s- strongly') the boys join in the like-minded atmosphere: Jusu by talking (lines 2 and 4) and Saku by his supportive laughter, which the father also joins in with.

It is worth noticing that the speech of the younger son, eight-year-old Jusu, represents a bold and masculine mode of talk that consists of laughing at the weaknesses of players. However, mutual, warm encouragement continues between the TV watchers. The father looks at Jusu (line 6) and laughs in a friendly fashion with Saku after Jusu has continued his talk. In an educational sense, the lesson that Jusu gets is that it is favourable to admire physical power and look down on weakness and laziness. The father gives positive credence to this kind of masculinity through his encouraging response and thus inspires the continuation of this masculine mode of talk. It is noteworthy, however, that what is not encouraged is admiration for breaking the rules of ice hockey.

In addition to the warm father–son interaction, the participants also construct other kinds of settings. The next extract illustrates how an asynchronic interactional framework takes shape.

Extract 2

10	Jusu:	((in a cosy tone of voice)) Father do you remember when (0.5) erm
11		when Lehterä got two plus ten [because,
12	Father:	[Look, (0.3) <u>Sasha</u>
13		((Sasha is a nickname of ice hockey player Barkov.))
14	Father:	<u>Look,</u>
15		((Rises eagerly as if going to stand up and glances rapidly
16		at the boys.))
17	Father:	<u>O:h my: Go:d o:h [my: Go::d.</u>

Jusu starts his cosy chat with a personal address ('Father'), but does not get a response. Instead, he is sharply interrupted by his father's gradually growing exclamation at the incidents on the TV screen. The player, whose nickname is Sasha, excites the father's attention much more strongly than the cosy talk his son initiated. By shouting '<u>Look</u>' twice and then most emphatically '<u>O:h my: Go:d o:h [my: Go::d</u>', the father throws himself into the ecstatic world of the ice hockey experience. Thus, the stimulation of the TV programme overrides the ordinary rules of conversation, which include listening to the other party and answering questions.

Although watching ice hockey is the father and sons' joint hobby, the ecstatic style of the father does not inspire the boys to join in the mood. Regarding Jusu's position as a child, it is significant whether he gives up speaking and asking questions or not. We can see his choice in the next extract. The square bracket before his first word ('Dad', line 18) means that he starts his talk simultaneously with his father's emphatic shouting ('<u>O:h my: Go:d o:h [my: Go::d</u>'). Because of this overlap, I repeat line 17 from the end of the previous extract.

Extract 3

17	Father:	<u>O:h my: Go:d o:h [my: Go::d.</u>
18	Jusu:	[Dad,=
19	Father:	=Now did you see when he came from there.=
20	Jusu:	=Dad (1.0) how when Lehterä got two plus (0.5) ten
21		((The father is getting up from the sofa as if leaving somewhere,
22		but then he stops to listen to Jusu's question.))
23	Jusu:	when Ohtamaa came headlong towards him
24	Father:	°mhy°
25	Jusu:	against Kärpät ((another team)) do you remember.
26	Father:	<u>No.</u> (0.5) [I wasn't there. ((a slightly rude tone))
27	Jusu:	[Don't you remember.

Even if it seems very difficult to get his father away from the immediate game of ice hockey, Jusu repeats the friendly address again ('Father' in line 10 and 'Dad' in lines 18 and 20). It is noteworthy that in Jusu's speech, the previously used word 'Father' is changed to the closer address 'Dad'. The difficulty in the address can be seen after Jusu's first 'Dad' (line 18), when the father ignores this address and instead continues his own mode of talk by exclaiming 'Now did you see when he came from there'. Although the father's body language suggests that he is oriented to leaving the room, Jusu calmly continues his question (lines 20 and 23). At first, his question produces only a quiet sneer (°mhy°) from his father. Jusu does not comply with this response; he continues his question with some additional information and repeats a straight question ('do you remember', line 25). Eventually, this repetition succeeds in gaining the father's attention, even if the response is uttered somewhat rudely.

Unlike the father, Jusu's elder brother, Saku, seems to be in the same world as Jusu, as seen in the next extract.

Extract 4

28	Saku:	He surely tackled him (1.0) but it was °elbow down.°
29		((Jusu gets up from the sofa.))
30	Jusu:	He went like this from there a[nd, ((Acts falling down.))
31	Father:	[Who. ((blurting tone))
32	Jusu:	That Atte [Ohtamaa once.
33	Saku:	[Ohtamaa Kärpät. ((name of a team)).
34	Father:	So you mean Lehterä. ((Starts leaving the room.))
35	Saku:	Yeah.

36	Father:	[It was wrong. ((criticizing the penalty))
37	Jusu:	[Yea he came like this and then Lehterä just skated away °from there°.
38		((acting energetically with his whole body))
39	Father:	Ye:s. (he had to organize game) ((while walking away))
40	Saku:	What.
41		((The father answers something unclear while walking from the room.))
42	Jusu:	Surely he'll do the same in Sunday's game.

In the first line of the extract, Saku marks his little brother's question as sensible by adding some details to its premises. In addition, the reciprocal, like-minded and simultaneous speech (lines 32–33) creates a sense of community between the boys. Although the father is leaving the room, the boys' team spirit also inspires him to join in the cosy father–son chat (lines 34, 36 and 39). As part of this chat, the father also comments on the issue in question ('It was wrong', line 36) in a way that is possible to understand as the first constructive response to the question Jusu has asked most persistently (lines 10, 18, 20, 25 and 27).

It is interesting how easy-going the chat between the brothers seems to be. In addition to the joint simultaneous talk and like-mindedness mentioned previously, Jusu even acts out with his whole body the tackling situation his elder brother described. The cosy chatting also continues when the father returns to the room.

Extract 5

43		((for a while only voices from the TV until the father returns
44		and talks at the door))
45	Father:	They fired Ville Nieminen. ((a famous ice hockey player))
46	Saku:	Yeah they did (.) for <u>what</u>. ((eagerly))
47	Father:	Well he was all shit of course.
48	Saku:	Yep.
49	Jusu:	I hope he'll join Tappara. ((a favourite team))
50	Father:	Surely won't come () ((explains in a cosy manner))
51	Jusu:	Why,
52	Jusu:	not [because well,
53	Saku:	[there are so many tough guys.=
54	Jusu:	=he was all jo:ker.
55	Saku:	°Well I don't know°
56	Jusu:	Surely he is.
57	Jusu	Why doesn't Tallberg play.
58	Saku:	°I dunno.° ((cosy manner))

Thus, when father returns, he tells them something that is newsworthy for an ice hockey fan: a famous player has been fired. Both boys are excited about discussing the topic. The explanation that the father gives ('Well he was all shit of course', line 47) is surprising, because it does not represent the mode of talk of an ordinary parent. It sounds more like the bad language that parents of young children often try to forbid. Here the 'bad talk', however, represents a masculine mode of talk that is suitable when discussing ice hockey. Instead, chatting between the boys seen in the previous extract conforms to so-called good manners regarding both vocabulary and turn-taking.

As a whole, the father–son interaction seems to be hierarchic in the way that the position of the father is clearly higher in status than his sons. The father determines the rules of interaction and states in a very powerful way how things are. His expressions are also more varied and bolder compared to those of the boys. The level of reciprocity and sense of community varies greatly during the interaction.

Mother–Daughter Interaction

At the beginning of the mother–daughter case, the mother lies on a sofa and watches the British TV series *Heartbeat*. Her 12-year-old daughter, Mari, moves around in the room and occasionally chats with her mother (Picture 7.2). From her mother's perspective, Mari also often moves in front of the TV.

Mari, who is recovering from an illness, is choosing clothes in order to go to a school party. In the plot of the TV programme, the daughter of a

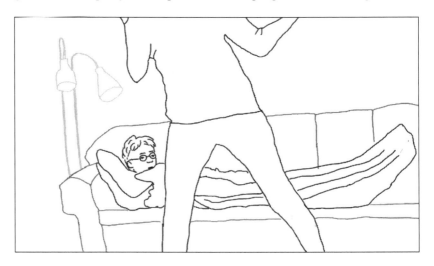

Picture 7.2   Mother–daughter interaction during a TV series episode

family angrily leaves home and her parents dispute the seriousness of the situation: the mother is graver than the father. While the TV shows a girl walking briskly accompanied by rhythmic music, Mari enters the space between her mother and the TV.

Extract 6

1	Mari:	Is this good.
2	Mother:	Ye↑:s.
3	Mari:	((dancing towards mother)) Look how these fit well together.
4	Mother:	M↑m ((Daughter continues dancing.)) Very good.
5	Mari:	Mother, ((hands wide open and raised)) (1.0) new Escada perfume must
6		be bought for me. >It is< obviously I am addicted to this (perfume).
7		((hands childishly, eagerly raised at the word 'addicted'))
8	Mother:	>Well there's now< (.) there are also other perfumes.
9	Mari:	No: (.) I want Escada perfume because Escada is made for the young.
10	Mother:	Mh↑y
11	Mari:	So that's it. ((while dancing energetically from the room))

Although Mari's question about her choices of clothes ('Is this good') obviously disturbs her mother's TV watching, her mother answers in an easy-going way and with a friendly rising intonation ('Ye↑:s'). The easy-going atmosphere also continues in the conversation, even when Mari demands a contentious acquisition. The mother respects the initiative of her daughter, even though she does not agree with her child's demand. The mother avoids straightforward confrontation by showing her disagreement in a cosy way, in the form of a supplementary idea ('>Well there's now< (.) there also are other perfumes', line 8) as well as by responding in a minimal, neutral and friendly way ('Mh↑y', line 10) to the argument her daughter has adopted from an advertisement ('Escada is made for the young', line 9). The maintenance of a friendly atmosphere requires, however, that the mother does not express her stance in a clear way but simply maintains the friendly fluency of the conversation.

Mari's ending of the conversation ('So that's it', line 11) that she utters while dancing energetically from the room is interesting. It indexes the disputed demand as valid, but is, on the other hand, uttered in a light and possibly playful way. The mother–child conversation seems to have produced a sense of cooperation and communion despite the fact that the mother's concentration on watching TV has been disturbed. Prioritizing the child over the TV becomes even clearer in the next part of the conversation.

Extract 7

((Mari comes whistling back into the room. She walks across the front of TV,
rattles something and walks back humming loudly (obviously to draw her
mother's attention). Continuing to hum, Mari comes back with a bag. She
watches the TV series for a while: the girl who has run away from home has a
quarrel with her friends and leaves them by light motorcycle))
18   Mari: We:ll it isn't so cold there=five degrees.
19   Mother: Yes. (2.0) °no but° cold rain after all.
20   Mari: I'll take an umbrella. (1.0) ((Starts humming again.))
21   Mari: They'll surely come very soon.
22   ((Mari leaves while her mother watches TV, but soon comes
                back
23   singing the word 'beautiful' and dancing energetically. She
24   sits down on her mother's feet.))

Thus, Mari seems to succeed in taking the role of the main character who
evidently gets her mother's attention whenever she wants, regardless of
what her mother is concentrating on. However, how her mother responds
to Mari's comment on the weather ('Yes. (2.0) °no but° cold rain after all',
line 19) is not merely aimed to please her daughter. That is to say, she also
warns her child in a caring manner just as a good mother should. Mari also
acknowledges the reasonableness of her mother's concern by responding
that she will take an umbrella.

Although the conversation runs as an easy-going dialogue, it is interesting
how far the mother accepts her daughter's attention-seeking, allowing it to
interrupt her viewing. Sitting down on the mother's feet is an example
of the type of interruption the mother overlooks. The attention-seeking
interruptions also continue in the next extract. In the lines marked with
arrows (→), the pacing of dialogue grows faster for both participants.

Extract 8

25   Mari: How awful. ((looks at her mother))
26   Mother: ((Glances at Mari and asks)) What,
27   Mari: What happened.
28   ((Mari gets up, but stays close, dancing and coughing twice.))
29   ((Mother momentarily turns her gaze from the TV towards
                Mari.))
30   Mari: →   Are you worried.
31   Mother:→   About you? ((Mother's gaze turns again towards Mari.))
32   Mari: →   Mh↑y
33   Mother:→   I am if you [()
34   Mari:→   [Surely I can take Panadol ((a pain killer)) with me.
35   ((Mother nods.))
36   Mari: Mmhm

37	Mari:	Shall I take.=
38	Mother:	=°Sure you can take°.
39		((Mari leaves dancing and humming to continue her work.))

It is interesting that Mari looks at her mother when she says 'How awful' (line 25). When specifically referring to the TV drama, it would be natural to look at the screen. Therefore, acting as if horrified is not actually about TV drama; it serves to maintain the communication and relationship between the mother and daughter. The mother's responsive question ('What') makes the communication reciprocal. After this response, it is possible for Mari to utter her own question ('What happened') as if desired by her mother. It is noteworthy that her mother does not start answering and Mari does not wait for an answer but gets up and starts to dance (line 28). Thus, both understand that the function of Mari's question is something other than information-seeking. The function of this dialogue is maintaining the mother–daughter relationship.

Mari also continues seeking attention with other devices: by coughing and asking, 'Are you worried' (lines 28 and 30). Note that the mother reacts to Mari's coughing by momentarily turning her gaze towards her and offering a counter-question ('About you?', line 31). This question is logical, because the previous dialogue has already turned the topic to the participants' personal relationship. In addition, the coughing and question happens in the context of Mari's convalescence. With her personal question ('Are you worried'), Mari also succeeds in associating with the role of the mother without mentioning it, because the question includes 'a category bound activity' (Watson, 1983, pp. 39–42; Stokoe, 2004, p. 112) of being worried about one's own child that is culturally connected to the mother's category. Furthermore, the fact that the pace of the dialogue grows faster (in the lines marked with arrows) supports this interpretation, because the interaction seems to run as a routinized ritual in which both participants orientate without any hesitation to talk about the mother's worries concerning her child.

Even if the ritual maintains the mother–daughter relationship, there is a minor disturbance when Mari does not recognize her mother's nod (line 35) at the expected moment. The participants, however, easily correct this misunderstanding by an extra question–answer pair (lines 37–38), restoring their seamless cooperation.

The Procession of Volume and Rhythm

The difference between the masculine and feminine modes of interaction can be further analysed by examining how volume and rhythm varies in the

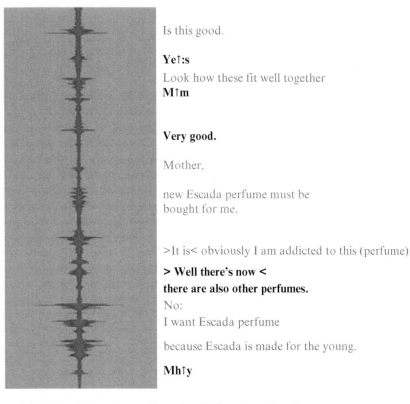

Is this good.

Ye↑:s
Look how these fit well together
M↑m

Very good.

Mother,

new Escada perfume must be
bought for me.

>It is< obviously I am addicted to this (perfume)

> Well there's now <
there are also other perfumes.
No:
I want Escada perfume

because Escada is made for the young.

Mh↑y

Figure 7.1   Variation in volume level of mother–daughter interaction

train of the interactions. In the next two figures, it is possible to see graphic
visualizations of the variation of volume in the first parts of the analysed
cases. I present the visualization of the mother–daughter conversation
first, because it is easier to analyse (Figure 7.1).

It is clearly seen from the variation of column width that in mother–
daughter interaction both participants follow the same dialogical rhythm.
That is, the duration between each turn is almost as long and the rhythm
is easily maintained. As seen previously, there is one exception outside this
first phase in which the rhythm of the dialogue is faster. However, both
participants orientate to this faster pace as a joint, reciprocally understood
interactional ritual. Thus, the fast pace is not an exception to this feminine
dialogue that favours a synchronism of pace. The father–son conversation
differs radically from this joint synchrony, as can be seen in Figure 7.2.

Although the procession of the father–son interaction is difficult to
describe graphically, it is easy to notice that the rhythm of the conversation

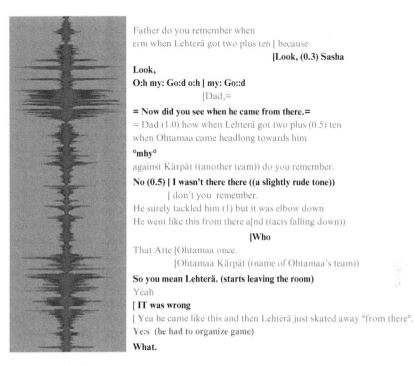

Father do you remember when
erm when Lehterä got two plus ten [because
                                  [Look, (0.3) Sasha
Look,
O:h my: Go:d o:h [my: Go::d
                [Dad,=
= Now did you see when he came from there.=
= Dad (1.0) how when Lehterä got two plus (0.5) ten
when Ohtamaa came headlong towards him
°mhy°
against Kärpät ((another team)) do you remember.
No (0.5) [I wasn't there there ((a slightly rude tone))
          [don't you remember.
He surely tackled him (1) but it was elbow down
He went like this from there a[nd ((acts falling down))
                             [Who
That Atte [Ohtamaa once.
          [Ohtamaa Kärpät ((name of Ohtamaa's team))
So you mean Lehterä. (starts leaving the room)
Yeah
[IT was wrong
[Yea he came like this and then Lehterä just skated away °from there°.
Ye:s (he had to organize game)
What.

Figure 7.2   Variation in volume level of father–son interaction

is much more arbitrary than the mother–daughter dialogue. Very long
'branches of a tree' typify the TV-inspired shouting by the father.

From the point of view of the child, it is essential that in both cases
the interaction with his or her parents creates a sense of togetherness and
well-being. This may be accomplished either by harmonious reciprocal
dialogue (as in the mother–daughter case) or by the joint focus on the TV
programme (as in the father–son case). The father–son interaction seen
above is, however, highly parent-centred in the way that it allows criticism
from the perspective of child-centred ideals.

DISCUSSION

The analyses have revealed a number of differences between the two
cases that resemble Tannen's (1991) division between women's favouring
the language of personal relations and men's favouring the language of
independence. I have also identified some aspects from the two cases that

Table 7.1   Masculine and feminine aspects of interaction

Father–son interaction	Mother–daughter interaction
Atmosphere that encourages the child's bold performance	Atmosphere that emphasizes emotions and togetherness, and the child's appearance
Parent-centred interaction; the excellence of the parent's judgement, the parent does not always listen to his child	Child-centred interaction; the initiatives of the child are responded to with understanding
The parent uses a variety of styles to express himself; the child mostly speaks in a moderate way	The child uses a variety of styles to express herself; the parent mostly speaks in a moderate way
The TV programme overrides the reciprocal rules and rhythm of conversation	The TV programme does not override the rhythm of conversation
Togetherness through a joint area of interest, comparing personal knowledge, enthusiastic overlapping talk and accepting gestures	Togetherness via an easy-going reciprocal dialogue and also by discussing the mother's concern about her child
Clear-cut methods to express judgements; the importance of qualified knowledge	Ambiguous methods to express judgements; the importance of taking care of the participants' personal relationship
Varied and arbitrary volume level and rhythm of dialogue	Harmonious rhythm and volume level of dialogue

draw a more vivid picture of how the differences may actualize in mundane interaction. The variation of different aspects can be seen in Table 7.1.

The aspects mentioned in the table indicate a clear difference between two kinds of interactional modes, which may be called masculine and feminine. The father–son setting encourages the son into a bold performance including the use of physical power, and the mother–daughter setting encourages the daughter to express her own emotions, think about her appearance, and also take care of a reciprocal relationship. The power relations also clearly differ in the two settings. The father seems to be the self-evident authority, whereas the mother is a parent who carefully listens to everything her daughter says. This difference applies both to the intellectual status of the participants and the ways the parents control the trajectory of interaction. By the intellectual status, I refer to the potential to utter unconditional assertions in a way that the other party self-evidently accepts. By control over the interactional trajectory, I refer to the potential to decide the rules of interaction as well as the variety of modes and the rhythm of interaction. It is striking that the father's variation of tones and volume of utterances is much more versatile that that of the mother's. The masculine interactional mode makes it familiar for the son to speak in a way that does not compete with his father's varying tone of voice, whereas in the feminine interactional mode, the mother seems to be a calm speaker while the daughter uses a great variety of expression. Noticing the stereotypical gender division in the two cases, it is possible to argue that the cases illustrate the large variation of practices that may actualize gender socialization in everyday family interaction.

From the point of view of the child, it is essential that the child-centeredness of the mother allows her child to interrupt her TV watching. The mother seems to avoid all kinds of straightforward turns of talk that could provoke disputes, whereas the daughter favours bolder utterances but softens them with a playful ambivalence. By contrast, for the father, the occurrences on the TV screen are much more important than the child's initiatives. To some extent, this difference relates to the type of TV programme: a British drama series is not as intensive as an ice hockey match. Thus, if the mother of a family happens to be a more passionate ice hockey fan, interactional practices may turn contrariwise. However, the concepts of masculinity and femininity still apply in the sense that men usually favour ice hockey more than women.

Is it justifiable, then, to appreciate feminine parenting over masculine parenting in the context of the current child-centred ideals in the Western world? This argument is applicable from the feminine perspective, but from the masculine perspective, the situation is more complicated. From the masculine interaction, it seems natural to emphasize the virtue of straight and open talk, and moreover it may seem odd that the mother maintains friendly rituals without clearly voicing her own parental judgements. Thus, Tannen's (1991) perception that women favour the language of personal relations and men the language of independence gains some support. If we conceptualize feminine and masculine practices as collateral cultures, it is unfair to argue univocally which one is better. Both masculine and feminine practices seem to work, at least in some families.

What is also important from the point of view of the child is that both feminine and masculine interaction in the context of watching TV seems to generate meaningful togetherness between the parents and children. In the mother–daughter interaction, the element that generates togetherness is reciprocal dialogue in which the status of the daughter is at least formally equal – or even superior – to that of her mother. Instead, in the father–son case, an atmosphere that emphasizes a strong masculine performance is jointly appreciated, despite the fact that the father is the more central actor.

The father's attention seems to be especially important to the younger (eight-year-old) son. In addition, the interest in comparing knowledge on ice hockey teams and players seems to be enjoyable to both the father and the sons, although the father holds a higher status than his sons.

However, if questioning the desirability of the strict gender socialization seen above, the results seem problematic. If trying to change traditional gender division, parenting should somehow change. There are two possibilities to actualize the change. The first option is to favour some kind of general 'ideal', such as child-centredness, regardless of the parent's gender. The other option is to conceive masculine and feminine practices as alternative resources for every parent, and to encourage both fathers and mothers to master both types of practices to some extent. Obviously, this would probably apply to different occasions of family interaction.

The analysis performed in this chapter proves that masculine and feminine practices still exist in some aspects of today's late modern society. In addition, the analysis has demonstrated how gender socialization may be actualized in and through the small choices made by family members when watching TV.

NOTE

*   This chapter is based on Suoninen, E. (2015), 'Isä–poika- ja äiti–tytär-vuorovaikutus television äärellä', in A.R. Lahikainen, T.Mälkiä and K. Repo (eds), *Media lapsiperheessä*, Tampere: Vastapaino.

REFERENCES

Gee, J.P. and M. Handford (eds) (2012), *The Routledge Handbook of Discourse Analysis*, London: Routledge.
Goodwin, C. (2007), 'Participation, stance and affect in the organization of activities', *Discourse & Society*, **18** (1), 53–73.
Gordon, C. (2009), *Making Meanings, Creating Family: Intertextuality and Framing in Family Interaction*, Oxford: Oxford University Press.
Hutchby, I. and R. Wooffitt (1988), *Conversation Analysis*, Cambridge, UK: Polity Press.
Potter, J. and M. Wetherell (1987), *Discourse and Social Psychology*, London: Sage.
Raudaskoski, P. (2011), 'When lives meet live: Categorization work in a reality TV show and "experience work" in two home audiences', *Text & Talk*, **31** (5), 619–41.
Ridgeway, C.L. (1999), 'The gender system and interaction', *Annual Review of Sociology*, **25** (1), 191–216.
Sacks, H. (1992), in G. Jefferson (ed.), *Lectures on Conversation: Vol. II*, Oxford: Blackwell.

Stokoe, E.H. (2004), 'Gender and discourse, gender and categorization: Current developments in language and gender research', *Qualitative Research in Psychology*, **1** (2), 107–29.

Tannen, D. (1991), *You Just Don't Understand – Women and Men in Conversation*, New York: Ballantine Books.

Tannen, D., S. Kendall and C. Gordon (2007), *Family Talk: Discourse and Identity in Four American Families*, Oxford: Oxford University Press.

Tovares, A. (2007), 'Family members interacting while watching TV', in D. Tannen, S. Kendall and C. Gordon (eds), *Family Talk: Discourse and Identity in Four American Families*, Oxford: Oxford University Press, pp. 283–309.

Watson, R. (1983), 'The presentation of victim and offender in discourse: The case of police interrogations and interviews', *Victimology*, **8** (1–2), 31–52.

8. When a computer dominates a child's attention*

Eero Suoninen

INTRODUCTION

Parents know how tiring it can be to get a child immersed in computer use to move his or her gaze away from the screen, and many parents are concerned about the dangers that the increased use of computers can cause to their children. They are afraid that children may forget other important activities, become addicted to computer use or join dubious social networks. It is difficult for parents to control children's computer use precisely because children are often much keener to play with computers than to discuss the rules of playing. In addition, the fact that children are usually more skilful computer users than their parents makes traditional parental control demanding. Despite this difficulty, many parents try to regulate, for example, under what circumstances and for how long their children can use the computer.

In this chapter, I analyse the interaction that takes place in the context of computer usage. I focus my attention on the discussion and debate between the parent and child in a situation where the child is strongly attached to computer use and the parent would like to the child to do something else. Today, this kind of tensional situation in which parents and children argue over child's computer time may be common and challenging in most Western families.

DATA AND METHODOLOGY

Family interaction has usually been studied through surveys and interviews that rely on subject recall. However, there are two important exceptions. The first is the American family research centre 'Everyday Lives in Families' (e.g., Goodwin, 2007; Ochs and Kremer-Sadlik, 2013), which analysed videotaped data on everyday family life collected from American middle-class homes. This type of data makes it possible to analyse the details of naturally occurring interaction, which may be important from the point of view of joint action. The publications mentioned above demonstrate the importance of multimodal analysis that includes language, gestures and other extra-linguistic activities when studying family interaction. The research centre also cooperates with a Swedish research project that analyses the use of media and relationships resulting from the use of computers (Aarsand, 2007).

The second significant exception is an American socio-linguistic research project that audio-recorded everything that was said by four American families over one week. By the means of these recordings, the face-to-face interaction of dual-income families were analysed in the home context as well as in some other relevant contexts (e.g., Gordon, 2007, 2009; Tannen, 2007; Tovares, 2007). The variation of frames, positions and values were analysed from the interactional perspective. Tovares (2007) focused her analysis on the family as a small community that interacts while watching TV. She demonstrated how family members expressed themselves by intertextual repetition of phrases from the televisual text. The research work on this project demonstrates the importance of analysing longer trains of interaction when trying to understand the formation of positions in the local family culture.

In this chapter, I apply the ideas mentioned above: I consider the multimodality of interaction and analyse longer interactional processes. The video-recorded data were gathered in 2011–12 as a part of the research project 'Media, Family Interaction and Children's Well-Being' (described in Appendix 1 at the end of the book). Originally, my intention was to identify how different parenting styles – such as child-centred, authoritarian or negotiating – differ from each other in the context of disputes over the use of computers. However, all the parents in our data seemed to display features from a variety of parenting styles. Thus, I focused my analysis on the variation of aspects of parenting styles and especially the way they arise at different stages of the interaction process. By analysing this variability, it is possible to gain access to the mutual negotiations that include both the parent's and the child's participation. From this perspective, I analyse in detail the strategies through which the parent and child negotiate the use of the computer and their relations to other family practices.

How is it possible to describe the above-mentioned strategic nature of interaction in methodological terms? I interpret the negotiation over computer use as operating on three levels, consisting of (1) position-taking, (2) frameworks and (3) cultural discourses. Position-taking refers to the choices made by the participants in their turns in relation to the conversation process. The concept of position is also suitable for examining the kinds of combinations of positions constructed between conversationalists (Suoninen and Wahlström, 2009). By the concept of framework, following Goffman (1974), I mean the way of explaining 'what is going on' in a given activity, for example playing together (a play framework) or a parent educating her or his child (an educational framework). By the discourses, I refer to terms and phrases that are frequently used in public discussions, for example 'child-centeredness' and 'the importance of setting boundaries for children'. For an everyday language user, discourses are culturally given in a certain epoch (e.g., Foucault, 1986, p. 107). However, because of the general nature of discourses, in practice they can be actualized in many different ways. The concept of strategy brings together the aspects of the above-mentioned levels (position-taking, interactional frameworks and discourses) in the way they permeate the parent and child's everyday activities. Thus, the interaction is analysed as an active pursuit and argumentation containing choices that relate to the local and cultural contexts. Whether the strategic choices are intentional or naturally made is, however, excluded from the analysis.

This methodological approach combines the traditions of discourse analysis (e.g., Wetherell, 2001; Suoninen and Wahlström, 2009), frame analysis (Goffman, 1974), discursive psychology (e.g., Edwards and Potter, 1992) and conversation analysis (e.g., Stokoe, 2011), and to some extent also features of multimodal analysis (Goodwin, 2007) and new rhetoric (Billig et al., 1988). According to the common understanding among these traditions, my aim is to look at the interaction process as it unfolds turn by turn for the participants themselves. From this perspective, it is essential to analyse how each speaker makes sense of the previous turn of talk in his or her next turn (Sacks et al., 1974, p. 728) and what kinds of accounts they give in the tensional moments of interaction (Edwards and Potter, 1992). In the concrete analysis of this chapter, the main focus is on the positions that participants take and the frameworks they orient towards.

The analysis focuses on one multistage interaction process selected from the data corpus of 26 video recordings of families' afternoons. I chose these recordings because this family case includes the most intensive negotiations about computer use. Focusing on one case allows the analysis of a long interaction process between the same participants. At the end of this chapter, however, I make some remarks about the larger data corpus.

ANALYSIS

The analysis follows the course of the original interaction process between a mother and son as it unfolds, including all the moments that necessitate rapid choice-making from the participants. In the analysed interaction process, the 12-year-old son is immersed in computer use and his mother suggests to him things that would require him to stop using the computer. The son's enthusiasm for spending time on the computer has been a recurrent problem for the parents, and they have tried to alleviate it by setting a time limit and some other conditions, such as doing homework before gaming. It is, however, difficult to assess whether the computer time has already been spent or the other conditions met. In general, the family has difficulties in agreeing on what kind of computer use is reasonable in relation to the boy's other obligations.

Conversational Tensions and Who is to Blame

The interaction process starts from a situation in which mother returns home after the working day before leaving again to partake in her hobbies. When mother arrives, her 12-year-old son, Timo (name changed), is sitting in the corner of the room playing a computer game (Picture 8.1).

Prior to the first data extract, the mother and Timo talked for a while about the research cameras and a text message from the father in which

Picture 8.1   The position of the son from his mother's perspective

he inquired whether 'you are at home normally'. The choice of word 'normally', which is repeated at the beginning of the first line of Extract 1, refers to the researcher's instruction to act as normally as possible when the recording is taking place. The first extract begins at the phase of conversation in which some tension begins to develop between the parties. Some notation marks (explained in Appendix 2) have been used in the extracts to make visible the nuances of interaction.

Extract 1

1	Mother:	I'm sending dad a message that sure we are quite normal <u>unfortunately</u>
2		(1.0) ↑but that it's football ((Timo's hobby)) today then. (0.8)
3		And you could for example try to send a <u>mes</u>sage to Henry erm (1.5)
4		that he is (.) if he's coming tomorrow.
5	Timo:	= >Yes<
6	Mother:	It it (.) do you have () number
7	Timo:	(1.0) ↓no.

The first line already hints at the tensional situation, because mother uses the wording '<u>unfortunately</u>'. Even if this quip was intended to be humorous, both parties remain serious. In the second line, the mother reminds Timo about his hobby. She also suggests that Timo should take care of his own hobby with his mobile phone. This proposition threatens Timo's ability to continue his computer use.

Next, the mother starts suggesting to Timo that he should send a message related to his hobby. It is noteworthy that the mother does not present her suggestion as a direct command. For example, she does not say that 'send Henry a message to check if he will come tomorrow', let alone 'stop playing and text Henry'. Instead, she expresses her suggestion cautiously: 'And you could for example try to send a <u>mes</u>sage to Henry erm (1.5) that he is (.) if he's coming tomorrow'. The mother marks on the topic delicately in many ways, such as by using the conditional tense ('you could'), mitigating the impression of an unconditional compulsion ('for example') and extra hesitations ('erm', two pauses and the correction of wording 'that he is (.) if he's coming'). Marking the proposal as delicate makes sense from the mother's point of view, because it may diminish the risk of an open dispute and improve the likelihood of the acceptance of her proposal (Van Nijnatten and Suoninen, 2014).

At first glance, Timo seems to accept his mother's suggestion by answering 'Yes' (line 5) with a fast speech rhythm and without any delay. An immediately positive answer is usually considered indicative of an unproblematic response, because it smoothly follows the preference organization of the interaction (Schegloff, 2007). The position combination that is constructed between the participants is: the mother suggests sensitively – the son accepts the suggestion. However, both Timo's gaze and his body position are clearly oriented towards the computer game, and his answer is minimal (a quick, monosyllabic 'Yes'). Thus, a suspicion remains that this is only a formal compliance to the preference structure of the conversation, and not an indicator of cooperation.

The mother's choice in the next turn is exceptionally interesting, because it reveals how she interprets Timo's ambiguous 'Yes'. After the mother's question and Timo's ambiguous answer, one could expect her evaluation of Timo's unclear answer in the 'third turn' (Drew and Heritage, 1992, pp. 39–41). The mother's response is also interesting in relation to the variation of culturally given discourses in the late modern epoch. Her situation seems contradictory; using the wording of Michael Billig and colleagues (1988), the situation is 'ideologically dilemmatic'. It would be ideal for the mother to be 'child-centred' and listen to her child and show him confidence. This could be done, for example, by saying 'It's great that you're going to take care of the matter'. On the other hand, however, parenting also means taking care of your child, including guaranteeing that important duties get done. In her third turn (line 6), however, she does not indicate whether she takes Timo's affirmative response as a promise to take responsibility for the phone call, nor does she express her worries about the unclear nature of her son's response. Instead, she seems to turn a blind eye to the ambiguous nature of Timo's answer, and by doing so, she marks the answer as being acceptable enough. Instead of criticism, the mother solves the interactional and ideological dilemma by asking (line 6) Timo a practical question about the telephone number he needs to complete the task. With this move, she invites her son away from the game framework and towards cooperation in the practical framework without indicating the impression of mistrust.

The son again gives a one-word answer, but now it is negative ('no' with a falling intonation) and given after a one-second delay. Therefore, unlike Timo's first response, it is not even formally preferred. Usually, some kind of account is added to the non-preferred response (Schegloff, 2007), which could be in this case, for example, Timo's explanation why he has not got the telephone number, or why the number is not necessary. Thus, the overall picture of Timo's position becomes clear: even though he answers the questions, his cooperation is only formal and does not express commitment to the activities discussed.

At the end of the extract, the mother has a similar choice situation as two lines earlier: she can accept her son's responses or take a more critical position towards his avoidance of responsibility. Her choice is seen in the next extract.

Extract 2

```
8              (1.2)
9    Mother:  I tried to phone you but your phone is somewhere again and you
10             [didn't answer.
11   Timo:    [I know ((sharply)) (0.8) my phone is somewhere ↑again↓.
12             ((irritated tone, the word 'again' melodically))
```

Thus, after a 1.2 second pause, the mother presents a more critical comment ('I tried to phone you but your mobile phone is somewhere again and you didn't answer', lines 9–10). When she previously asked 'do you have () number' (Extract 1, line 6) and got a negative answer that denies responsibility, one could expect her evaluation of Timo's immediately preceding negative reply in the third turn. Still, the mother again avoids a straightforward comment on Timo's reply by slightly changing the focus of the talk. However, the mother starts to show general dissatisfaction with her son's continuous neglect in taking care of his things. She invites Timo into the interactional setting in which the mother criticizes her son's lack of responsibility – the son gives an account. A valid account could consist of reasons for the lack of responsibility or an explanation of its insignificance.

The other party may, however, either accept an invitation to give an account or reject it. In this case, Timo chooses the latter option with his strong counter-critique. His response (line 11) consists of two parts, the sharply uttered 'I know' that overlaps the mother's speech and the melodically uttered 'my phone is somewhere ↑again↓' that ironically imitates the mother's tone of voice. Signs of Timo's irritation are therefore striking: roughly overlapping speech, downgrading the value of the mother's turn by the response 'I know' and ironizing the mother's way of speaking by imitating her melodic style.

Ironic imitation, in turn, produces the position of unreasonable nagger for the mother. By the choice of the word 'again', Timo hints at the narrative of the habitual nagging mother. By this turn of talk, he displaces the narrative about himself as a son who does not do his part, which was hinted at by his mother. In Timo's narrative, 'the bad guy' is his mother, and thus there is no need to blame himself. Timo's position-taking changes the interactional setting to the mother as a habitual nagger – the son as a critic of his mother's unreasonable nagging.

The Practical and Educational Frame or Gaming and Individual Psychology

Despite her son's irritation, the mother does not give up.

Extract 3

```
13              (2.0)
14   Mother:    And still you tell me that you'll send a message to Henry. ((criti-
                cizing tone))
15              (1.0)
16   Timo:      °I already forgot it.° ((friendly tone))
```

The mother's interactional difficulty can be seen in her pause that is longer than ordinary (line 13). Although her next turn ('And still you tell me that you'll send a message to Henry', line 14) is more critical than previously, she is not provoked by Timo's ironic counter-position. Rather, the mother's speech is an evaluation of the longer conversation flow calling for logical consistency: how can you promise to phone, if you do not know where the phone is? As in Extract 1 and 2, the mother therefore bypasses evaluating Timo's previous problematic turn. This repeated practice of turning a blind eye is reasonable because if mother had accepted her son's invitation to discuss who is to blame, the conversation would have resulted in a fruitless quarrel.

In the context of the mother's rational speech, the son changes his speech to a quieter and more cooperative tone of voice and offers an account ('°I already forgot it.°', line 16). Thus, son's speech includes some kind of apology for his behaviour. The variation on the cooperation level is essential, because it indicates that the son is not oriented only to the game framework but also – at least momentarily – to the ordinary interaction framework.

Despite the softening of the tone and the apology, the content of Timo's account is problematic for the mother. After all, it offers only a thin psychological explanation (forgetting) for the illogicality of Timo's behaviour, but not any idea of how to fix it. The parent's dilemma, therefore, moves back to the familiar dimension: how far should you understand the expressions of your child when he or she concentrates on a computer game without moving her or his gaze from the screen?

Extract 4

```
17              (2.0)
18   Mother:    Is it in that in that small Donald Duck backpack or,
19   Timo:      = >No.<
20              (1.5)
```

21	Mother:	in a schoolbag=when have you last used it (1.0) if I were you
22		I would <u>sea</u>rch for the phone a little.
23	Timo:	I thought I'd search for the phone.
24	Mother:	You thought so. ((ironic tone))
25		((Mother searches, Timo keeps concentrating on the computer game.))

Again, the mother seems to respond to Timo's problematic turn in the way seen in previous extracts. She follows a strategy of turning a blind eye by bypassing the evaluation of the previous problematic turn, and instead changes the focus to a practical framework.

After the mother's practical move ('<u>Is it</u> in that in that small Donald Duck backpack or', line 18), Timo utters a minimal, one-word response ('>No.<', line 19) that, again, omits his personal responsibility to do his part. After the repetition of this minimal response, it is logical that the mother should try to somehow change her communication style. This takes place as a combination of a practical frame ('in a schoolbag=when have you last used it', line 21) and an educational frame ('if I were you I would <u>sea</u>rch for the phone a little', lines 21–22). Starting her turn of talk in a practical frame is a sensible attempt, because maintaining practical cooperation sometimes softens the delicate aspect of taking the position of educator (Suoninen and Lundán, 2005). Accordingly, Timo seems to orient to cooperation a little better than previously by saying 'I thought I'd search for the phone' (line 23). This is, nevertheless, a problematic account that resembles the forgetting explanation we saw in Extract 3 (line 16). Although Timo refers to a plan to search for the phone, his mother sees a boy who is concentrating intensely on something else. Thus Timo's account seems more like an excuse not to take responsibility for searching for his phone. The mother displays this kind of understanding by responding in an ironic way 'You thought so' (line 24).

Because of a shortage of space, one minute has been omitted from the dialogue. During this time, the mother continues searching for Timo's phone while Timo concentrates on his computer game. The mother still continues the practices of the educational frame by explaining how rational searching is done (for example, calling Timo's mobile phone with another phone) and by systematically asking Timo to recall the places where he used the phone.

After Timo's answers again shorten to a minimal one-word level, the mother must decide how far it makes sense to continue this one-sided discussion. The turning point can be seen in the beginning of the next extract. The mother utters her turn in a loud voice and without any pause after Timo's repeated minimal response.

Extract 5

```
26  Mother:  Where can you have put it what do you need the phone for
27           [if you constantly lose it.
28  Timo:    [I do::n't know.
29           ((crowing tone))
30           (1.5)
31  Mother:  °hmy°
32           ((Mother continues searching in another room while Timo
             continues playing.))
33           ((Then she starts talking in commanding tone.))
34  Mother:  Now stop the game and start to look for your phone a bit=I'm
             really=it is an
35           expensive phone it may erm so where have you left it ag[ain.
36                                                              [I know.
```

In this extract, the mother no longer hides her irritation. She starts in a question form, but an irritated and loud voice and blaming wording ('Where can you have put it') and a genre of emotional exclamation ('what do you need the phone for if you constantly lose it') do not invite Timo to answer, but rather to explain why he does not take care of his phone. Thus, the mother takes a strongly critical position, inviting Timo to reflect and fix the problem. However, Timo's response does not include explanations or promises to fix the problem. Instead, he again gives a minimal answer leaning on a psychological state of mind ('I do::n't know', line 28) as if the mother's critical turn had been a simple ordinary question. In this case, the asynchrony of the conversation only gets worse.

After a few moments (lines 34–35), the mother's frustration bursts again out in the form of a lecture that consists of four elements: order giving ('Now stop the game and start to look for your phone a bit'), outburst of emotion ('=I'm really='), highlighting economic realities ('it is an expensive phone') and reproachful exclamation ('so where have you left it again'). In this short lecture, the mother, therefore, takes a number of different positions in a row – an authority that sets limits, an emotional human being, an economic adviser and a critic of irresponsibility – inviting her son to give a large collection of accounts. The multiplicity, however, turns out to be unsuccessful in this tensional situation, because the son considers himself justified in choosing which part of the lecture to reply to. His response ('I know', line 36) is a valid reply to the reminder of the price of the phone, but it completely ignores all the other elements of the mother's turn that would be much more important from the point of view of joint understanding. Therefore, the multifaceted nature of the mother's turn made it easy for Timo to override the essential idea of the mother's talk – to stop the game and search the phone – without actually breaking conversational rules.

Timo's word choices are also interesting. When the mother twice strongly criticizes Timo's withdrawal from his responsibilities, he persistently keeps on gaming by means of psychological vocabulary (lines 28 and 36). After the latter of those ('I know'), the mother eventually changes from the lecture framework to straightforward order-giving.

Extract 6

```
37   Mother:   The:n switch the g[ame off
38   Timo:                    [Yes I am switching. ((empathetically, but
                 continues playing))
39   Mother:   So. ((pushing tone, walks a little further))
40   Mother:   You say that you know but nothing happens.
41             ((Timo continues playing.))
42   Timo:     Sure you know me. ((cosy tone))
```

When the mother now presents an order to end the game ('The:n switch the [game off'), Timo agrees straight away ('Yes I am'). The mother's order does not make it easy for Timo to bypass his own responsibility, as previously, by giving a psychological account like 'I know', 'I thought so' or 'I forgot'. The order strongly invites Timo to accept, even if his promises would be empty. Actually, he continues the game in spite of his own promise and the mother's additional pushing ('So. . . You say that you know but nothing happens', lines 39–40).

Because of Timo's failure to actualize his promise, he faces growing pressure to give an account, which he eventually does (line 42). However, the content of the account, 'Sure you know me', is at first sight surprising, because it cancels out the previous promise without seemingly rational logic, which could be, for example, a reference that the phase of the game makes it impossible to switch off the game at once. In terms of the analysis, it is particularly interesting to consider in what sense the utterance is sensible.

When Timo's reference to a psychological response like 'I know', 'I thought so' or 'I forgot' is not enough, he seems to move to a heavier psychological account that not only refers to the moment's psychological state but also to his individual personality. Personal qualities, therefore, glue the son to the computer. With this account, Timo constructs for himself the position of the involuntary agent. Although the account seems far-fetched, it is perhaps a very pure form of appeal to the modern individualistic discursive ethos. Timo's mother also apparently accepts the report, or at least turns a blind eye by abstaining from objections. The individualistic ethos is practically connected to a child-centred discourse (e.g., Doddington and Hilton, 2007), according to which parents must listen carefully to their children as unique personalities. Because children are skilful ethnographers of their own culture, they quickly learn to use the discursive climate for their own purposes. 'Sure you know me' seems a rare turn in a conversation, but it closely resembles the more common phrase 'It's most important to be yourself' used today especially by young people.

So far, Timo appears to be the winner of all the previous rounds of dispute. He has succeeded in justifying his intensive concentration on the game framework by conducting a conversation framework on a minimal level and by giving psychological accounts. The mother has tried hard to get a joint focus on the educational framework, but has nonetheless stuck to the practical framework in which she has searched for his mobile phone alone. However, mother returns to the topic.

The Solution of the Discursive Dilemma by the Combination Statement

After the mother has been searching for a mobile phone in another room for about a minute while the boy has continued gaming, she returns to the problematic issue.

Extract 7

```
43   Mother:   ((shouts from downstairs)) I found it but you must pick it up.
44   Timo:     Yes, ((yet continues playing))
45             (5.0)
46   Timo:     ((Because immersed in the game, is startled by the sound of an
               opening door,
47             raises his hands up and shouts annoyed.)) I am coming right
               away. (1.0)
48   Timo:     Here I have, ((waving angrily hands in the air and gesturing
               towards
49             the screen))
```

At the beginning of the extract, the mother seems to have invented a way to solve the dilemma. She utters a two-part proposal according to which Timo's involvement could also take place naturally: 'I found it [meaning Timo's mobile phone] but you must pick it up'. The fair proposal successfully invites the son to give a positive response ('Yes', line 44). The problem remains, once again, that Timo's formal conversational cooperation does not make him do what he promised, or to clarify what he means by his acceptance. After a moment, Timo, who has immersed in gaming, quails at the sound of an opening door and moves angrily, because his game has been halted (lines 46–49; see Picture 8.2).

In spite of Timo's irritation, he again claims that he has accepted his

Picture 8.2   Irritated gestures of the son after the halt of the game

mother's order ('I am coming right away', line 47). On the other hand, his gestures give the impression that he cannot quit the game. Even if he looks irritated, this is the first time in the negotiation when he has turned to face his mother. Timo's irritation could be understood as an interactional move that invites the mother either to take a provoked counter-position to Timo's illogicality or to account for her disturbing the game. The mother, nevertheless, chooses a different strategy.

Extract 8

50	Mother:	So I found it but you must pick it up.
51		((Timo continues waving angrily towards the screen.))
52	Timo:	(1.0) mhy.
53	Mother:	Let it stay there.

54	Timo:	Yes I sure let [you see because,
55	Mother:	[(Now this is) the most important matter in the world.
56	Timo:	((while standing up)) I'll sure let this stay on pause see. ((dissatisfied tone))
57	Mother:	Well '<u>so</u> what' ((says in English))
58	Timo:	Would you like it to stay on pause. ((cosy tone while walking downstairs))

The mother determinedly repeats her proposal (line 50). Her voice is strong but cosy. Timo's deep irritation continues. However, the unprovoked but still purposeful line of the mother gradually softens Timo's behaviour so that in the end they leave the room talking with each other cosily.

Why, then, did the mother construct this combination of speech ('<u>I found the phone</u>]' + '<u>you must pick it up</u>') and hold on to this double formulation determinedly? This formulation is not functional concerning practicality. The phone is in fact in Timo's school backpack, from which the mother could get the phone effortlessly herself or bring the whole backpack to Timo when she enters the room. Instead of the practical frame, the meaningfulness of the proposal is based on the educational framework. The son is taught in a concrete way to take care of his own responsibilities, and that justifies the interruption in the use of the computer. In addition, the mother solves a challenging discursive conflict: how to be at the same time a parent who is child-centred but also able to set limits. '<u>I found it</u>' refers to a child-centred mother who has helped her child to continue his game, and '<u>but you must pick it up</u>' refers, in turn, to a mother who is able to set limits on her child's behaviour.

Another interesting phenomenon is the son's above-mentioned strong and emotionally laden gesturing. With strong gestures (lines 56 and 58), he created an impression that pausing the game would cause some dramatic problem. Actually, in some games this can be the case (e.g., there no pause option available), but in this case the impression appears deceptive. In spite of the misleading nature of the impression, it could justify the continuation of the game if the parent took it to be true. In this case, however, the mother seems to understand the operation of the computer well enough not to take these misleading hints seriously, and it turns out that son's outburst was just an attempt to continue his computer time.

Table 8.1   The variety and combinations of strategies

Mother's strategies	Son's strategies	Outcomes of the combination
Friendly suggestion	Minimal response: accepting without actualizing	Only formal cooperation Competing frameworks
Sharpening criticism	Psychological accounting Counter-critique	Neutralizes the child's responsibility Constructs the mother as the bad guy
Turning a blind eye and changing to a practical framework	Minimal response: accepting without actualizing	Only formal cooperation Parenting without a co-actor
Lecturing	Psychological accounting	Unproductive hassle
Double strategy: a fair directive	Angry acceptance Trying to bluff	The child softens to cooperate

DISCUSSION

This chapter analyses the variety of strategies that a mother and son apply when negotiating over the pausing of the son's computer use. The mother and son's strategies differed greatly and – importantly – collided with each other in many unproductive ways. Table 8.1 collects the mother and son's main strategies and the outcome of the combination of these strategies.

When analysing the overall process, the mother's progression differs greatly from that of the son's. The mother's train of strategies consists of friendly suggestion, sharp criticism, turning a blind eye and changing to a practical framework, lecturing and balanced direction. Thus, we see both an empathetic mother who considers her child's perspective and an authoritarian mother who tells her child what he should do. The son's train of strategies consists of minimal response, referring to psychological accounts, counter-critique and trying to bluff. Although all of these strategies seem to function in favour of maximizing gaming time, the skilful use of very different strategies is worth analysing. However, the outcome of negotiations depends on the combination of both parties' strategies. The right-hand column of Table 8.1 collects the outcomes of the combinations during the analysed interactional process.

The first outcome mentioned in the table, formal cooperation, is possible because of the difference between the formal side and substantial side of conversation. Thus, it seems possible to keep interaction going by answering questions and agreeing to suggestions without thinking about their substance. The beginning of the analysed episode illustrates the fact that friendly talk is not always successful. If conversational cooperation is only formal, it may actually operate in concealing the most essential source of trouble: the struggle between competing frameworks, here gaming and other frameworks.

When the conversation is not successful from the point of view of the mother, she gradually sharpens her criticism about her son's lack of responsibility. However, he is skilful enough to neutralize his responsibility by referring to his personal psychological world: his thoughts, plans and even personality. The child's leaning to his or her own psychological state is difficult to contradict, because who could be thought to be a better expert of his or her own mental life than the person themselves? Referring to one's psychological state also resonates with the generally known discourses of individuality and child-centred ideals, which give the psychological talk a powerful cultural soundboard. In addition, the son succeeds in opposing his mother's criticism through his ironic mimicking, giving the impression of a constantly nagging mother who could be the bad guy of the story.

In this difficult interactional situation, the mother starts to turn a blind eye to the son's troublesome turns of talk and instead changes the topic to a practical framework to ensure that important things get done. However, the son again succeeds in preventing practical cooperation by continuing with minimal responses that include accepting without actualizing the accepted activities. Thus, the mother seems to 'act parenting' without her child's important co-acting. When frustrated, the mother invokes the strategy of lecturing, and the unproductive hassle gets even worse.

Eventually, the mother finds a key to solve the problem: a double strategy that combines the parent and child's responsibilities in a balanced way. She does this by mentioning in one turn of talk her own contribution (she finds her son's missing mobile phone) and the son's responsibility to do his part (to pick the phone up). This double strategy, however, does not succeed right away. At first, the son's response is – like after many previous turns of the mother – an empty 'yes' as a device to buy more gaming time. After the mother's determined repetition of her double strategy, the son's reaction grows angrier and gives the impression that there is some dramatic obstacle to pausing the game. On the other hand, he starts to communicate face-to-face with his mother for the first time during the whole negotiation episode. Following a short dialogue, the son pauses the game and softens his behaviour to friendly cooperation.

I have analysed one multifaceted dispute concerning the desire of a boy to continue gaming. Concentrating on one long episode made it possible to analyse the procedural nature of the interaction. The analysis illustrates the fact that it is fruitless to name good and bad strategies, either from the point of view of the mother or son, because the outcome of negotiations always depends on the turns of both participants. In addition, the success of any strategy also depends on the previous phases of interaction. Thus, the parent's successful double strategy, which balanced the parent and son's obligations, would hardly be as successful in other phases of the interaction process. On the other hand, the innovative combination of different culturally known discourses can be worth trying in many tensional negotiations.

The analysis also illustrated the particularly intensive nature of computer gameplay. Because of the invasion of ICT devices into the home, this quality may cause widespread challenges to today's Western families. In a way, the computer seems to be a third actor in the discussion between the mother and child. When a child intensively listens and watches a computer, the parent has great difficulties discussing issues that would restrict the use of computer. In this situation, the parent has the following options: (1) to force the child to interrupt gameplay to create the conditions for other activities, (2) to wait for a suitable moment, when the child is not immersed in the game or (3) to ask when it would be a suitable time for other things.

The first option is risky. A parent may show themselves to be inconsiderate, because he or she does not take the specificity of the situation into account at all. However, strong interference can be in many situations a better option than a superficial conversation in which only one party is intellectually involved. The latter two options aim at the appropriate timing of the conversation. Ideally, the family will have some common undisturbed time every day during which the family members can discuss what's going on and compare the perspectives of each other. This shared undisturbed time, such as easy-going mealtime conversation, is nevertheless a luxury that has become less common in most families. Thus, in many cases, the best everyday option for solving asynchrony may be to plan together the most appropriate moment for common discussions. This option creates the best possible interactional context for conversations. In addition, a mere discussion on timing can teach parties to understand one another's worlds.

When the complexity of rival activities increases, parent–child asynchrony may escalate to become a nerve-racking experience for both sides. If the participants are unable to solve the escalation through ordinary everyday conversations, there will be a strong need for meta-level discussion about the common rules of home life. Although it is impossible to give exact instructions for meta-level conversations, it is worth emphasizing that they take place in a context that does not include rival activities, such as seen in the data extracts of this chapter. If both participants engage in reciprocal negotiation, then the variety of parents' strategies identified in this chapter – the cautious approaching of tensional issues, turning a blind eye, switching to a practical framework, demonstrating parental authority and combining child-centred and parent-centred ideals – may represent the most useful competences for the parent.

NOTE

* This chapter is based on Suoninen, E. (2015), 'Kun tietokone vangitsee lapsen huomion', in A.R. Lahikainen, T. Mälkiä and K. Repo (eds), *Media lapsiperheessä*, Tampere: Vastapaino.

REFERENCES

Aarsand, P. (2007), *Around the Screen. Computer Activities of Children's Everyday Lives, Linköping Studies in Art and Science No. 388*, Linköping: Linköping University.

Billig, M., S. Condor and D. Edwards et al. (1988), *Ideological Dilemmas: A Social Psychology of Everyday Thinking*, London: Sage.

Doddington, C. and M. Hilton (2007), *Child-Centred Education. Reviving the Creative Tradition*, Thousand Oaks, CA: Sage.

Drew, P. and J. Heritage (1992), 'Analyzing talk at work: An introduction', in P. Drew and J. Heritage (eds), *Talk at Work: Interaction in Institutional Settings*, Cambridge, UK: Cambridge University Press, pp. 3–65.

Edwards, D. and J. Potter (1992), *Discursive Psychology*, London: Sage.

Foucault, M. (1986), *The Archaeology of Knowledge*, London: Tavistock.

Goffman, E. (1974), *Frame Analysis*, Cambridge, MA: Harvard University Press.

Goodwin, C. (2007), 'Participation, stance and affect in the organization of activities', *Discourse and Society*, **18** (1), 53–73.

Gordon, C. (2007), '"I just feel horrible when she does that": Constituting a mother's identity', in D. Tannen, S. Kendall and C. Gordon (eds), *Family Talk – Discourse and Identity in Four American Families*, Oxford: Oxford University Press, pp. 71–101.

Gordon, C. (2009), *Making Meanings, Creating Families: Intertextuality and Framing in Family Interaction*, Oxford: Oxford University Press.

Ochs, E. and T. Kremer-Sadlik (2013), *Fast-Forward Family – Home, Work, and Relationships in Middle-Class America*, Berkeley, CA: University of California Press.

Sacks, H., E.A. Schegloff and G. Jefferson (1974), 'A simplest systematics for the organisation of turn-taking for conversation', *Language*, **50** (4), 696–735.

Schegloff, E.A. (2007), *Sequence Organization in Interaction: A Primer in Conversation Analysis, Vol. 1*, Cambridge, UK: Cambridge University Press.

Stokoe, E. (2011), 'Simulated interaction and communication skills training: The "conversation analytic role-play method"', in C. Antaki (eds), *Applied Conversation Analysis*, Basingstoke, UK: Palgrave Macmillan, pp. 119–38.

Suoninen, E. and A. Lundán (2005), 'Encountering an uneasy child', in N. Kelly,

C. Horrocks and K. Milnes et al. (eds), *Narrative, Memory and Everyday Life*, Huddersfield, UK: Huddersfield University Press, pp. 223–9.

Suoninen, E. and J. Wahlström (2009), 'Interactional positions and the production of identities: Negotiating fatherhood in family therapy talk', *Communication and Medicine*, **6** (2), 199–209.

Tannen, D. (2007), 'Power maneuvers and connection maneuvers in family interaction', in D. Tannen, S. Kendall and C. Gordon (eds), *Family Talk – Discourse and Identity in Four American Families*, Oxford: Oxford University Press, pp. 27–48.

Tovares, A.V. (2007), 'Family members interacting while watching TV', in D. Tannen, S. Kendall and C. Gordon (eds), *Family Talk – Discourse and Identity in Four American Families*, Oxford: Oxford University Press, pp. 283–309.

Van Nijnatten, C. and E. Suoninen (2014), 'Delicacy', in C. Hall, K. Juhila, M. Matarese and C. van Nijnatten (eds), *Analysing Social Work Communication: Discourse in Practice*, London: Routledge, pp. 136–72.

Wetherell, M. (2001), 'Editors' introduction: Minds, selves and sense-making', in M. Wetherell, S. Taylor and S.J. Yates (eds), *Discourse Theory and Practice: A Reader*, London: Sage and Open University Press, pp. 9–13.

9. The sticky media device*

Eerik Mantere and Sanna Raudaskoski

INTRODUCTION

The dynamics of day-to-day interaction are based on various shared norms of conduct. These common rules are intertwined with the moral structures that members of society are expected to follow. In this chapter, we show how a parent's smartphone use can bring additional ambiguity and difficulty to communicating with his or her child and in fact challenge the conventional normative and moral structures of social actions. Because parent–child interaction is so crucial for the development of children, the challenges posed to it by ubiquitous media devices are one of the pressing issues of our time.

In this chapter, we introduce a new concept, namely the 'sticky media device', which depicts how a media device appears to a person seeking face-to-face interaction with its user. Hence, it refers to a situation in which problems can be seen in acquiring the smartphone user's orientation for face-to-face interaction, which, even if momentarily gained, readily returns back to the device.

ADJACENCY PAIRS AND MORAL ACCOUNTABILITY

In his research on social order, the founder of ethnomethodology, Harold Garfinkel, discovered that members of the same culture share normative assumptions about what is the 'normal' way to act in a given situation. The intersubjective understanding and explaining of day-to-day social activities are in fact only possible through these shared assumptions (Garfinkel, 1967; Heritage, 1984).

As we grow up and are socialised in the conventions of a certain community and culture, these shared expectations become the unconscious guideline for our behaviour with others. At the same time, they guide the moral stances taken by the participants in each interaction. When we greet someone we know, the expectation is that they will greet us back. If that is not the case, we see it as an exception to the norm of polite behaviour, come up with explanations and often become disgruntled: 'What's up with him? He didn't even say hi to me'.

According to conversation analysis, which is the study of naturalistic interaction based on ethnomethodology, social action is realised through adjacency pairs. These pairs – like issuing and returning a greeting or a question and answer – are routinely expected to appear together (e.g., Sacks et al., 1974; Schegloff, 2007, pp. 13–21). Together, the people of any culture construct the dynamics of conversation in such a way that the preferred response to the 'first-pair part' of an adjacency pair is a response that does not cause trouble or difficulty for the ongoing interaction (Brown and Levinson, 1987). In other words, the preferred response (the 'second-pair part') to a first-pair part like an invitation would be accepting the invitation. A response that is not in alignment with the interactional expectations – in other words a dispreferred second-pair part – usually manifests with moments of silence in or between the turns the speakers take. In addition, articulations of hesitation or other sounds that delay the giving of a response are characteristic of a dispreferred turn, which is often produced with mitigations and accounts (Schegloff, 2007, pp. 58–60). Conversation analysis focuses on the detectable ways people produce, reproduce and orient to the normative structure of interaction, not on what people 'really want' or 'really mean'.[1] It is in these formal structures that the meaningful social action is carried out. As children, when we learn the conventions of interacting with others and taking part in conversation, at the same time we learn the norms of appropriate behaviour. We become habituated and adapted to the common customs and moral obligations of everyday actions.

Request is one of the fundamental social actions in human interaction and adjacency-pair practices. At an early age, we learn that requests should always be answered and the expected answer is acceptance. When rejecting a request, we learn to give accounts and explanations. A request does not always have to be in the form of a question. Depending on the context, a variety of utterances can be understood as requesting something (Schegloff, 2007, p. 8). Already at the age of three, we can interpret social situations so skilfully that we can discriminate between direct and indirect requests (Wells, 1981, p. 43). Children usually acquire this interactive know-how mainly from their parents, though other adults and children also play their part. While growing up, we become increasingly knowledgeable of the ever-increasing number of rules necessary for understanding how to truly be adept in the social world of adults.

One example, especially relevant for the analysis to follow, is the marked difference between the act of request and its close cousin, the command.

When uttering an imperative command, or a directive, the action is more about informing than asking, and there is the presumption that the person giving the directive has a legitimate right to regulate and control the actions of the other. A request, on the other hand, does not directly order someone to do something; it also takes into account the possibility that the other may decline (Craven and Potter, 2010). One way that this is seen in day-to-day conversations is that requests are usually preceded by so-called pre-sequences (Schegloff, 1980; 2007, pp. 28–9) that function as ways to protect the 'faces' (Goffman, 1955) of the participants from the discomfort that a rejecting response might cause. It is common, for example, to ask 'Do you have any plans for the evening?' before inviting someone to go see a movie together. It is important to note that this so-called 'face work' is not merely done out of shyness or indecisiveness on the part of the requester; it generally serves the interests of both participants.

DATA AND METHODS

The phenomenon of the 'sticky media device' will be elaborated on with the help of transcribed excerpts from the dataset of the project 'Media, Family Interaction and Children's Well-Being', conducted at the University of Tampere, Finland. The data were collected during 2010 and 2011. The parts of the data utilised in our chapter are the video recordings made in the homes of 26 families with children. They were performed with four – or, in rare cases, three – video cameras installed upon tripod stands. The positioning of the cameras was planned together with the aid of the parents in attempt to cover the most relevant locations from the viewpoint of parent–child interaction and digital media use. In most cases, they were installed in different rooms and have therefore created a dataset that is quite unique in its nature. It often covers simultaneous but different scenarios taking place in two or more separate but sometimes also partly connected rooms within a household. The dataset consists of 665 hours of video footage, which is the sum total of the recordings of all the video cameras, but the data actually only cover a 186-hour time span.

The families taking part in the research were recruited through kindergartens and primary schools in both high- and low-income areas. In each family there was a five- or a 12-year-old child who was later interviewed for a variety of aspects relating to media use and well-being. The cameras were turned on for one day from the time that this focal child came home to the time they went to sleep. The day of the recording was always chosen to be what the parents considered a 'normal day', and the family was instructed to spend the day as usual. This chapter will concentrate on a short episode in which a child of 12 is seeking her mother's attention while the mother is simultaneously using a smartphone. In the excerpts we present, the child makes several requests to her parent. Answering the requests requires the mother to at least momentarily disengage from the ongoing interaction with her smartphone.

We focus on what is commonly referred to as 'talk-in-interaction' and base our analysis on the principles of Garfinkel's ethnomethodology and the tradition of conversation analysis. This means that we look at the data as if we were merely trying to see them more clearly and not in an attempt to interpret them with preconceived concepts and theories that offer hypotheses about the reasons and 'real meanings' behind the observable interaction of the participants. The idea is that the way each participant in the conversation is feeling or thinking about something they themselves or someone else has said or done is only relevant if it is produced as an observable action – be it verbal or non-verbal. Whatever is going on in the inner lives of participants – if not seen in any way in the actual interaction – would necessarily be analysed by the researcher only through preconceived notions and general theories. These theories might be useful in another kind of study utilising, for example, the hypothesis-testing methodology of experimental psychology, but they do not really contribute much in the analysis of how actual real-life interaction episodes are produced by people living their daily lives.

It is not assumed beforehand what elements will turn out to be relevant in a given social situation. Careful turn-by-turn study of the progression of a communication episode can reveal the ways that participants themselves relate to what is happening between them, but very little should be assumed before actually having gone through the case with painstaking care. This accuracy is made possible by the tradition of transcription in conversation analysis. Even coughing, silences and breathing are transcribed, as it might be the case that they turn out to play a role in the construction of the interactive episode.

Repeated viewing of the corresponding video material, together with an accurate transcription of it, revealed to us a collection of patterns and aspects we call the 'sticky media device'. Even though these elements are also present in many other places in the data, we chose this original case of a 12-year-old and her mother for analysis and presentation due to its particular richness in various aspects of the phenomenon in question. In addition, we are able to perfectly see and hear both the mother and the child; they are the only people in the apartment during the conversation, and their interaction is not affected by anything outside our field of interest. There are no pets or other family members joining the situation halfway through, and the aspects of the sticky media device can be exceptionally clearly shown and explained by the analysis of the chosen case.

THE CASE OF A MOTHER, A DAUGHTER AND A SMARTPHONE

Here, we elucidate a situation in which a daughter is requesting her mother to participate in a joint activity and has to compete for attention with her mother's smartphone. The facets of this interactive event are explored through the use of five data excerpts, each being a direct continuation of the former. The excerpts show how difficult it can be for a child to get the attention of their parent when the parent is simultaneously using a smartphone (cf. Radesky et al., 2014). At first, the 12-year-old Anu (the name has been changed) and her mother are sitting at the kitchen table facing each other going about their own businesses. The mother finished eating about 20 minutes before the beginning of the excerpt. She has remained at the table to go through some advertisements and is now doing something with her smartphone. Anu is drawing pictures of supermodels in her notebook. Anu asks her mother to evaluate the drawing and the mother complies, but only after extra effort is applied on Anu's part.

Extract 1

1	Anu:	eihän tää oo nii hirvee,
		this isn't so terrible is it,
2		(1.1)
3	Anu:	#äiti#,
		#mother#,
4		(2.1) ((the mother looks at the picture))
5	Mother:	[mt' ↑ei::. se on ihan (.) kiva.
		[th' ↑no::. it is quite (.) nice.
		[((the mother's gaze returns to the screen))
6		(7.5) ((the mother continues to tap her smartphone but glances
7		at the daughter as Anu browses through the drawings))

The extract begins by Anu inviting her mother to participate in a joint activity. After finishing a drawing of a supermodel, she looks at the drawing, wipes it with her hand (as if removing the residue of coloured pens) and asks her mother: 'this isn't so terrible is it' (line 1). The turn is designed in a way that it invites the receiver to produce a particular kind of response, in this case the recipient's agreement to the negation 'isn't. . .is it'. The question is a first-pair part of an adjacency pair and anticipates some kind of an answer to follow. As Sacks (1987, p. 57) remarks, if the question is built in such a way as to exhibit a preference between 'yes' and 'no' responses, this is the choice that should be preferred by an answerer. This holds true for both 'yes' and 'no' preferred answers. A preferred answer should also be produced instantly after the first pair part. Here Anu produces her question in a way that obliges her mother to evaluate the picture, and the expected response would be something like 'no, it is not (so terrible)' (cf. Sacks, 1992, p. 414; Heritage, 2002).

However, the mother does not produce any answer in the first 'transition relevant place' (TRP),[2] that is, in the place where the answer should usually be produced, immediately after Anu's question (the 1.1-second pause in line 2). Anu works further to gain her mother's attention and uses the summons 'mother' (line 3) as a means to allocate attention and oblige her mother to answer. Now the mother raises her head and leans forward towards the notebook, looks at the picture (which is upside down from her perspective), and answers: 'th' ↑No::. it is quite (.) nice' (line 5). The mother's gaze returns to the screen of the phone when she ends the first stretched word 'no'. The mother says the rest of the utterance ('it is quite nice') when she is again looking at the screen of her smartphone (Picture 9.1).

Thus, the mother fails to answer in the first interactional place expected (line 2), but after Anu's summons produces an utterance that – from the perspective of normative sequence organisation in talk-in-interaction – is 'right'; it is the preferred answer. Then again, in the production of the turn there are classical marks of dispreferred answers: delaying the answer, sucking teeth (th), stretching the word 'no' and the micro pause before the

Picture 9.1   The mother's gaze is back on the screen at the end of the word 'no::' (line 5)

word 'nice' (cf. Pomerantz and Heritage, 2012). One might say that these are all connected to mother engaging in the task of evaluating the picture that Anu is showing to her and thus are actually part of her producing a preferred second-pair part to Anu's request. Obviously it is the case that the mother could not evaluate something she hasn't looked at so it is reasonable to assume that at least part of the delay before the mother begins the word 'no' is due to the task of evaluating. However, missing the first TRP as well as all the other classical signs of dispreference still go unexplained. In this case the fumbled answer is not in fact connected to the sequential dynamics of conversation and the content of the utterance (i.e., making a choice between a preferred 'no' and dispreferred 'yes' answer), but is actually caused by the fact that mother's attention is divided: she is orienting both to the interaction with Anu and to the simultaneous interaction with her smartphone (cf. Haddington and Rauniomaa, 2011).

Schegloff (2007, p. 62) mentions that on top of the groundings of preference found within a single sequence in talk-in-interaction, like the aforementioned classical dispreferred markers, preference is also constructed based on the progression of the course of action taking place. There are sequences, like for example the summons–answer, that are designed to mobilise the attention of one or more recipients for some further action. Whether this predicted future action will actually take place or not is contingent on the success of the summons sequence in attracting the attention of the recipient. Some sort of 'go-ahead' response is preferred, since it provides space for the next step to be taken. Here Anu succeeds in getting her mother to evaluate the drawing, but can only catch her attention for a minimal time. This is obvious by the way her mother already turns back to the phone while producing her reply.

Anu invites her mother to participate in the joint activity in a situation where the mother's attention is preoccupied with the smartphone. The mother has not only directed her gaze at the screen but is also using the device with both of her hands. As mentioned, while answering Anu's question, the mother goes back to using her smartphone, most likely to continue the activity that was interrupted by Anu's request, and Anu begins to browse through her notebook.

However, even though the mother did not stop using her phone, Anu's request to evaluate the drawing and mother's answer to it – albeit accomplished by Anu's extra interactional work – did create a communicational space that Emanuel Schegloff and Harvey Sacks (1973, pp. 324–5) call the 'continuing state of incipient talk'. By this term, they mean, for example, a situation within family life where everyone can be passing time in the same room and each be going about their own business, but may also initiate conversation or continue previous topics with others, even after longer gaps, without having to specifically begin or end the conversation each time. By being in the shared space, the individuals present assume that everyone recognises the possibility of this kind of frame of interaction and no one treats sudden utterances by others as weird or non-normative.

In our example, the mother may orient to the possibility of a continuing state by glancing over to Anu while still using her smartphone (lines 6–7). Hence, when Anu asks her mother to look at and evaluate one of her drawings, her mother's agreement generates a social reality in which she in principle can and would be interested in evaluating Anu's pictures. From what follows, it can be interpreted that the first sequence that began the conversation removed obstacles for new and more specific requests to be made. Thus it functioned as a kind of a 'presequence'; it was preliminary to a more demanding request (cf. Schegloff, 2007, pp. 28, 62).

Extract 2

6		(7.5) ((the mother continues to tap her smartphone but glances
7		at Anu when she browses through the drawings))
8	Anu:	selaa näitä tästä eteenpäin?
		browse through these from here onwards?
9		(1.3) ((Anu stands up and walks towards her mother))
10	Anu:	[ja s:ano mulle mikä näistä on susta <hianoin>.
		[and te:ll me which one you think is <the nicest>.
11		[((Anu walks next to her mother, places the notebook on the
12		table and her hand on mother's shoulder))
13	Mother:	.hhh (.) oh[hhhhh

After asking her mother to go through the drawings (line 8) Anu positions herself right next to her mother, placing the notebook on the table immediately adjacent to her mother's smartphone, which is the current focus of her mother's gaze. While still walking, she continues to speak: 'and te:ll me which one you think is <the nicest> (line 10). However, the mother does not reply to Anu's request but sighs loudly (line 13, Picture 9.2) while still keeping her gaze on the screen of the phone. The sigh might be an expression of the mother's problematic situation of having to take part in two rival activities – that is, continuing what she is doing with her phone and starting to do what Anu requests.

Anu's request for the mother to begin looking and evaluating her drawings would require her mother to handle the notebook and put the smartphone away. In other words, the mother would have to stop whatever she is currently engaged in with the smartphone. Anu's next turn, which is a more precise request than the earlier one, overlaps her mother's sigh.

Picture 9.2   The mother's sigh

Extract 3

```
13  Mother:   .hhh (.) oh[hhhhh
14  Anu:               [sanot (.) ykkösestä viiteen kuinka monta tähteä
                       [tell (.) how many stars out of five you
15             annat tälle?
               give to this one?
16             ((Anu taps her mother's shoulder while speaking))
17             (2.0) ((the mother looks at the picture, starting to lay her
18             phone aside with her right hand, but draws it back close to her
19             body, grabs it with both hands and turns her gaze back on it))
```

When Anu takes her turn in line 14, she is in fact not only making her request more precise but also transforming it: '[tell (.) how many stars out of five you give to this one?' (lines 14–15). Here Anu is no longer asking her mother to take hold of the notebook and browse through it (in order to see which one is the 'nicest') but suggests that she should concentrate on one specific picture. While talking, Anu is holding one hand on the notebook and rhythmically, but lightly, tapping her mother on the shoulder with the other. This functions as an efficient focuser and the mother turns her gaze towards the picture, simultaneously starting to put her smartphone on the table. However, still looking at the picture, mother pulls the smartphone back, very close to her body, soon refocuses her gaze on it, and again takes hold of it with both hands (Picture 9.3). Thus, despite the momentary orientation towards the notebook, prompted by Anu's taps on her shoulder, the mother still does not produce an answer but actually returns to attending to the device.

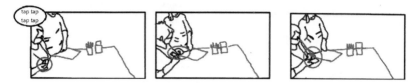

Picture 9.3   The 'sticky' phone will not disengage from the mother's fingers

However, Anu does not give up, but nudges her mother strongly on the arm saying: 'mother?' This can be seen in Extract 4 (line 20) and Picture 9.4.

Extract 4

    20   Anu: äiti?
                      mother? ((nudging her mother's arm))

Anu's nudge as an embodied directive is an extreme way for the child to get the attention of the parent in talk-in-interaction. However, rather than just a single occurrence in an action sequence constructed by an adjacency pair, embodied directives are more like trajectories of action in progress (Goodwin, 2006; Cekaite, 2010). The trajectory leading to the nudge is co-constructed with verbal and embodied practices, and it is in the service of the whole 'project' of the activity that is going on, not only of the adjacent actions (cf. Levinson, 2013). From the four excerpts above, it can be seen that the nudge is related to Anu's many attempts to get her mother's

Picture 9.4   Anu nudges her mother's arm

attention to focus on the notebook instead of the smartphone. The physical touch and the word 'mother' uttered with a pleading intonation get the mother to finally release the smartphone and concentrate on the picture Anu is trying to show her. This is shown in Extract 5.

Extract 5

```
21              (0.4)
22   Mother:   oh-
               wel- ((the word is cut just a bit short and ends with holding
23             of the breath))
24             (0.8) ((mother puts the mobile far from her, on the edge of the
25             table and looks at the picture))
26   Mother:   @tää on must muuten niinku (.) tosi makee?@
               @I think this is otherwise like (.) really cool?@
27   Anu:      m-hm?
```

The single dialogue-particle 'well' (line 22), which Anu's mother utters just before she moves the smartphone far from herself, manifests a transition to a new activity (cf. Sorjonen, 2002). The mother's 'well' ends with a cut sound and the typical way of producing this word is replaced by a holding of the breath at the end. This makes it seem like there is some kind of complex relation to the transition. The mother then puts the smartphone on the table as far from herself as she can, focuses on the picture and produces a verbal evaluation: 'I think this is otherwise like (.) really cool' (line 26). In her next turn, Anu acknowledges her mother's evaluation with an approving minimum input: 'm-hm?' (line 27). For the following ten or so minutes, not included in the data excerpt, the mother goes through Anu's pictures, evaluating them with an upbeat style. She praises one of costumes that Anu has drawn as being just as stylish as those in the 'Supermodel' TV show that Anu was watching earlier that day. During this time, Anu keeps chuckling, smiling and laughing regularly.

CONFLICTED BY TWO SEPARATE INTERACTIONS

An interactive situation can have various interactive resources that are relevant for the ongoing action. These resources can be conceptualised as semiotic fields (Goodwin, 2000). A semiotic field describes a collection of aspects of the human body and its environment that are significant to a specific social action. This collection can consist of elements, such as speech, gestures, posture, material and technological objects, arrangements in space, and so on. Goodwin emphasises that speech cannot be dissected from the other material and bodily components of the interaction: they all co-create the semiotic fields through which interaction takes place. In interaction, many different semiotic fields can be simultaneously present, but they may not all be active at the same time. Those semiotic fields that the participants are currently orienting towards form the 'contextual configuration' of the ongoing social action (Goodwin, 2000, p. 1490).

Changing the contextual configuration requires orienting towards new semiotic fields. In our example, while trying to get her mother to attend to the joint activity, Anu also had to try to alter the contextual configuration that her mother was currently acting in. A central semiotic resource in that contextual configuration was the screen of the smartphone. At first, Anu asked for the evaluation of just one picture. When Anu later asked for more thorough participation, the initial request functioned as kind of a 'foot in the door' (Freedman and Fraser, 1966), as part of a course of action requesting the mother to join a more long-term joint activity (cf. Schegloff, 2007, p. 62; Levinson, 2013, p. 126).

In the usage of a smartphone, the action taking place is structured in turns undertaken by both the device and the human being. This is true even if the device is not being used to engage in interaction with another person, such as in chatting via an application. The use of a smartphone – or any other ICT device – has a structure of 'adjacency pairs' so that even the machine is in a way 'expecting' certain relevant actions from the user at certain relevant times (Suchman, 1987). This means that the device always reacts in some way to the user's actions. Even an absence of reaction is a response. The information from the device directs the action, just as other participants' actions do in a human–human interaction. Although it is the human participant that reads the meaning into whatever the technologies do or display, this interpretation work resembles what people do when encountering each other, and is in this way interactionally bonding (Raudaskoski, 1999, p. 17).

In order to challenge her mother's current action, Anu has to get her mother's attention away from the smartphone. Anu's mother is required to change her posture and direction of gaze to signal to Anu that she is attending to the same participation framework with her daughter and the notebook (cf. Goodwin, 2000, p. 1500). This cooperative stance (Goodwin, 2007, p. 62) is not accomplished easily; it takes plenty of work from Anu. She uses – among other things – several deictic expressions like 'here', 'these' and 'this one', and thus builds a competing focus of attention to the smartphone (cf. Goodwin, 2007, p. 55). In the progression of the episode, Anu's verbal requests evolve to be more and more imperative, while at the same time she adds other modalities into them: she moves next to her mother, taps on her mother's shoulder, nudges her and positions the notebook in her mother's field of vision.

THE STICKY MEDIA DEVICE

Most of us have found that communication with a person using an ICT device – like a smartphone, tablet or computer – can sometimes be quite frustrating. We might have to wait for the response or feel we have not been heard at all. We might also get unclear or incomplete responses. The conversational counterpart's orientation is not easily taken from their device, and while their attention may be momentarily disengaged, it nevertheless might return back to the device without delay. This is a common phenomenon, but to date no detailed description of it has been made, so we suggest that naming it will serve both scientific and lay communities. We call it the phenomenon of the 'sticky media device'. The concept depicts the situation from the viewpoint of the person who is inviting the user of the media to engage in face-to-face interaction.

The stickiness of the smartphone shows in the interaction between Anu and her mother particularly clearly when the mother begins to put away her smartphone for the first time (Picture 9.3). She cuts her movement short and pulls the smartphone back close her body, takes hold of it again with both hands and focuses her attention on it once more. It genuinely looks like the smartphone cannot easily be dislodged from the mother's hands. In extracts 4 and 5, Anu's actions become increasingly demanding. After this, the sticky smartphone is finally released. The stickiness of a device can be conceptualised as a difficulty to change the contextual configuration. As discussed earlier, the device and its user form an interactive relationship. The contextual configuration that the mother is orienting to has been formed in relation to the events taking place with the smartphone and what the mother – and the device – predict will happen next (cf. Arminen, 2005, p. 203; Raudaskoski, 2009, pp. 145–76). This interactive relationship requires the user to engage in cognitive processing, and disengaging from it might not happen easily – especially if the task at hand is unfinished.

With a media device the rhythm of the interaction is different from non-technology-mediated human interaction. Also, by and large, only very simple actions can be executed with a media device without it starting to hamper other consecutive activity. In face-to-face interaction, the pauses between and within turns are subject to precise social control, and having too many or too long pauses is considered problematic for the joint activity. Any action with the smartphone that requires even slightly longer orientation by the user influences the simultaneous conversation in the form of stammering, hesitation, delays and repetitive beginnings. In fact, the simultaneous performance of several different conscious activities rarely truly takes place. Instead, people synchronise concurrent activities with an overlap, one immediately after another, and this has an effect on construing of all of the ongoing activities (Levy and Gardner, 2012).

In the analysed episode, the overlap of activities is seen, for example, in the slowness of the mother's turn-taking. As stated earlier, while we learn the order of interaction, we also become aware of the moral aspect connected to that order. If our counterpart in an interaction does not join us in the same participation framework, in spite of our invitation, it is considered to be a breach of the shared rules of social conduct, and the counterpart is seen as morally accountable and usually causing some irritation. It is nevertheless worth noticing that Anu does not in any direct way appear to lose her temper with her mother and, for example, walk away from the situation. Anu seems to attribute the troubles in the interaction to her mother's simultaneous use of the smartphone, just as we do. As researchers, we do not know what Anu's mother is doing with her smartphone, but the situation is the same for Anu: the details of the interaction between her mother and the smartphone are no more readily available to her than to the researchers watching the video recordings (see Chapter 11 for more discussion on the bystander's position).

Still, Anu can clearly see that her mother is focused on the smartphone and even though she does not get a reply from her mother before summoning her (Extract 1, line 3) – and regardless of her mother's gaze returning to the screen even before delivering an answer (Extract 2, line 10) – Anu acquiesces in the situation. Anu does not in any recognisable way treat her mother's first reply as a dispreferred action, but it is interesting to note that nor does she treat it as a clearly preferred one (cf. Schegloff, 1992). Anu seems to be capable of understanding that her mother's fumbled conversational turns relate to the presence of the smartphone: the problems in preference organisation of talk-in-interaction originate in the mother's difficulty in changing the object of her orientation, and are not really connected to the contents of the requests that Anu is making. This vagueness would not be present if the mother was not in the midst of using a smartphone.

Then again, the way Anu nudges her mother while snapping at her ('mother?' on line 20) actually shows some moral indignation: it is the duty of her mother at this point to give at least some kind of a reply. Anu's turn is reminiscent of the behaviour of some children in an experiment performed by Michael Tomasello's research team (Tomasello, 2014). They found that if a prize was gained through collaboration and one of the children took more than their fair share of the bounty, the other child would execute a very simple protest, consisting of a short verbal outcry or just a mere motion of a hand. There was no need to elaborate on the nature of the perceived moral transgression; it was immediately understood what kind of behaviour was expected by the one who had taken more than they were supposed to (Warneken et al., 2011). In our present example, the divergence from the norm – not paying attention to Anu and not giving a reason why – comes to be treated as if it would be obvious to both Anu and her mother what should be done. In the aforementioned experiment, the addressed child did not protest but gave up the extra candy without argument (ibid.). Similarly, Anu's mother did not protest the nudge. Even though it is clear that we cannot see inside her head and claim to know why she acted the way she did, the comparison here is tempting. We know that adults are aware of the shared social norms of their societies and Anu's mother's rapid agreement to comply after receiving the nudge can therefore reasonably be proposed to be connected to her knowing very well what she should do. In fact, she starts to put her smartphone away less than 0.1 seconds following Anu's nudge, thus making it inconceivable that she would at this point be unclear about the proper cause of action.

The central function of social norms is to aid in interpreting the behaviour of others. Shared norms help us to see the social world, not as utter chaos, but as something that can be understood and influenced in predictable ways. This order is threatened if others do not play by the common rules (Heritage, 1984, pp. 95–101). Therefore, every instance of interaction also contains a moral stance – and with it an affective stance – towards the activity (Goodwin, 2007, pp. 65–9). The person invited into interaction has to either take part in it or offer some sort of explanation for their default. While Anu's mother is interacting with her smartphone, she repeatedly fails to fulfill the fundamental requirements of human interaction and delays responding to Anu's requests. This 'failing' is understood co-constructively, and hence Anu's demand for a reply and the nudge embodying it are justified by the jointly comprehended moral and affective stances.

Each time a turn produced by a user of a smartphone is delayed, contains pauses or inconsistencies, is manifold in its meaning, or is left unfinished or started again, it makes the interpretative task of the receiver of the turn more challenging. Do these aspects relate to the shared social activity of the participants of the interaction, or do they exist solely due to one of the participants having their orientation directed towards their smartphone? We claim that when one of the participants in conversation simultaneously uses a smartphone, from the perspective of the ongoing talk-in-interaction, it is harder to identify whether their turns are preferred or dispreferred. If sticky media devices make the deciphering of joint activity in families more difficult, it means that their constant presence can cause difficulty, awkwardness, annoyance, arduousness and discomfort in family interaction. In one family of our personal acquaintances, the father has an inventive method for acquiring the attention of his children when – even though they are sharing the same physical space with him – they are very much absorbed in the games they are playing on their smartphones: he calls them with his own phone and produces his social act as part of the contextual configuration that the children are already orienting to. Would Anu also have gained the attention of her mother more rapidly if she had called her mother across the kitchen table?

DISCUSSION

Many of the elements of the conversation we have presented here are recognisable to most people in today's developed world. Mobile phones, and especially smartphones, have become an integral part of people's day-to-day lives. They have radically changed the conventions and temporal structures of our everyday activities: things are negotiated and rapidly agreed upon through mobile connections, and it is generally expected that others are available for this ongoing planning and restructuring of daily coordination (Ling, 2004). People become easily disgruntled when they are unable to reach someone through a mobile connection.

On top of phone calls, today's smartphones provide a variety of interactive social media and other applications for their users. The devices act as hubs for a plethora of applications and connections to distant others. At the same time, some new norms have developed about how the members of a society are expected to respond to these multiple ways of being contacted. Between friends, it can already begin to be a cause of concern if a message is not answered within a minute. In families, arguments can arise if one of the parents cannot be reached when there is a need to reorganise the immediate plans of the household. In the crossroads of such socially normative expectations, individuals find themselves having to decide, over and over again, how to conduct their lives with the media devices that accompany them (cf. Raudaskoski, 2009, pp. 76–9). Are they going to be available all the time? Do they immediately need to know what their friends have published on some social media site?

In our data example, Anu's mother eventually stretched out to place the smartphone as far away from herself as she could – on the very edge of the table, away from her space of action. This gesture in a way brings to mind the classical Stanford marshmallow experiment, where some children used the same tactics as a means of self-control: putting the marshmallow physically further away makes it easier to resist the temptation to eat it (Mischel and Ebbesen, 1970). As mentioned earlier, portable media devices are socially normative and are expected to be 'always on' (Turkle, 2008) in order for everyone to be continuously reachable. In addition, they also contain countless media and entertainment possibilities that can easily be tempting, or even addictive, to people of any age (Cheever et al., 2014). Reviewing the dataset (see Appendix 1) as a whole revealed that some kind of presence of media devices is commonplace during the daily face-to-face interactive situations within families. Nevertheless, as our example shows, the role of media devices in interaction might not be unproblematic. Every media device can bring a parallel and rival contextual framework for ongoing activities. They also create the presence of at least two concurrent but divergent normative worlds. One is the world of norms connected to the interactive processes with the device and the other is the normative world of face-to-face social interaction.

Considering the norms of face-to-face interaction, in the case examined, Anu was relatively patient with her mother's difficulty in transiting into the shared activity, even though she had to do a lot of interactional work to disengage her mother from the 'sticky' smartphone. Through the examined case and other similar occurrences present in the data, we can conclude that media devices break the traditional social norms of interaction and introduce interpretive complexity into face-to-face interaction.

Over the last two decades, portable screen media devices have radically changed various social and societal practices. We who have lived in the era before mobile phones can in some sense compare the current situation to what came before. Those who are born today, who grow up surrounded by different media devices, actually learn what social skills mean in this very environment. Parent–child interaction is crucial for the development of children, and therefore the challenges that media devices pose to this interaction is a question of the utmost importance.

Earlier, we discussed how the knowledge of what is socially appropriate is learned simultaneously with the skills of interaction. The question here is one of intersubjectivity, not merely as a skill of the individual, but something that is built turn by turn through a contextual configuration, always in a certain time and in a certain place in joint activity with others (Pontecorvo et al., 2001, p. 346). As previously mentioned, social norms are first and foremost learned in order to understand and function in a social world. It is disturbing and even threatening when other people do not act according to common rules, and therefore the situated activities always also have moral and affective aspects (Goodwin, 2007, p. 71). But if the ubiquitous presence of screen media devices can break these traditional normative rules, and thus produce ambiguity and interpretative variance, it may have an effect on the development of children's social and emotional skills. Today's children encounter conflicting norms in their daily lives: for example, they might first learn the practices of requesting and answering a request, but then notice that these practices might not be applicable after all, at least when a smartphone is present in the interaction.

Reviewing the data, some grand questions come to mind. Older children can already interpret interaction to a large extent, but what about when a crying baby is waiting to receive attention from a parent who is interacting with a sticky media device? Attachment theory suggests that it is in interaction with the caregiver that children form their understanding of being worthy of receiving help and care, and whether other people can be expected to offer aid or not (Bowlby, 1969, 1973, 1980 [1982]). If a child must compete for parental attention with media devices from infancy, can this endanger the formation of secure attachment? Could sticky media devices turn out to be developmental risk factors?

NOTES

*   This chapter is based on Mantere, E. and S. Raudaskoski (2015), 'Kun matkapuhelin vie vanhemman huomion', in A.R. Lahikainen, T. Mälkiä and K. Repo (eds), *Media lapsiperheessä*, Tampere: Vastapaino, pp. 205–26.
1. We might, for example, invite our boss to a party purely out of courtesy, even though we might not really consider them a friend or actually want them to attend. The boss might decline the invitation pleading work overload instead of saying that they are really not interested in the party at all.
2. Transition relevant place (TRP) is a name given to such a moment in interaction where the speaker can change without it being perceived as an interruption. It is usually marked by a pause after the latest utterance. In these moments, it is common to non-verbally and rapidly 'negotiate' who will be the next speaker, but if the next speaker has already been addressed, it is expected that they will take the next turn. If they do not do this quickly, it is commonly interpreted to mean that a dispreferred second-pair part – for example, declining an invitation – is to follow (Clayman, 2012).

REFERENCES

Arminen, I. (2005), *Institutional Interaction. Studies of Talk at Work*, Aldershot, UK: Ashgate Publishing Ltd.
Bowlby, J. (1969), *Attachment and Loss. Vol. 1: Attachment*, London: Hogarth Press.
Bowlby, J. (1973), *Attachment and Loss. Vol. 2: Separation: Anger and Anxiety*, London: Hogarth.

Bowlby, J. (1980 [1982]), *Attachment and Loss. Vol. 3: Loss: Sadness and Depression*, reprint, New York: Basic Books.

Brown, P. and S. Levinson (1987), *Politeness: Some Universals in Language Usage*, Cambridge, UK: Cambridge University Press.

Cekaite, A. (2010), 'Shepherding the child: Embodied directive sequences in parent–child interactions', *Text and Talk*, **30** (1), 1–25.

Cheever, N., L. Rosen, L. Carrier and A. Chavez (2014), 'Out of sight is not out of mind: The impact of restricting wireless mobile device use on anxiety levels among low, moderate and high users', *Computers in Human Behavior*, **37**, 290–97.

Clayman, S.E. (2012), 'Turn-constructional units and the transition-relevance place', in J. Sidnell and T. Stivers (eds), *The Handbook of Conversation Analysis*, Chichester, UK: John Wiley and Sons, pp. 150–66.

Craven, A. and J. Potter (2010), 'Directives: Entitlement and contingency in action', *Discourse Studies*, **12** (4), 419–42.

Freedman, J. and S. Fraser (1966), 'Compliance without pressure: The foot-in-the-door technique', *Journal of Personality and Social Psychology*, **4** (2), 195–202.

Garfinkel, H. (1967), *Studies in Ethnomethodology*, Englewood Cliffs, NJ: Prentice Hall.

Goffman, E. (1955), 'On face-work: An analysis of ritual elements in social interaction', *Psychiatry*, **18** (3), 213–31.

Goodwin, C. (2000), 'Action and embodiment within situated human interaction', *Journal of Pragmatics*, **32** (10), 1489–522.

Goodwin, C. (2007), 'Participation, stance and affect in the organization of activities', *Discourse and Society*, **18** (1), 53–73.

Goodwin, M.H. (2006), 'Participation, affect, and trajectory in family directive/response sequences', *Text and Talk*, **26** (3–4), 513–42.

Haddington, P. and M. Rauniomaa (2011), 'Technologies, multitasking and driving: Attending to and preparing for a mobile phone conversation in the car', *Human Communication Research*, **37** (2), 223–54.

Heritage, J. (1984), *Garfinkel and Ethnomethodology*, Cambridge, UK: Polity Press.

Heritage, J. (2002), 'The limits of questioning: Negative interrogatives and hostile question content', *Journal of Pragmatics*, **34** (10–11), 1427–46.

Levinson, S.C. (2013), 'Action formation and ascription', in J. Sidnell and T. Stivers (eds), *The Handbook of Conversation Analysis*, Chichester, UK: John Wiley and Sons, pp. 103–30.

Levy, M. and R. Gardner (2012), 'Liminality in multitasking: Where talk and task collide in computer collaborations', *Language in Society*, **41** (5), 557–87.

Ling, R. (2004), *The Mobile Connection. The Cell Phone's Impact on Society*, San Francisco, CA: Morgan Kaufman Publishers.

Mischel, W. and E. Ebbesen (1970), 'Attention in delay of gratification', *Journal of Personality and Social Psychology*, **16** (2), 329–37.

Pomerantz, A. and J. Heritage (2012), 'Preference', in J. Sidnell and T. Stivers (eds), *The Handbook of Conversation Analysis*, Chichester, UK: John Wiley and Sons, pp. 210–28.

Pontecorvo, C., A. Fasulo and L. Sterponi (2001), 'Mutual apprentices: The making of parenthood and childhood in family dinner conversations', *Human Development*, **44** (6), 340–61.

Radesky, J.S., C.J. Kirstin and B. Zuckerman et al. (2014), 'Patterns of mobile device use by caregivers and children during meals in fast food restaurants', *Pediatrics*, **133** (4), e843–e849.

Raudaskoski, P. (1999), 'The use of communicative resources in language technology environments. A conversation analytic approach to semiosis at computer media', dissertation, University of Oulu, Faculty of Humanities.

Raudaskoski, S. (2009), *Tool and Machine. The Affordances of the Mobile Phone*, Tampere: Tampere University Press.

Sacks, H. (1987), 'On the preferences for agreement and contiguity in sequences in conversation', in G. Button and J.R.E. Lee (eds), *Talk and Social Organization*, Clevedon, UK: Multilingual Matters, pp. 54–69.

Sacks, H. (1992), in G. Jefferson (ed.), *Lectures on Conversation. Vol. II*, Oxford: Blackwell.

Sacks, H., E. Schegloff and G. Jefferson (1974), 'A simplest systematics for the organization of turn-taking for conversation', *Language*, **50** (4), Part 1, 696–735.

Schegloff, E. (1980), 'Preliminaries to preliminaries: "Can I ask you a question?"', *Sociological Inquiry*, **50** (3–4), 104–52.

Schegloff, E. (1992), 'Repair after next turn: The last structurally provided defense of intersubjectivity in conversation', *American Journal of Sociology*, **97** (5), 1295–345.

Schegloff, E. (2007), *Sequence Organization in Interaction: A Primer in Conversation Analysis. Vol. 1*, Cambridge, UK: Cambridge University Press.

Schegloff, E. and H. Sacks (1973), 'Opening up closings', *Semiotica*, **8** (4), 289–327.

Sorjonen, M.-L. (2002), 'Recipient activities: The particle no as a go-ahead response in Finnish conversations', in C. Ford, B. Fox and S.A. Thompson (eds), *The Language Turn and Sequence*, New York: Oxford University Press, pp. 165–95.

Suchman, L. (1987), *Plans and Situated Actions: The Problem of Human–Machine Communication*, New York: Cambridge University Press.

Tomasello, M. (2014), 'What makes humans unique?', lecture presented as Albert Magnus Professor Lecture, University of Cologne, 15 May, accessed 30 May 2016 at https://youtu.be/RQiINQiAn4o.

Turkle, S. (2008), 'Always-on/always-on-you: The tethered self', in J. Katz (ed.), *Handbook of Mobile Communications and Social Change*, Cambridge, MA: MIT Press, pp. 121–37.

Warneken, F., K. Lohse, A.P. Melis and M. Tomasello (2011), 'Young children share the spoils after collaboration', *Psychological Science*, **22** (2), 267–73.

Wells, G. (1981), *Learning Through Interaction: Vol. 1: The Study of Language Development*, Cambridge, UK: Cambridge University Press.

10. Together individually

Sanna Tiilikainen and Ilkka Arminen

INTRODUCTION

Digital society pervades all aspects of our social life and entails an evolution in our social processes, relationships, and activities (Sawyer and Winter, 2011; Beath et al., 2013; Hess et al., 2014). The use of multiple ICTs in social settings is altering the ways in which people interact with each other, not only in cyberspace, but also while located in the same physical space in intimate settings (Castells et al., 2007; Van Dijk, 2009; Shove et al., 2012; Scheepers and Middleton, 2013).

People are still doing the same things at home as previously (tending to their personal relationships, taking care of their personal interests, doing homework and work brought home from the office) but – enabled by ubiquitous information and communication technologies (ICTs) such as smartphones, laptops and tablet computers – they now incorporate these various technologies into their everyday lives. This technologically mediated lifestyle means that their preferred ways of interaction are increasingly enabled by and dependent on the technology they use (Scheepers and Middleton, 2013). The expanding salience of ICT in the home increases the complexity of social interaction, and requires families to develop new skills to master multiple ongoing engagements simultaneously. Over time, the new ways of interacting may become mutually accepted and commonplace, thus affecting the social contract of family members – that is, the general social expectations people have of each other as individuals, members of the family, or as a part of society (see Beck and Beck-Gernsheim, 2008).

This chapter focuses on the current ways families spend time together at home with and around ICT as instances of the socialization process of children. In the socialization process, family members work towards a mutually accepted social contract of family togetherness. Today, this social contract also entails knowledge about the accepted and unaccepted uses of ICT when other family members are present in a shared physical space. To understand and describe the emergent social contract of spending time together at home with children, we studied instances of face-to-face interaction in the home from a 150-hour corpus of video recordings. According to our findings, the present conduct of spending family time with and around multiple ICT devices is relevant to the development of socialization patterns. This suggests that the socialization of the children may be evolving because of the emergent tensions and opportunities present in our digitalized and individualized society.

We are nevertheless adamant that the inclusion of ICT in family time does not pull families apart, as feared, but instead allows emerging individualized togetherness. According to our findings, we are not all becoming lonely: the relentlessly ongoing connection to the digital world does not lead to us being 'together alone' in a shared physical space – the new kind of solitude suggested by Turkle (2011) – but rather to being 'together individually' as a new form of individualized togetherness.

The rest of this chapter is organized as follows: in the next section, we present the theoretical background, followed with the data, method, analysis and findings. After discussing the findings, we conclude the chapter with a summary of our findings and a few thoughts on potential future ways of being 'together individually' with and around ICT.

BACKGROUND: DIGITALIZATION, INDIVIDUALIZATION AND THE GENESIS OF 'TOGETHER INDIVIDUALLY'

Digitalization refers to a process of transformation that synthesizes the possibilities of ICT (comprising the Internet, ubiquitous smart devices and digital social network services and applications) into everyday life (Hess et al., 2014). These possibilities enable new means of social interaction during both work and leisure (Yoo, 2010; Scheepers and Middleton, 2013). Digitalization can also have unintended consequences. People often adapt ICTs for their own purposes and end up using them in novel ways while also changing their own practices in the process (Ilmonen, 2004). In this way, digitalization may also alter the practices related to the social relationships of the users if the users perceive that the new applications add value to them, despite the changes they impose (Rogers, 1962; Norman, 1999; Ilmonen, 2004; Castells et al., 2007).

Digitalization is not the only factor affecting social interaction in the home, however. Another developmental undercurrent, individualization, has been affecting the social contract in the home since the 1960s (Harari, 2014). Individualization is a process of social change in which the acceptability of making personal choices increases while the pressure to follow norms and traditions diminishes. These changes allow enhanced individuality and the differentiation of social practices (Giddens, 1991; Beck et al., 1994; Beck and Beck-Gernsheim, 2008). In the digitalized society, these individualized practices are often carried out and even enabled by ICT use. In this way, though individualization and digitalization are independent phenomena, they are in practice often simultaneously present in social settings around the use of ICT, creating the conditions for the emergence of their joint effects. For example, individualization is relevant to the adoption of new technologies, generating an atmosphere open to the emergent individual ICT user's needs and circumstances. Furthermore, it provides the impetus to alter traditions and incorporate new technologies into social settings. On the other hand, digitalization promotes individualization by offering new expressive vehicles through which to carry out individualized practices.

In this chapter, we explore the interplay between digitalization and individualization in the context of families spending time together at home with and around ICT. Family life is an area of complex and meaningful social relationships that have undergone profound changes with individualization, opening up negotiations and differing options of togetherness (Beck and Beck-Gernsheim, 1990). In an individualized family, everybody wants to feel socially fulfilled while also leading a personally meaningful life, and this demands altruism and negotiation from all parties to keep family together (ibid.). The dual demands of personal fulfilment and the need for compromise to ensure the happiness of others create widespread tensions within individualized families, resulting in various attempts to reduce these tensions with purposeful solutions (Beck and Beck-Gernsheim, 1990, 2008; Giddens, 1990; Beck et al., 1994; Chambers, 2012).

Using case examples, we demonstrate how ICT can both contribute to the emergence of such tensions within families and also be used as a solution for mitigating them. Well-established social conducts, such as the ways of spending time together at home with the family, often include established elements that give meaning to the action for the participants and contribute to the formation of the shared experience (Giddens, 1991). These kinds of social conducts tend to be resistant to change (ibid.). People may, however, start reconsidering their traditions if, for example, a new technology comes along promising some kind of perceived advantage through its adoption (Ilmonen, 2004). In the digitalized society, ubiquitous ICT devices pervade all the elements of life, including family togetherness. It is at moments when ICT devices are used during the family's time together that family members must make decisions as to whether they also accept the potential changes in their social conduct of being together.

Children also need to be socialized into the acceptable ways of using ICT in the digitalized society. Traditionally, the parents have been in a leading position in the socialization of children into the social conduct of the family (Giddens, 2009). With the inclusion of ICT devices in family life, however, the socialization processes are affected by the ubiquitous and interactive nature of ICT (Tiilikainen and Tuunainen, 2014). We begin by exploring the emerging ways of socializing children with and around ICT, drawing on Castells's (2000, p. 21) vision about the process of socialization in the digital age:

> [In a network society] the process of socialization becomes customized, individualized, and made out of composite models. The autonomous ability to reprogram one's own personality, in interaction with an environment of networks, becomes the crucial feature for psychological balance, replacing the strengthening of a set personality, embedded in established values.

In an individualized and digitalized society, the socialization of children towards the acceptable use of ICT as a part of social situations is a complex process including not only the parents and the children but the demands of ICT too (Tiilikainen and Tuunainen, 2014). The resulting socialization process is a hybrid between the individualized family values and the values inscribed in and put forth by the ICT (and media content) used (ibid.). Family values and the values put forth by ICT may contradict one another, and this can increase tensions and conflicts between the parents and children over the use of ICT in social situations (ibid.). The parents hope that ICT-embedded values will support their family values and the socialization of their children while helping to ease the tensions within the families arising both from the individual demands of the family members and the use of ICT (ibid.).

The theoretical framework on which this chapter is grounded builds on the premise that the use of ICT during family togetherness brings forth emergent tensions between the togetherness and the individual interests of the family members, and thus the use of ICT have either to be managed and made a part of the collocated togetherness or rejected. We theorize that doing this is a part of the individualized composite socialization process (see Castells, 2000) for the children towards the mutually agreed social contract (see Ilmonen, 2004; Beck and Beck-Gernsheim, 2008) of the family, because during these negotiations the children learn about acceptable and discouraged ways of using ICT in social situations. Simultaneously, the emergent situations brought about by ICT and the processes of negotiating over them force the parents to constantly evaluate and reorient their responses and actions around ICT. Figure 10.1 presents our theoretical framework.

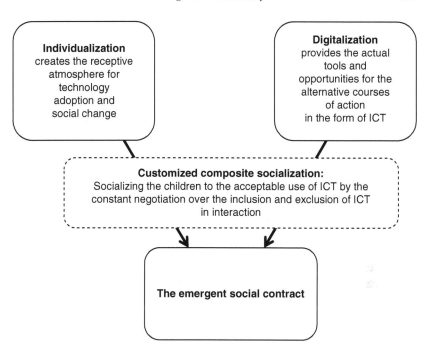

Figure 10.1   The theoretical framework for studying the socialization of children and the social contract included

DATA AND ANALYSIS

This chapter uses qualitative video material from 26 families in Finland between May 2011 and January 2012; it was collected for the 'Media, Family Interaction and Children's Well-Being' project. The data contain 665 hours of video recordings, comprising either a capture of just one family member present, children without their parents or all the family present. Because our interest in this chapter is the socialization of children, we selected for our analysis 150 hours of recordings in which all the family or at least one parent and one or more of the children was present. During the analysis, we used multimodal techniques: we broke down the video material into sequences of interactions to reveal the interactional organization of the action and the role of the physical surroundings and ICT in it (see Heath et al., 2010). We combined the visual analysis with interaction and conversation analysis to form a picture of the social action in its physical environment and to capture both the spoken and non-spoken (gesture-based) socialization techniques present in data (see Goodwin,

2000; Streeck et al., 2011; Arminen, 2012). Our goal in the analysis was to find instances where a member of the family (either a child or a parent) used ICT during the moments of family togetherness to see how the other family members present reacted. We paid special attention to the examples given by the parents about how to use – or not to use – ICT, to the attempts to use ICT made by the children and the ways the parents received these attempts in order to understand how the children are socialized into ICT use and the social contract being formed in the process.

FINDINGS

According to our findings, both ICT use and the negotiations over ICT use between the children and the parents are ubiquitous in the data. Across the families studied, the social conducts and rules regarding the acceptable or unacceptable uses of ICT as a part of family togetherness in a shared space are situated and based on the reflexively achieved patterns of social interaction in the families. Each family has its own code of conduct regarding ICT use during family togetherness, and there appears to be no discernible similarity between families. Most of the families appear to have a rule of not using ICT devices during mealtimes, but there are also families where mobile phones are used during meals, in particular, if family members eat at different times or in separate groups. However, we found evidence for acceptable and unacceptable ways of using ICT devices during family togetherness based on the negotiation processes present in data. We call the emergent social contract formed in these negotiations 'together individually', because we find it contains elements from both being together and simultaneously tending to individual interests. Using our theoretical framework (see Figure 10.1) and our empirical evidence, we argue that the children are socialized into the 'together individually' contract as follows: individualization creates a receptive atmosphere for new ways of doing things and ICT provides the means for alternative courses of action, so the ongoing negotiations make both the parents and the children learn and relearn the boundaries of possible and acceptable ways of using ICT devices during family togetherness in a shared physical environment. As a result, the emerging social contract of 'together individually' comprises individualized and digitalized elements. Below, we provide examples of these elements with three cases from the data.

Case 1: Producing Togetherness with ICT

Mobile ICT devices afford convivially concurrent engagements in which participants can flexibly engage and disengage in their activities, as in

Picture 10.1   The daughter finds a way to invite the mother to share amusing content[1]

Case 1. Here, after turning the bedroom TV off, the mother has started reading a book, the son is playing with toys and the daughter is using her newly acquired mobile phone. When the daughter starts moving towards the mother, her eyes catch her daughter's movement. She attends to the daughter's mobile phone for a while, but then focuses back on her book. The daughter is very amused by her mobile phone, and manages to get her brother's attention. Then the daughter laughs and pushes her mobile into her mother's field of vision, thus getting her attention for a moment of shared laughter. After this moment of togetherness, the mother raises her book up again as a kind of interaction shield (see Ayass, 2014) and returns to reading (Picture 10.1).

Case 1 shows how the mobility of ICT can be used to produce and reproduce family togetherness in a shared physical space: the child moves to be within an arm's distance of the mother, and then pushes the mobile device towards the mother, introducing repeated calls for togetherness into the situation. While the mother is committed to reading her course book, being physically but not socially present, the child uses her mobile app to invite moments of togetherness by pushing the device into her mother's field of view. The child does this several times, but still within limits that become evident in the interaction. In Case 1, the child explores the limits of acceptable ways of entering the private space of her mother, whose responses teach the child about the possibilities and limits of ICT in initiating togetherness. Enabled by ICT and its versatile content, the child is trying to shift the situation from the personal time of her mother to the togetherness of the family based on the child's playfulness with the ICT content. In this situation, both the mother and the child have to negotiate how to manage the emerging tension between the interests of the mother, the child and the social contract of the family regarding the conduct of togetherness. In Case 1, this tension is resolved by the mother accepting several rounds of sharing the ICT content with the child. At the end of Case 1, the mother simply refuses further togetherness and resumes her individual commitment (reading). The child accepts this, although her mobile phone still has the potential for initiating more moments of sharing, because of the unlimited variety of content available. Case 1 shows how in 'together individually', although ICT has the potential for producing and reproducing family togetherness, the moments of togetherness over sharing the ICT content have to be achieved collaboratively; individual wishes for private moments set limits on togetherness. Case 1 shows how 'together individually' may be reproducible with and around ICT, but it still has to accommodate individual wishes too.

Case 2: Juggling the Demands of Family Togetherness and ICT Simultaneously

Changes in family sociality often raise worried voices about new conducts tearing down family traditions and togetherness (see Turkle, 2011, 2015). Our data shows how family members (parents and children) still opt to spend time together at home, albeit in an altered form. The essential part of the togetherness in 'together individually' is achieved non-verbally through visual cues in the shared physical space: this multimodal multiactivity is carried out simultaneously with individualized technology use. This allows the establishment of individual freedom within family togetherness, but the demands of the togetherness have to be monitored at all times. To achieve this, the participants can move between focused social activity in the shared physical space and peripheral awareness, as in Case 2. Here, the family (the father and three children) is gathered on the living room sofa to watch the TV show *South Park*. The eldest son has been communicating with text messages, and he receives one just as the punch line of a joke is building up in the show, forming the social experience of sharing humour together with the family in the shared physical space. The son briefly glances at the phone, but puts it away, prioritizing shared humour with his family. He then focuses on the TV show, first smiling and then laughing. After the gag, he returns to messaging, still switching back between the TV and the phone message. Strikingly, all other family members have not attended to the messaging with its alert tones. The son, on the other hand, has to juggle to find balance between the engagements (Picture 10.2).

Case 2 demonstrates how during family togetherness in a shared physical space, the ICT use of an individual can connect him with further social

Picture 10.2 The oldest son juggles between private and family engagement

worlds outside the home. In Case 2, the outer social world is connected only to the son receiving the messages and therefore for the family togetherness it represents his individual, private engagements. The other members of the family have to decide whether this is acceptable in the context of family togetherness or not. Even though traditionally everybody is expected to focus on the same thing during moments of togetherness (Goffman, 1961), such as watching TV, Case 2 demonstrates how, by not attending to the extracurricular ICT use of an individual, the family members choose to accept the momentary extracurricular activities of the son receiving the message. Other family members (the father, both other children) ignore the son's incoming messages. By doing this, the father is respecting his son's privacy and also indicating to the other children that the behaviour is acceptable.

Consequently, the use of ICT is combined with family togetherness seamlessly. The son receiving the messages, on the other hand, delays the emergent demands of the ICT device, prioritizing the engagement in togetherness in the physical world according to the situational demands. The son demonstrates mastery of the social conduct of the family by delaying the reading of his message until the shared laughter has passed, thereby showing respect for the social contract of the family. Case 2 shows how in the 'together individually' contract, family togetherness in a shared physical space can accommodate momentary individual ICT engagements too. However, in the case of conflicting demands of ICT and family togetherness, both individual behaviour and family norms become accountable.

Case 3: Directing Togetherness with ICT

In the 'together individually' contract, the participants have to be able to smoothly reallocate their focus between their personal commitment and other engagements in order not to neglect anyone. In Case 3, the family (a mother, a father, a baby, a son and a daughter) is gathered in the living room. There is an ice hockey game on TV; the father, holding the baby, watches TV with the children who eat ice cream; the mother is looking at housing ads on a laptop. When the father shifts his attention to the baby, she responds with babbling. Simultaneously, the son has been trying to challenge the others to participate in an ice-cream-eating contest. When the father comments on the baby's babbling, the mother starts turning to attend to them; at the same time their son starts turning, gazing at his mother already before the mother's eyes settle on the baby. When the mother starts to turn back towards her laptop, her son seizes the moment to initiate the appeal for an ice-cream-eating contest again. While the mother turns her head, her gaze passes her son, who has just started to relaunch his contest appeal. All the time, the mother's finger on a keyboard has reserved her return back to the laptop. The son's gaze and utterance make it necessary for her to turn back and acknowledge her son's plea. This brief mother/son dialogue also catches the attention of the daughter, who initiates an inquiry concerning possible plans to move to a new apartment. After the parents briefly explain that they are not moving yet, they all return to their original positions oriented towards the TV or laptop (see Sacks and Schegloff, 2002) (Picture 10.3).

In Case 3, the mother uses ICT to pick up an emergent topic to discuss based on the parents' interests, departing from the frame of the ice hockey game on TV. The mother has been quietly browsing the laptop on the side, occasionally commenting on some housing ads. By doing this, she shows the children that it is acceptable to introduce parallel topics alongside the other members' ongoing engagement with the sport on TV during the family time together (as opposed to concentrating on one thing only). The father and the children have to decide whether or not and how to integrate the new engagements as a part of the family togetherness.

Case 3 contains an orientation to topical cohesion and continuity (Sacks, 1987). The parents juggle their focus between the TV, housing ads, and their children. The son aims at introducing yet another new frame – the ice-cream-eating contest. By monitoring his mother's attention, he manages to get an acknowledgement of his idea but does not succeed in engaging others in it. His sister instead succeeds in returning the conversation to the family's housing plans, thereby also showing her grasp of her parents' topical relevancies. In this way, she is teaching her brother

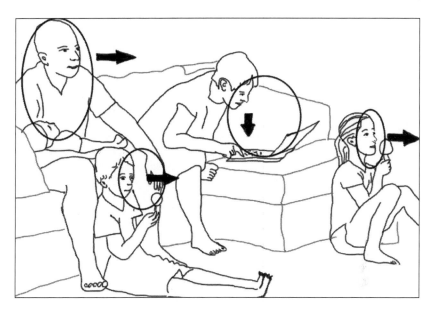

Picture 10.3   Orderliness of concurrent family engagements

that topical cohesion and continuity outweigh unconnected topics. The emergent togetherness has an internal orderliness: the topics introduced have to be either related to the content introduced or disclosed properly before moving on to the next topic. In this way, the media augmentation of family togetherness does not change the principles of topical cohesion and continuity (ibid.). Case 3 shows how the 'together individually' contract may be complex, but not chaotic.

DISCUSSION

Our results show how families manage the inclusion of ICT into their time together at home by the formation of the emergent, accountable social contract of 'together individually'. Our results also show how the children are socialized into this social contract with constant negotiations over the acceptable and unacceptable uses of ICT during family togetherness in a shared physical space. Figure 10.2 summarizes the genesis of the 'together individually' social contract.

According to our findings, 'Together individually' is an emergent and accountable form of social contract, because it is formed and maintained through constant negotiations and it contains both individualized and

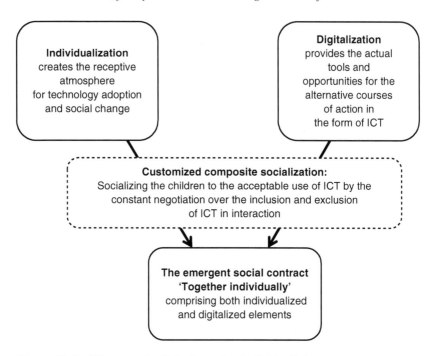

Figure 10.2   The genesis of the 'together individually' contract

digitalized elements (see also Morgan, 1996, 2011). Despite being emergent, the 'together individually' contract is accountable too. The three cases selected from the data provide evidence for our arguments and demonstrate the defining characteristics of the 'together individually' contract.

The previous generation of immobile desktop computers raised worries about the isolating effects of IT use, potentially resulting in people being 'together alone' (Turkle, 2011). However, mobile ICTs are not confined to one place; they can be used anywhere. Our results demonstrate how in the 'together individually' contract, the family members gather in a shared space, carrying their mobile ICT with them to where they naturally want to spend time within the home. The mobility of ICT devices is essential for being 'together individually'. Since concurrent face-to-face engagements are dependent on the physically shared location, the ICT used have to be either mobile or located in a place where families spend time. Any distance from the shared physical location is usually enough to block attempts at casual sharing. An increased bonus of the contract is that the children are using technology within the physical and emotional proximity of their parents, so small children can rely on immediate parental support in the case of frightening content, and the parents can easily keep an unobtrusive eye on their children's media use. In previous research, the mobility of ICT has also been associated with socially isolating effects, harming the engagement and commitment to conversation and the formation of empathy towards others (Turkle, 2015). Our results show how the opposite effects are possible, too: first, mobile ICT can also bring family members together, provide points for initiating conversation and assist in sustaining the conversation on the chosen topic or change the topic if appropriate (cf. Aaltonen et al., 2014). In our data, this appears to be especially important for teenagers and their parents, who are offered topics to talk about during family togetherness.

Second, our results show how the parents socialize their children during the use of ICT, teaching them to use it in a way that shows respect for family togetherness and the feelings of others, thus teaching empathy to the children in the process. Both of these effects are dependent on the shared physical location and the presence and socialization work of the parents, however: those children who grow up alone with ICT or whose parents fail to take their children into account when using the devices themselves may not be learning about the social skills related to the considerate and empathetic use of ICT during time together with family and friends (see Turkle, 2015). Our cases show how social skills and empathy are a prerequisite for being 'together individually' at home. In summary, 'together individually' is an emergent, accountable social contract, an achievement that has to be constantly maintained and renewed by negotiation over the use of ICT in a way that is mutually acceptable. Reaching the state of 'together individually' can open the door to the beneficial effects of ICT use, facilitating togetherness and conversation. We suggest that more attention should be paid to the formation and upkeep of 'together individually' as well as the socialization of children into the 'together individually' contract in the future, to encourage the positive effects of the increasing use of ICT in social situations, both during leisure time and at work.

CONCLUSION

In this chapter, we have analysed the socialization of children into the social contract we call 'together individually'. This contract involves the use of ICT as a part of family togetherness in a physically shared space at home. We have defined 'together individually' as an emergent and composite form of social contract comprising both individualized and digitalized elements that must be constantly maintained and negotiated concerning the use of ICT. Using three cases from the data, we have demonstrated how 'together individually', despite being emergent and complex, also has distinct characteristics that reveal how the family members balance their togetherness and individual wishes with the use of ICT.

First, we demonstrated how ICT can be used to produce togetherness, but in a way that takes the wishes of each individual into account, too. Second, we showed how ICT can be used for extracurricular social activities during family togetherness, but the demands of the family togetherness have to be monitored at all times. Third, we revealed how ICT can be used to direct togetherness by either complementing conversation or introducing new topics of conversation, but the resulting conversations must have an internal order and not be chaotic.

Through our results, we also demonstrated how the parents socialize their children into successfully engaging in the 'together individually' contract by showing them examples of what can and cannot be done with ICT during family togetherness. Finally, we suggested that paying more attention to achieving and maintaining the 'together individually' contract could be a way of encouraging the positive effects of ICT, both during leisure and at work.

NOTE

1.   Due to space restrictions, we are limited to one picture per case, and we cannot show in detail the embodied orchestration of the participants' conduct in each individual case.

REFERENCES

Aaltonen, T., I. Arminen and T. Raudaskoski (2014), 'Photo sharing as joint activity in conversation with an aphasic speaker', in M. Nevile, P. Haddington, T. Heinemann and M. Rauniomaa (eds), *Interacting with Objects: Language, Materiality, and Social Activity*, Amsterdam: John Benjamins, pp. 125–44.

Arminen, I. (2012), 'Ethnomethodology in the analysis of discourse and interaction', in C. Chapelle (ed.), *The Encyclopedia of Applied Linguistics*, Chichester, UK: Blackwell Publishing Ltd, pp. 2051–6.

Ayass, R. (2014), 'Using media as involvement shields', *Journal of Pragmatics*, **72**, 5–17.

Beath, C., N. Berente and M.J. Gallivan (2013), 'Expanding the frontiers of information systems research: Introduction to the special issue', *Journal of the Association for Information Systems*, **14** (4), i–xvi.

Beck, U. and E. Beck-Gernsheim (1990), *The Normal Chaos of Love. Contemporary Sociology*, Cambridge, UK: Polity Press.

Beck, U. and E. Beck-Gernsheim (2008), *Individualization, Theory, Culture and Society*, London: Sage.

Beck, U., A. Giddens, and S. Lash (1994), *Reflexive Modernization: Politics, Tradition and Aesthetics in the Modern Social Order*, Cambridge, UK: Polity Press.

Castells, M. (2000), 'Materials for an exploratory theory of the network society', *The British Journal of Sociology*, **51** (1), 5–24.

Castells, M., M. Fernandez-Ardevol, J.L. Qiu and A. Sey (2007), *Mobile Communication and Society. A Global Perspective*, Cambridge, MA: MIT Press.

Chambers, D. (2012), *A Sociology of Family Life: Change and Diversity in Intimate Relations*, Cambridge, UK: Polity Press.

Giddens, A. (1990), *The Consequences of Modernity*, Cambridge, UK: Polity Press.

Giddens, A. (1991), *Modernity and Self-Identity. Self and Society in the Modern Age, Corrosion*, Cambridge, UK: Polity Press.

Giddens, A. (2009), *Sociology*, Cambridge, UK: Polity Press.

Goffman, E. (1961), *Encounters: Two Studies in the Sociology of Interaction*, Indianapolis, IN: Bobbs-Merrill.

Goodwin, C. (2000), 'Action and embodiment within situated human interaction', *Journal of Pragmatics*, **32** (10), 1489–522.

Harari, Y. (2014), *Sapiens: A Brief History of Humankind*, New York: Random House.

Heath, C., J. Hindmarsh and P. Luff (2010), *Video in Qualitative Research: Analysing Social Interaction in Everyday Life*, London: Sage.

Hess, T., C. Legner and W. Esswein et al. (2014), 'Digital life as a topic of business and information systems engineering?', *Business and Information Systems Engineering*, **6** (4), 247–53.

Ilmonen, K. (2004), 'The use of and commitment to goods', *Journal of Consumer Culture*, **4** (1), 27–50.

Morgan, D. (1996), *Family Connections: An Introduction to Family Studies*, Cambridge, UK: Polity Press.

Morgan, D. (2011), *Rethinking Family Practices*, Basingstoke, UK: Palgrave Macmillan.

Norman, D.A. (1999), 'Affordances, conventions and design', *Interactions*, **38** (3), 38–42.

Rogers, E.M. (1962), *Diffusion of Innovations*, New York: Free Press.

Sacks, H. (1987), 'On the preferences for agreement and contiguity in sequences in conversation', in G. Button and J. Lee (eds), *Talk and Social Organisation*, Clevedon, UK: Multilingual Matters, pp. 54–69.

Sacks, H. and E.A. Schegloff (2002), 'Home position', *Gesture*, **2** (2), 133–46.

Sawyer, S. and S. Winter (2011), 'Special issue on futures for research on information systems: Prometheus unbound?', *Journal of Information Technology*, **26** (2), 95–98.

Scheepers, R. and C. Middleton (2013), 'Personal ICT ensembles and ubiquitous information systems environments: Key issues and research implications', *Communications of the Association for Information Systems*, **33**, 381–92.

Shove, E., M. Pantzar and M. Watson (2012), *The Dynamics of Social Practice*, Thousand Oaks, CA: Sage.

Streeck, J., C. Goodwin and C. LeBaron (2011), *Embodied Interaction: Language and Body in the Material World*, Cambridge, UK: Cambridge University Press.

Tiilikainen, S. and V.K. Tuunainen (2014), 'Reinforcing family values with web design – case Yle "P2" children's website', *Selected Papers of the IRIS*, pp. 50–64.

Turkle, S. (2011), *Alone Together: Why We Expect More from Technology and Less from Each Other*, New York: Basic Books.

Turkle, S. (2015), *Reclaiming Conversation: The Power of Talk in a Digital Age*, New York: Penguin Press.
Van Dijk, J. (2009), *Network Society*, 3rd edition, Bodmin, UK: MPG Books.
Yoo, Y. (2010), 'Computing in everyday life: A call for research on experimental computing', *MIS Quarterly*, **34** (2), 213–31.

PART III

Conclusions and discussion

11. The influence of parental smartphone use, eye contact and 'bystander ignorance' on child development

Sanna Raudaskoski, Eerik Mantere and Satu Valkonen

INTRODUCTION

Digital technologies and media have changed the daily lives of families around the world by creating new interactional contexts and relational patterns (e.g., Ólafsson et al., 2013; Wartella et al., 2013). The familial use of digital media has quickly renewed the structure, function and mentality of family interaction. Smartphones are the flagships of new digital media and the number of smartphone owners (Smith, 2015), as well as the frequency of smartphone use (Rosen, 2012; ebrand Finland, 2015; Turkle, 2015), has been increasing rapidly. The shift from the 'computer age' to the 'smartphone age' is a reality all over the world (Carson and Lundvall, 2016).

A common response to criticism of new technology states that technologies have always been met with suspicion and horror stories that in hindsight have turned out to be exaggerated. The hampering effects of smartphone use on simultaneous face-to-face interaction have been dubbed the phenomenon of the 'sticky media device' and concern has been raised about parental smartphone use in particular (see Chapter 9 in this book). But why should using a smartphone differ in this regard from reading a book or making dinner? Can parental attention not be 'stuck' on various things and so lead to absent or confusing responses to a child?

In this chapter, we illustrate the central mechanisms of smartphone use that, from the point of view of small children, set the parental use of the smartphone significantly apart from many other activities in the visible home environment. There is a point to be made that, for example, television and magazines do not create a similar interactional structure with their user based on turn-by-turn actions (cf. Mantere and Raudaskoski, Chapter 9 in this book), but we also argue that there are other as yet uninspected elements in the equation that are crucial for understanding what the spread of smartphones into the everyday lives of families can mean for a developing child. Compared to the handling of other objects in the home environment, the use of smartphones is exceptional in two major ways: (1) it catches the gaze and thus draws the caregiver away from the participation framework and (2) it conveys exceptionally few signs of the activity that the caregiver is engaged in.

We start off the chapter by considering the meaning of gaze in early interaction, focusing on how it paves the way for attachment and social skills. After that, we discuss the affordances of environmental artefacts and their part in the process of socialization. Following this, we introduce the new concept of 'bystander ignorance', which illustrates the role of smartphone use from the point of view of another person in the same physical space with the smartphone user. We approach bystander ignorance by considering the situational aspects of parental smartphone use relevant to a small child. To conclude, we discuss the possible influences of bystander ignorance on child development and highlight the need for further studies.

THE ROLE OF EYE CONTACT IN EARLY ATTACHMENT

> Making eye contact is the most powerful mode of establishing a communicative link between humans. During their first year of life, infants learn rapidly that the looking behavior of others conveys significant information. Human infants prefer to look at faces that engage them in mutual gaze and that, from an early age, healthy babies show enhanced neural processing of direct gaze. (Farroni et al., 2002, p. 9602)

The quality of the parent–child relationship has endured in the history of the human sciences as the paramount factor in child development (e.g., Bowlby, 1969; Valsiner and Connolly, 2005). Studies in the field highlight that making eye contact is the most powerful mode of establishing a communicative link between humans. For people with well-functioning eyesight, gaze is one of the major aspects of forming a system of attachment between a caregiver and child. Moreover, early sensitivity to a mutual gaze is arguably the basic foundation for the later development of social skills.

In the early weeks and months of a baby's life, eye contact with others 'maintains life' by tempting the child into curiosity and activity. It is essential for the development of humans to understand that faces can reflect internal states of social partners, at the hub being the importance of processing information about eyes and eye-gaze direction (e.g., Robson, 1967; Tomasello, 1999a; Farroni et al., 2002; Ayers, 2003). At all ages, a gaze shared between two persons is a way of showing a willingness to begin a mutual encounter (Goffman, 1963, pp. 91–5; Argyle and Dean, 1965, p. 291; Kendon, 1967). Eye contact is also the beginning of relating to objects, which forms a model for how the child becomes familiar with the world. Thus, among human beings, gaze seems to function to provide information, regulate interaction, express intimacy, exercise social control, and facilitate task goals (Kleinke, 1986).

The links between eye contact and emotional responsiveness have been reported in a number of studies (e.g., Ainswort et al., 1971). The sensitive responses of parents to a child's signals can strengthen the child's positive emotional states and modulate negative ones, forming a specific style of attachment (Bowlby, 1969; Ainsworth, 1979). Infants needing care in order to survive seek proximity to the parents or other caregivers and try to establish communication with them. Repeated experiences become encoded as expectations and then as mental models of attachment, which give children a sense of security called the secure base (Siegel, 1999). Thus, with small children, the direction of the gaze is linked to whether the caregivers are emotionally available. Emotional availability has been called the 'connective tissue of healthy socioemotional development' (Easterbrooks and Biringen, 2000, p. 123). According to earlier studies, emotional availability, coherent behaviour and adequate stimulation can be associated with the development of an emotionally and socially competent child, whereas the experience of emotional unavailability, incoherent behaviour and inconsistent reactions in the early years of life may lead to ambivalent emotional reactions in later social relations. Parental under-attuning can be connected to the fragmentation of children's attention, uncertain mutuality, ambivalent emotionality, and insecure relationships (Kreppner, 2005).

Koulomzin et al. (2002) found that the attachment styles of one-year-old infants could already be predicted by the behaviour the infants showed while playing with their mothers at the age of four months. By coding specifically the gaze, head orientation, facial expression and self-touching/mouthing behaviour, they concluded that compared to children who ended up having insecure/avoidant attachment style, the future-secure infants spent more time focusing their visual attention on the face of the mother than those with a future-avoidant attachment style.

LEARNING SOCIAL SKILLS

The long-standing social psychological concepts of the 'looking-glass self' (Cooley, 1902) and the 'generalized other' (Mead, 1934) state that the development of the self is based on children's understanding of how others perceive them, and a person's self grows out of interpersonal interactions and the perceptions of others. A child's perceptions of how parents or other caregivers acknowledge his or her initiatives determine the child's view of themselves.

Studies show that long before children are able to speak, they encounter an interactionally organized social world (e.g., Goffman, 1964; Tomasello, 1999a, p. 71; Levison, 2006, p. 40), even just after their birth (e.g., Meltzoff and Moore, 1977; Stern, 1985). Early-appearing forms of communicative actions are carried out through visible bodily behaviour, including, for instance, pointing gestures and gaze (Liszkowski, 2006; Lerner et al., 2011). It has been argued that even if human children had an evolutionary based biological readiness for interaction, the actual process of developing communicative skills conforms to the requirements of the observable order of interaction and participation in it (Levinson, 2006, p. 54; Lerner et al., 2011, p. 57).

Interaction is characterized by an expectation of the next relevant action and its close timing (Levinson 2006, p. 46). Significant for understanding the issues that shape the child's emerging social skills is the orientation that children – and those with whom they interact – have on the production and recognition of mutual understandings. This view of development brings into focus the subtle changes in association produced by the child, which are often shown to be highly sensitive to the communicative sequence in which they occur (Gardner and Forrester, 2010). Already young infants comprehend normative expectations of face-to-face interaction and find even short temporary violations of these expectations upsetting (Mesman et al., 2009). However simple an action may appear, it is a sequentially organized, locally realized practical activity with an emergent structure that provides the resources for the recognition and production of actions relevant to it. Thus, what is glossed as 'socialization' takes place as conduct situated in these constituents of the toddler's everyday life (Lerner et al., 2011, p. 57; Keel, 2016)

The learning of social skills is complex, and the meaningful layering of gaze, gesture, talk and other resources are very much part of the communicative framework at any age. Local sequential issues are always inextricably linked to wider issues of the child's emerging membership within society (Gardner and Forrester, 2010). We stress here Mantere and Raudaskoski's notion of how the use of smartphone hampers the smooth sequential progression of interaction and the timing of relevant next actions (see Chapter 9 in this book). Thus, there is a point to be made that the use of the smartphone creates a competing participation framework (Goffman, 1981) that has an effect on simultaneous face-to-face interaction.

As said earlier, gaze orientation gives the infant fundamental information about the caregiver's emotions and involvement, which, accordingly, influences the baby's feelings of safety and security. The opportunity to recognize another's intention to approach or avoid is one of the principal mediating factors governing social interaction. Research has shown that approach-oriented emotions like joy, love and affection are usually expressed with a direct gaze, whereas avoidance-oriented emotions such as sorrow, bewilderment and disgust are displayed with an averted gaze. Because gaze direction conveys important information about a person's thoughts and emotions and specific gaze behaviours tend to co-occur with particular facial displays of emotion, these gaze behaviours might also influence how such facial displays are perceived by others (Adams and Kleck, 2005, pp. 3–4).

Thus, a caregiver looking at the screen of the smartphone may produce a facial expression of joy, but it is not synchronized with eye contact, and this produces ambivalent information about the caregiver's affective state in relation to the bystanding baby. In addition, because the attention fluctuates between the face-to-face situation and the smartphone, it is unclear to others which level of awareness about the participation framework should be expected of them. Babies do not yet comprehend the frame of action produced by parental smartphone use, and cannot interpret the multiple actions.

The question we want to raise is that if theories of human development unquestionably argue for the importance of eye contact in the early development of children, what are the possible effects of frequent smartphone use by parents? What happens if, due to smartphone use, a parent or another significant caregiver is misattuned, withdrawn, rejecting, and does not produce a response to the excited, crawling, playing child who is unable to engage the caregiver's eyes? Following the interaction order and the sequential progression of face-to-face activity would be difficult for anyone – let alone young children – when one of the members is simultaneously oriented towards an activity with a smartphone.

THE AFFORDANCES OF ARTEFACTS AND IMITATIVE LEARNING

Human babies start imitating the facial expressions of others almost immediately after birth. Initially, the brain of a newborn is not capable of organizing sensory-motor information of a degree much higher than the movement of the eyes, but other forms of imitative behaviour manifest as the brain matures: facial movements and increasingly sophisticated movements of the hands are followed by the rest of the body all the way up to complicated modulations in posture, conveying exact social information with the fine-tuning of a fraction of a second (e.g., Vygotski, 1966; Stern, 1971; Meltzoff, 1996; Valsiner and van der Veer, 2000).

Babies who are learning to interpret their environment come across different kinds of objects and artefacts: they grasp, suck and manipulate them and thus become aware of their affordances (Gibson, 1979). This is called the direct learning of affordances. However, even physical objects are usually encountered in a social framework, and thus most human affordances are in fact 'social' (e.g., Reed, 1996, pp. 124–5; Ingold, 2000, pp. 21–2). Children are selectively exposed to objects by other individuals, and then begin to use them as reference points in deciding how to interact with the objects in question (Tomasello, 1999b, p. 165).

The ability to process gaze information is pivotal when drawing conclusions of behavioural intentions from the non-verbal behaviour of others. Monitoring the caregiver's direction of gaze tells the child where the caregiver's focus of attention is. Already very early on in their lives, infants begin to tune in to and attempt to reproduce both the adults' goal and their behavioural means: the artefacts come to embody what Tomasello calls 'intentional affordances' (1999a, p. 84; 1999b, p. 166). Children learn about the artefacts' conventional or cultural affordances. As human children observe other people using cultural tools and artefacts, in Tomasello's words (1999a, p. 81; 1999b) they often engage in the process of 'imitative learning' in which they attempt to place themselves in the 'intentional space' of the other, discerning the other's goal – that is, what they are using the artefact 'for'. In this process, children come to know not only the sensory-motor affordances, but also the intentional affordances – in other words, the intentional means that other people have in the world through artefacts (Tomasello, 1999a, pp. 84–5).

The visible bodies of participants provide systematic, changing displays about the orientation and goal-relevant actions. In addition to the participants' placement, the ability to perceive something meaningful is always tied to access to relevant material surroundings. Rather than standing alone as a self-contained domain, visual phenomena are constituted and made meaningful through the way in which they are embedded within a larger set of practices (Goodwin and Goodwin, 1996; Goodwin, 2001). By engaging in imitative learning, the child joins the other person in affirming what the object is used for: hammers are for hammering and pencils are for writing (Tomasello, 1999a, p. 84). Usually in these kinds of situations of imitative learning, there is a plethora of visual, auditory or even other types of information instantly available for the child to maintain the sense of what is going on in the social setting. Children's embodied engagement with an environment of intentional affordances is shaped into meaningful actions through interaction with an experienced practitioner – a caregiver – through the structure of mutual accessibility created in the joint participation framework (cf. Goffman, 1981; Fogel, 1993, pp. 89–98; Goodwin, 2007, p. 59). This kind of joint attention, in which multiple actors are attending the same object in the environment, is a key aspect in the organization of human intersubjectivity (Tomasello, 1999a, p. 62).

Traceable courses of actions also play a part in the process of learning the emotional states of others, that is, the affective relationships between actors and intentional affordances (cf. Ingold, 2000, p. 23). The mental states of people physically near to us are not their individual business alone. They are highly relevant to all sharing the space with them. One has to be aware of all the semiotic resources (Goodwin, 2000) to make sense of the relationship between mental states and objects of actions in order to determine whether some action, or any action, on our part is befitting or outright vexatious.

We argue that unlike most artefacts in the human environment, smartphones serve poorly as intentional affordances for small children. The smartphone – and its use – does not include such clues that enable the 'intentional stance' (Dennett, 1987) of the user to be easily traced. Because we do not readily see what activity a user is performing with a smartphone, we can neither easily interpret the phase of their action: they serve poorly as a basis for the framework of joint attention. Next, we will theoretically conceptualize this phenomenon by introducing 'bystander ignorance'.

BYSTANDER IGNORANCE

A caregiver using a smartphone draws back from the participation framework, which in practice means that his or her gaze and attention averts from the child and the surroundings, and fastens onto the screen of the device. The interactional nature of most applications used by the smartphone leads to a situation where it is not easy to take one's eyes from the screen. At the same time, the traceable hints of the sequences and goals of smartphone activity, which can be anything from playing a game to closing a deal with a customer, become unclear. This notion leads to the central issue of our chapter: caregivers starting to use a smartphone to a large extent stop giving hints of the goals of their actions to the child watching them, and the child cannot infer from the posture and gestures of the caregiver or the shape and state of the smartphone which action the caregiver is currently performing. This aspect of smartphone use is by and large missing in other forms of solitary activity that a parent might become absorbed in. Having recognized this special aspect, we have named it 'bystander ignorance' and define it thus: the exceptional level and quality of unawareness that a person interested in pursuing face-to-face interaction with a smartphone user has about the aspects of the activity that the user is currently engaged in.

It is surely also a case with other object-aided actions that the action could be interpreted by the bystander to fall into more than one category. For example, a parent going through papers on a desk might be working, paying bills or just tidying up. However, of all the objects within the modern household, it is exactly the smartphone that is the medium for the greatest number and variation of possible actions and it is simultaneously the object that offers the least number of cues to the bystander about the particular action taking place. The screen of the smartphone is smaller than that of a TV, laptop or even tablet computer, and unlike a TV or laptop, it is usually directly facing the eyes of the user at a close enough distance that the screen is unlikely to be seen by anyone else.

In many activities, such as making dinner or watching television, there are immediately available hints to the bystander about the phase of the activity. Children can trace the sequential progression of the activity and in time get acquainted with the appropriate norms of behaviour (see also Chapters 9 and 10 of this book). In the case of smartphone use, however, the categories of action are so supremely hidden to the bystander that in comparison to the use of other domestic objects, the opportunities for social learning and comprehensive socialization to different areas and sectors of life circumstances can be hard to discern.

Of course, seeing a parent using a smartphone will give information about smartphone use to the child, and surely there are already many norms and schemas that today's children learn about smartphone use. One norm that accompanies poor intentional affordances of smartphone use is the private nature of its use. When a child is old enough to understand the concept of privacy, this element also begins to contribute to bystander ignorance. Viewing another person's smartphone screen should be avoided (unless actively shared by the user). This being commonly assumed, the unprompted viewing of someone else's smartphone screen can be perceived as a breach of privacy. It is about accepting and normalizing the 'absent presence' that Kenneth J. Gergen (2002) talked about already in the early 2000s when mobile phones had become common. One is physically present, but is absorbed into a virtual world by mediating technology.

Gergen predicted that with the inevitable tendency towards ever more applications and functions in mobile phones, absent presence would proliferate in the future. He was right.

DISCUSSION

As discussed, in the early days of infancy, eye contact is of utmost importance in creating a secure attachment between the child and caregiver. However, young adults in the 2010s – and thus parents-to-be – are used to looking at their smartphones at least every 15 minutes and putting online textual interaction before face-to-face conversation (Turkle, 2015). We argue that within this world of 'conversational silence', where eyes are glued to the mobile screen, the production of relevant eye contact with children and timely, correct interactional turns is at risk.

Exploring the video data collected during the project 'Media, Family Interaction and Children's Well-Being' (665 hours in total; see Appendix 1) clearly shows that there is a process of increasingly complex imitation going on in the day-to-day lives of these families with children. Children can be seen imitating not only their parents, who may be preparing food or watering the plants, but also television characters, for example. Depending on their age, the children's performances varied from the imitation of bodily movements to the more sophisticated imaginative play of a professional or some other social identity. The imitative ability encompasses ever-greater complexity through the synergetic development of the brain in union with the practice-driven development of mental skill. What jumps out when observing modern family life is that among all the activities taken up by the primary objects of imitation (by the primary agents of socialization, i.e., the caregivers), there is one that stands alone in being shrouded in mystery when it comes to the child being able to see and follow the actual action of the caregiver. Whereas an undertaking of watering the plants is something that can be mimicked even by a two-year-old, the use of a personal smartphone by various means towards various ends is an activity that for a young bystander does not in fact open up as a process of doing something. 'What is mother doing with her smartphone?' asked one of the authors of their nephew. 'Talking', the child replied. 'And when she is not talking, what is she doing?' the researcher continued. 'I don't know', said the child. With the proliferation of smartphones into the everyday lives of families, children are in ever-increasing numbers observing their parents perform actions that do not look like actions, towards ends that they have no information about. The whole process of imitating the parents' smartphone use consists of taking the device in one's hand and looking at it. Here is the key issue: what is the practice of the skill of imitation leading towards in the ability to take roles in this imitative process? What are the quantity and quality of the actions to be imitated in the case of smartphone use? To the child undergoing the imitation of what he or she has seen, there is no recognizable sequence, no stages of planning, preparation, execution and completion, no evaluation and revision – there is indeed uniquely little to copy and hence uniquely few actions to be taken as a role expectation. 'Bystander ignorance' caused by the invisible procedures of another person's smartphone use can thus hamper the progression of social skills, and consequently may affect the development of children. In stating this hypothesis, we acknowledge the need for further empirical research, both in naturally occurring and experimental research settings.

REFERENCES

Adams, R.B. and R.E. Kleck (2005), 'Effects of direct and averted gaze on the perception of facially communicated emotion', *Emotion*, **5** (1), 3–11.

Ainsworth, M.S. (1979), 'Infant–mother attachment', *American Psychologist*, **34** (10), 932–7.

Ainsworth, M.S., S.M.V. Bell and D.M. Stayton (1971), 'Individual differences in strange situation behavior of one-year-olds', in H.R. Schaffer (ed.), *The Origins of Human Social Relations*, London: Academic Press, pp. 17–57.

Argyle, M. and J. Dean (1965), 'Eye-contact, distance and affiliation', *Sociometry*, **28** (3), 289–304.

Ayers, M. (2003), *Mother–Infant Attachment and Psychoanalysis: The Eyes of Shame*, New York: Routledge.

Bowlby, J. (1969), *Attachment and Loss. Vol. 1: Attachment*, London: Hogarth Press.

Carson, S. and A. Lundvall (eds) (2016), *Ericsson Mobility Report*, June, accessed 18 August 2016 at https://www.ericsson.com/res/docs/2016/ericsson-mobility-report-2016.pdf.

Cooley, C.H. (1902), *Human Nature and the Social Order*, New York: Charles Scribner's Sons.

Dennett, D.C. (1987), *The Intentional Stance*, Cambridge, MA: The MIT Press.

Easterbrooks, A.M. and Z. Biringen (2000), 'Guest editors' introduction to the special issue: Mapping the terrain of emotional availability and attachment', *Attachment and Human Development*, **2** (2), 123–9.

ebrand Finland (2015), 'Finnish youngsters and social media 2015', accessed 29 March 2016 at www.ebrand.fi/somejanuoret2015/ [in Finnish].

Farroni, T., G. Csibra, F. Simion and M.H. Johnson (2002), 'Eye contact detection in humans from birth', *Proceedings of the National Academy of Sciences of the United States of America*, **99** (14), 9602–5.

Fogel, A. (1993), *Developing Through Relationships. Origins of Communication, Self and Culture*, Chicago, IL: The University of Chicago Press.

Gardner, H. and M. Forrester (eds) (2010), *Analysing Interactions in Childhood. Insights from Conversation Analysis*, Chichester, UK: John Wiley and Sons.

Gergen, K.J. (2002), 'The challenge of absent presence', in J.E. Katz and M. Aakhus (eds), *Perpetual Contact: Mobile Communication, Private Talk, Public Performance*, Cambridge, UK: Cambridge University Press, pp. 227–40.

Gibson, J.J. (1979), *The Ecological Approach to Visual Perception*, Hillsdale, NJ: Lawrence Erlbaum Associates.

Goffman, E. (1963), *Behavior in Public Places: Notes on the Social Organization of Gatherings*, New York: Free Press.

Goffman, E. (1964), 'The neglected situation', *American Anthropologist*, **66** (2), 133–6.

Goffman, E. (1981), *Forms of Talk*, Philadelphia, PA: University of Pennsylvania Press.

Goodwin, C. (2000), 'Action and embodiment', *Journal of Pragmatics*, **32** (10), 1489–1522.

Goodwin, C. (2001), 'Practices of seeing. Visual analysis: An ethnomethodological approach', in C. Jewitt and T. van Leeuwen (eds), *Handbook of Visual Analysis*, Thousand Oaks, CA: Sage, pp. 157–82.

Goodwin, C. (2007), 'Participation, stance, and affect in the organization of activities', *Discourse and Society*, **18** (1), 53–73.

Goodwin, C. and M.H. Goodwin (1996), 'Formulating planes: Seeing as a situated activity', in Y. Engeström and D. Middleton (eds), *Cognition and Communication at Work*, Cambridge, UK and New York: Cambridge University Press, pp. 61–95.

Ingold, T. (2000), *The Perception of the Environment: Essays on Livelihood, Dwelling and Skill*, London and New York: Routledge.

Keel, S. (2016), *Socialization: Parent–Child Interaction in Everyday Life*, London: Routledge.

Kendon, A. (1967), 'Some functions of gaze-direction in social interaction', *Acta Psychologica*, **26** (1), 22–63.

Kleinke, C.L. (1986), 'Gaze and eye contact: A research review', *Psychological Bulletin*, **100** (1), 78–100.

Koulomzin, M., B. Beebe and S. Anderson et al. (2002), 'Infant gaze, head, face and self-touch at 4 months differentiate secure vs. avoidant attachment at 1 year: A microanalytic approach', *Attachment and Human Development*, **4** (1), 3–24.

Kreppner, K. (2005), 'Social relations and affective development in the first two years in family contexts', in J. Valsiner and K.J. Connolly (eds), *Handbook of Developmental Psychology*, Thousand Oaks, CA: Sage, pp. 194–214.

Lerner, G.H., D.H. Zimmerman and M. Kidwell (2011), 'Formal structures of practical tasks: A resource for action in the social life of very young children', in J. Streeck, C. Goodwin and C. LeBaron (eds), *Embodied Interaction: Language and Body in the Material World*, New York: Cambridge University Press, pp. 44–58.

Levinson, S.C. (2006), 'On the human "interaction engine"', in N.J. Enfield and S.C. Levinson (eds), *Roots of Human Sociality: Culture, Cognition and Interaction*, Oxford and New York: Berg, pp. 39–69.

Liszkowski, U. (2006), 'Infant pointing at twelve months: Communicative goals, motives, and social-cognitive abilities', in N.J. Enfield and S.C. Levinson (eds), *Roots of Human Sociality: Culture, Cognition and Interaction*, Oxford and New York: Berg, pp. 153–78.

Mead, G.H. (1934), *Mind, Self and Society*, Chicago, IL: University of Chicago Press.

Meltzoff, A.N. (1996), 'The human infant as imitative generalist: A 20 year progress report on infant imitation with implications for comparative psychology', in J.C.M. Heyes and B. Galef (eds), *Social Learning in Animals*, San Diego, CA: Academic Press, pp. 347–70.

Meltzoff, A.N. and M.K. Moore (1977), 'Imitation of facial and manual gestures by human neonates', *Science*, **198** (4312), 75–8.

Mesman, J., M.H. van Ijzendoorn and M.J. Bakermans-Kranenburg (2009), 'The many faces of the still-face paradigm: A review and meta-analysis', *Developmental Review*, **29** (2), 120–62.

Ólafsson, K., S. Livingstone and L. Haddon (2013), *Children's Use of Online Technologies in Europe: A Review of the European Evidence Base*, London: EU Kids Online/LSE.

Reed, E.S. (1996), *Encountering the World. Toward an Ecological Psychology*, New York: Oxford University Press.

Robson, K.S. (1967), 'The role of eye-to-eye contact in maternal–infant attachment', *Journal of Child Psychology and Psychiatry*, **8** (1), 13–25.

Rosen, L.D. (2012), *iDisorder: Understanding Our Obsession with Technology and Overcoming its Hold on Us*, New York: Macmillan.

Siegel, D.J. (1999), *The Developing Mind*, New York: Guilford Press.

Smith, A. (2015), 'U.S. smartphone use in 2015', *Pew Research Center*, 1 April 2015, accessed 29 March 2016 at www.pewinternet.org/2015/04/01/us-smart phone-use-in-2015/.

Stern, D.N. (1971), 'A micro-analysis of mother–infant interaction: Behavior regulation and social contact between a mother and her 3-1/2-month-old twins', *Journal of the American Academy of Child Psychiatry*, **10** (3), 501–17.

Stern, D.N. (1985), *The Interpersonal World of the Infant: A View from Psychoanalysis and Developmental Psychology*, New York: Basic Books.

Tomasello, M. (1999a), *The Cultural Origins of Human Cognition*, Cambridge, MA: Harvard University Press.

Tomasello, M. (1999b), 'The cultural ecology of young children's interactions with objects and artifacts', in E. Winograd, R. Fivush and W. Hirst (eds), *Ecological Approaches to Cognition: Essays in Honor of Ulric Neisser*, Mahwah, NJ: Lawrence Erlbaum Associates, pp. 153–70.

Turkle, S. (2015), *Reclaiming Conversation. The Power of Talk in a Digital Age*, New York: Penguin Press.

Valsiner, J. and K. Connolly (2005), *Handbook of Developmental Psychology*, London: Sage.

Valsiner, K. and R. van der Veer (2000), *The Social Mind. Construction of the Idea*, New York: Cambridge University Press.

Vygotsky, L.S. (1966), 'Development of higher mental functions', in A.N. Leontyev, A.R. Luria and A. Smirnov (eds), *Psychological Research in the USSR*, Moscow: Progress Publishers, pp. 11–46.

Wartella, E., V. Rideout, A. Lauricella and S. Connell (2013), *Parenting in the Age of Digital Technology: A National Survey*, Evanston, IL: Northwestern University, School of Communication, Center on Media and Human Development.

12. Family, media and the digitalization of childhood

Anja Riitta Lahikainen and Ilkka Arminen

THE DIVERSIFICATION OF FAMILIES BY MEDIA

The degree of digitalization in homes varies among families with children. First, the number of available ICT and media technologies differs from home to home. For example, the families participating in our project had between three and 11 devices, including televisions, computers, game consoles and DVD players. In addition, there were (smart) phones, which were not counted (Lahikainen et al., 2015, pp. 52–3). Second, ICT expertise varies between families. Third, parents' practices concerning the control and encouragement of their offspring to use ICT devices also varies. Consequently, ICT and media usage patterns and the consequent role of media in children's socialization in the home is dependent on many factors and is the result of the complicated intertwined processes of the parents' and children's decision-making.

The factors mentioned above consequently contribute to vast diversification in the socialization and digitalization of childhood (Repo and Nätti, 2015; see also Chapter 5 in this volume). One could use many different criteria for categorizing the families according to the role of media in the socialization of the offspring at home. Based on the results of our research project, we chose an eating metaphor when referring to the parents' use of media in the socialization of their children. The families could be divided into two groups: the *gourmets* are families where children's media use was carefully regulated mainly by arranging other types of joint activities with children, such as board games or outdoor activities, whereas the *gourmands* are permissive families who encouraged children's technology use and regulated it only loosely. This latter group seemed to prioritize learning how to use ICT media devices over other activities, and if the parents themselves were not very experienced in using technologies, this decreased the control even further. Making media accessible to the children was for some families a way of organizing otherwise chaotic situations, for example, when a mother alone prepared a meal for five children, including one-year-old twins.

Several factors characterize parental management of their children's media use at home: access to available media technologies is limited, the children have a few simple rules concerning the use of media, and parents watch over their children's use of media technologies. Parents are also accessible to their children and plan a daily programme. When media are ubiquitously accessible and there are several children in the family, it is more difficult for parents to manage daily home life and combine the different interests of the family members. The regulation of children's media usage becomes even more difficult when children get older.

When we tried to ascertain clear tendencies in the differences between the families examined, we discovered two prominent factors: the age of child and the type of media device. Younger children used computers less and watched TV more, relatively, compared to 12-year-olds. Among the older children, the time spent with computers (laptops, desktops, tablets, smartphones) was considerably longer than among the five-year-olds (Lahikainen et al., 2015, p. 52). The parent–child conflicts in the use of media tended to take place in front of the computer instead of in front of the television and they occurred more often with older boys than with girls.

It became very evident that the structuring of daily life, including the use of media, takes place within the frameworks of the family structure and the parents' position in working life. For example, a single mother with a baby and a five-year-old child is more dependent on online contacts with other adults than a working mother with older children and a husband. A five-year-old child easily gets less attention from the parent(s) if there are also younger children in the family.

MEDIA IN FAMILY INTERACTION AND SOCIALIZATION

Media can be used or abused in multiple ways from the point of view of socialization. The special feature of television lies in its capacity to offer its spectators the feeling of being part of a wider audience that shares experiences together (Kellner, 2005). This is true also for family audiences. We found that despite the appearance of new media technologies, sharing time together watching TV programmes like sports, competitions and games is still popular among families with children (Repo and Nätti, 2015).

Watching television together, however, need not mean that all family members are concentrating on it alone. The family members can come and go or do other things at the same time, such as surfing the Internet with a smartphone, tablet or laptop. Tolerance of multitasking seems to be growing. In particular, TV is such a mature media that its consumption is open to numerous parallel activities (see Chapters 7 and 10 in this volume).

At home in front of the television, children can learn and become socialized in a number of different ways. They observe their parents' responses to TV programmes, and in learning about their parents, they also learn what they like themselves. They learn to talk and exchange opinions, as described by Suoninen (see Chapter 7) and Tiilikainen and Arminen (see Chapter 10). Parents also mediate the impact of the programme contents by commenting on and interpreting the programmes, as described by Kallio in this book (see Chapter 6). Increasingly, also, web searches assist knowledge formation (see Chapter 3 by Susan Danby).

In addition, our findings concerning the uses of mobile phones and tablets highlighted that the devices are also used as uniting media and a means of contact between the child and the parent. They may function as a way of getting parental attention and gaining intimacy by being close (see Chapter 10).

The need to regulate children's use of media devices is clearly one consequence of the attraction felt toward the use of media by family members of all ages. According to the generational contract, the responsibility for the younger generations is delegated to the parents because of their superior knowledge and experience, whereas children are thought to have a limited responsibility (Mayall, 2002, pp. 27–8). Nobody, however, is in the position to control and limit the parents' use of media and communication technologies. Children try to interrupt their parents using media devices because they want their parents' attention (see Chapter 9). These attempts often fail (Mantere, 2014; Mantere and Raudaskoski, 2015).

Reasons for attempts at control seem to vary. Generally, adults are thought to have more rational reasons for controlling their children than the children controlling their parents. Usually, for example, it is thought that it is children – and not the parents – who are under the spell of media and communication technologies. It became evident in our project that parents may also become overwhelmingly interested in virtual worlds and online relationships; this may threaten the face-to-face encounters on which younger children are especially dependent (see Chapter 9).

Most media-related conflicts between parents and children, however, were due to a child's computer use and related disobedience. It was difficult for the child to stop playing or doing whatever else they were doing with computer technologies and to comply with the parent's wishes for the child to do something else (see Chapter 8). Unlike when watching television, knowing what someone is doing in front of a computer or the screen of a tablet or mobile phone is difficult. Therefore, understanding the actions of the user (a child or an adult) is very difficult for a bystander (a child/

parent). The diminishing accountability of ubiquitous media use (be it the parents' or children's) may increase the severity and difficultly of resolving conflicts.

Children do not necessarily want to exclude/isolate themselves from the flow of ongoing events at home, although the online attractions may win in a competition against everyday family life. For example, some children report that they would like their parents to be more interested in their online activities, unfortunately often without success (Noppari, 2014). New mobile devices, unlike desktops, enable simultaneous participation in other family activities besides online activities, thereby potentially improving the integration of media and technology use into other family activities. They may even add new ways of seeking the proximity/intimacy of the parent, a desire that has not disappeared among children (see Chapter 10).

The most obvious reason for parents to limit their children's media use is the necessity of getting children to perform other actions, such as eating, washing, brushing teeth, doing homework, taking part in extra-curricular activities and going to sleep on time. Parents have to schedule the children's time use, something that is difficult not only for a five-year-old, but also for a 12-year-old and even more so for an older child. The parents' scheduling of the family members' time has probably become more troublesome and time-consuming than before. With the increase in media usage at home, children's and parents' differing online interests and the proliferation of other leisure time options, the time shortage and conflicts about time usage are bound to become more pronounced.

Children Expecting Their Parents' Attention

There were other kinds of 'conflicts' too. Children were dissatisfied with their parents, and tried to get them to change their activities. Sometimes children desperately sought their parents' attention and tried to interrupt their actions, especially when the parent was concentrating on online activities (Mantere, 2014; Mantere and Raudaskoski, 2015).

In both cases mentioned above, conflicts arise when one party does not know what the other online party is doing. In both cases, the dissatisfied family member – the child or the parent – tries to defend the in-group relation of the family members against the online activities or sociability that are seen as outsiders. They remind the other of the priority of family intimacy over online relationships, activities and commitments. The out-group against which the family member occasionally fights is not a well-defined, stable group, or even a known group; instead, it is the bystander's ever-changing creation/image representing the unknown outward link of the other family member.

The type of conflicts described above can be interpreted at the level of the general functioning of the family institution in society, too. In the other words, in the longer historical perspective these conflicts can be seen as evidence of the permanent value of the family to its members, and of the family's ability to resist outside forces that threaten to disperse it. In this case, we deal with the dark side of media and communication technologies. This interpretation is further confirmed by other kinds of observations in our project. Family members use new media purposefully to promote family relationships and intimacy (Arminen and Weilenmann, 2009).

WHAT IS NEW IN FAMILY LIFE?

Thanks to the new mobile media, daily family life and interaction are no longer limited to the home. They move in space along with the family members. Messages with pictures, photos and music can be sent, short and long phone calls between family members can be made and taken throughout the day, and livecasts are becoming increasingly common. Connectedness can, in principle, be guaranteed. But the same is true for relationships to people outside the family too. The holders of media tools have the freedom to choose.

New media have enabled family members to introduce new patterns to interact both facially and from a distance, socially and individually, both in and outside family life (see Chapter 10). For example, mobile phone cameras provide extraordinary opportunities to document one's life outside the family for other family members and thus re-share experiences. As videophone technologies become more common, these opportunities are growing ever greater. Eventually, these developments may lead to new questions: how do families become accustomed to continuous changes occasioned by the adaption of brand new media applications and services, and how profound are the changes these socio-technological developments pose for family interactions?

CHILD–PARENT RELATIONSHIPS WITH MEDIA

Our main empirical data are video recordings of the daily life of families with children. The recordings have given us an opportunity for an extraordinary sharp holistic observation of daily family life and child–parent interaction in particular, both in relation to media at home and interaction when media are not present. In all 26 families that allowed the cameras into their lives, the cameras were positioned and the parents turned the cameras on and off according to the same principles, which guaranteed the systematic observations of families.

In general, family interaction is very rich and complex, full of parallel actions and semiotic objects, and it is deeply embodied, as demonstrated by the extracts of family interaction analysed in this book. The intimacy of family relationships developed in the family members' history and the mutual familiarity – as well as the history of mutual negotiations behind daily family life – constitute special features of this interaction, revealed through this project.

Socialization of the children at home seems to be embedded in all family activities, and media-related socialization forms a growing part of this process. Besides providing for their children, parents also have to oversee their children's homework, peer relationships and hobbies. Household chores were the most seldom shared activities during the days of research.

Privatization or Individualization Within the Family

Exposure to an increasing amount of new media services combined with increasing time shortage due to an active, individualized lifestyle increases the risk of the privatization/isolation of individual family members from each other, but it may strengthen the family members' online relationships with peers. The differences in tastes and priorities between family members may further add to the feeling of separation. Service and application designers also utilize this differentiation effectively in designing media platforms for increasingly narrow niches, and create tempting worlds to participate in, mainly individually, for all family members. The privatization of family members from each other may be the utmost latent consequence of a new media sphere, including the immediate ubiquitous accessibility of acquaintances online.

Media applications dynamically influence family relationships in many unexpected ways (see Chapter 3). Individualization and privatization of the children away from rest of the family at a too early stage may become a serious problem, challenging the depth of family relationships. However, the problem is not insurmountable as long as the cohesion of the family is maintained. The attractiveness of family relations is founded on a strong recalled history of family togetherness. We assume that up to now such family unities are still commonly formed, and new-born children have the opportunity to enjoy a close/intimate, bodily relationship with the parent(s) without the disturbing interference of media during the first months of life. Positive events shared together are also needed to continuously maintain the sense of mutual togetherness.

With the help of social media, a new and yet largely unknown connectedness is being achieved. It would be premature to assess its meaning for the growing child under the process of socialization and individualization. All we clearly know is that living an online life is a growing part of the daily life of ever younger age groups. We have provided an overview of daily family life with children and media and offered insights on how media are situated in the process of socialization in families. However, to learn and understand the long-term consequences of the digitalization of family life, we have to wait until today's babies grow up.

The Unpredictable Implications of Ubiquitous Technologies

New technologies are fiercely debated, both in everyday life and in academia. There are ongoing discussions on what is considered a technological or media disturbance, and what should be tolerated. It has also been noticed that the norms clearly vary between societies and cultures (Ling, 2012). In all, the considerations of the overall utility and potential harm of technologies are endless, not least in the education of children. Would it be beneficial to equip all schools with the latest technologies and gadgets for all pupils? Would this guarantee improved quality for education? As long as there is no consensus on these kinds of fundamental questions, we can hardly expect any clear answers for parents.

Again, we may seek help from research: can it solve our problems, and provide an objective, even a transcendent vision? One of the merits of our study is that we provide a reasoned answer as to why research can hardly provide such a vision. As technological applications have become part of the common repertoire of most people in most societies, they have simultaneously become tied to local circumstances indexically in so numerous and unforeseen ways that they are inseparable from multitude ways of living, as our study on family life shows. Consequently, technological development that is increasingly differentiated and serving a growing number of distinguished population groups shows a persistent tendency towards cultural differentiation (Arminen, 2007). The appropriation of technologies by no means leads to a uniform cultural and social development. Ubiquitous technologies afford seamless interaction between people and integration into differentiated global networks, and at the same time, we may be concerned on good grounds about the erosion of social relationships and family ties.

Those who have been concerned about social fragmentation have used concepts such as 'balkanization' (Van Alstyne and Brynjolfsson, 1996), the 'echo chamber' (Jamieson and Cappella, 2008), or 'filter bubble' (Pariser, 2011) to refer to various mechanisms of how the recent networking technologies of various mechanisms strengthen communication among small like-minded groups and prevent exchanges with outer groups. The fear is that this strengthens egocentric networks, and may lead to a balkanized world in which the tyranny of the like-minded prevails. Within families, we may see increased isolation between family members, immersion in online communities, decreasing joint family time and widening opinion gaps between family members.

Alternatively, we may speak of a heightened, connected presence, where ubiquitous technologies afford a social connection at any moment, accelerating social exchanges between people beyond the bounds of time and location (Licoppe, 2004; Arminen and Weilenmann, 2009). According to this vision, the remote or mediated relations and co-present relations are starting to merge, creating a condensed, intensified presence. This allows the emergence of the phenomenon of 'together individually', where family members' relationships are enriched and deepened by access beyond the immediate moment (see Chapter 10). The miniaturization of devices and their consequent pervasiveness is also seen as an advantage that enables communication and makes people increasingly accessible to each other. Furthermore, the mediatization of families does not necessarily endanger their ability to socialize; it may even enhance it. Lim (2016) has argued that the practice of 'transcendent parenting' is emerging and going beyond traditional parenting; it incorporates offline and online environments, making parenting ceaseless and all encompassing.

Pervasive, ubiquitous technologies pose new methodological challenges for research. As intriguing as our videotaped materials of the everyday life of families are, they actually lack access to the content of the mobile technologies. Unfortunately, mobile content often remains out of reach for most studies, both for technical and ethical reasons (see, e.g., Raclow et al., 2016). This limitation makes it very hard or sometimes impossible for researchers to decipher what people are doing with their laptops, tablets or smartphones. At times, this limitation can be turned into a strength. This is the case with the notion of the 'sticky media device' (see Chapter 9). The sticky media device describes purposefully the use of a device from the perspective of a bystander who does not have access to what is going on between the user and the device: the bystander's frustration may also be increased due to this lack of access to what is going on.

From an analytical point of view though, it remains a problem that without the mobile content we are not able to see why the person is tied to the online activity. The individual may be tied to work because of out-of-office-hours' duties posed by the employer, or due to a sudden family crisis that requires an immediate response, or to amusing Facebook posts. Indeed, we do not know whether the person has turned to browsing through amusing Facebook posts due to stress caused by one or the other of the two first scenarios. In any case, without access to the mobile content, our understanding of the reflexivity of user–device interaction remains shallow if we are not able to follow the user–device interaction in which the user's actions are redirected due to browsing through new information or to find out whether there is an ongoing person-to-person communication (Arminen, 2005). Consequently, observational studies or recordings of interactions tend to provide only limited, narrow and perspective-bound access to the participants' multidimensional social realities (which are still growing ever more complex in a technologically augmented world). Moreover, it is short-sighted to discuss ICT devices being addictive or posing a new stress factor to families: devices are mere vehicles that can open up access to other people or to numerous online realms, such as games, expert knowledge or social networks.

Finally, the fast and accelerating development of the technological world creates a flux in which it is increasing hard to predict the future. Exciting new technologies and applications come and go, and only a few are here to stay. For instance, mobile livecasting is becoming a huge success, but we cannot yet know whether it will continue to capture people's interest – and with what kind of consequences – or if it will be superseded by some new phenomenon. One of the new services may well impact the organization of social action and relationship formation and lead to cultural and political transitions that we may start to appreciate only afterwards. Nevertheless, in many respects, family life and its ties to social accountability will remain central and constant. The new media and technology developments will intensify social life, and add to the constant negotiations of individualized and digitalized forms of family life, but in its accountability family life will remain central.

REFERENCES

Arminen, I. (2005), *Institutional Interaction. Studies of Talk at Work*, Aldershot, UK: Ashgate.
Arminen, I. (2007), 'Mobile communication society?', *Acta Sociologica*, **50** (4), 431–7.
Arminen, I. and A. Weilenmann (2009), 'Mobile presence and intimacy – Reshaping social actions in mobile contextual configuration', *Journal of Pragmatics*, **41** (10), 1905–23.
Jamieson, K.H. and J.N. Cappella (2008), *Echo Chamber: Rush Limbaugh and the Conservative Media Establishment*, Oxford: Oxford University Press.
Kellner, D. (2005), *Media Spectacle and the Crisis of Democracy: Terrorism, War and Election Battles*, Boulder, CO: Paradigm.
Lahikainen, A.R., T. Mälkiä and K. Repo (2015), 'Ikkunoita perhe-elämään' [Windows into family life], in A.R. Lahikainen, T. Mälkiä and K. Repo (eds), *Media lapsiperheessä*, Tampere: Vastapaino, pp. 40–54.

Licoppe, C. (2004), '"Connected" presence: The emergence of a new repertoire for managing social relationships in a changing communication technoscape', *Environment and Planning D: Society and Space*, **22** (1), 135–56.

Lim, S.S. (2016), 'Through the tablet glass: Transcendent parenting in an era of mobile media and cloud computing', *Journal of Children and Media*, **10** (1), 21–9.

Ling, R. (2012), *Taken for Grantedness. The Embedding of Mobile Communication into Society*, Cambridge, MA: MIT Press.

Mantere, E. (2014), 'Ajan ja huomion saaminen vanhemmilta. Tutkimus lasten aloitteista yhdessä olemiseen ja vanhempien vastauksista keskustelunanalyysin ja kiintymyssuhdeteorian näkökulmista [Getting time and attention from parents. A study of childrens' initiatives for being together from conversation analytical and attachment theory point of view], MA thesis, Yhteiskunta- ja kulttuuritieteiden yksikkö, Tampere: Tampereen yliopisto.

Mantere, E. and S. Raudaskoski (2015), 'Kun matkapuhelin vie vanhemman huomion' [When a mobile phone catches parents' attention], in A.R. Lahikainen, T. Mälkiä and K. Repo (eds), *Media lapsiperheessä*, Tampere: Vastapaino, pp. 205–26.

Mayall, B. (2002), *Towards a Sociology for Childhood. Thinking from Children's Lives*, Buckingham, UK: Open University Press.

Noppari, E. (2014), *Mobiilimuksut: Lasten ja nuorten mediaympäristön muutos, osa 3* [Mobile kids: The Changing Landscape of Children's and Tween's Media Environment, Part 3], Journalismin, viestinnän ja median tutkimuskeskus, Tampere: University of Tampere.

Pariser, E. (2011), *The Filter Bubble: What the Internet is Hiding From You*, London: Penguin.

Raclow, J., J. Robles and S. DiDomenico (2016), 'Providing epistemic support for assessments through mobile-supported sharing activities', *Research on Language and Social Interaction*, **49** (4), 362–79.

Repo, K. and J. Nätti (2015), 'Lapset ja nuoret yksin ja yhdessä median parissa' [Children and youngsters alone and together with media], in A.R. Lahikainen, T. Mälkiä and K. Repo (eds), *Media lapsiperheessä*, Tampere: Vastapaino, pp. 108–31.

Van Alstyne, M. and E. Brynjolfsson (1996), 'Could the Internet balkanize science?', *Science*, **274** (5292), 1479–80.

13. Commentary: the need for evidence-based parenting support

Peter Nikken

The family is without question the most important environment for the child's development. Even before the child's birth, the parents' relationship provides the basic foundation for the child's future life; it is essential for establishing the child's identity, internalizing norms and values, gaining educational prospects, future careers, and so on. However, all around the world, the modern family environment is also increasingly dominated by technology and media use, which inevitably affects the parent–child relationship. Therefore, it is necessary that researchers from various disciplines – such as sociology, psychology, pedagogy, communication, law, economics and even history – pay attention to the child's development and the use of media in contemporary family life. Moreover, it is also highly necessary to make use of the scientific knowledge gained in these academic fields and to translate it into practical support for today's children and parents so that they can benefit from the media they use and avoid negative outcomes.

Children's media use is often perceived as potentially dangerous and thus researched from the risk paradigm. American guidelines for children's media use at home, issued by the American Academy of Pediatrics (AAP 2001, 2011), are a prime example. Basically, the guidelines advise parents to control their children's media use in volume and content: children under two years of age should use media as little as possible, whereas older children are advised to use screen-based media for no more than two hours a day, and in this time they should preferably consume 'quality media'. Other organizations and practitioners in other countries have followed these 2 × 2 principles, also advising parents to restrict media use as much as possible (see, e.g., Delfos, 2013; Australian Government, 2014; Kindergesundheid-info.de, 2016). An important argument for this stance is that the mere presence of devices and their use is seen as an interruption of the child's normal development. Media take time away from other beneficial activities, such as sleeping, reading, playing with toys, interaction with other children, communicating in real life (IRL), as well as having family meals. When children – especially young children – do not devote enough time to these basic social-emotional or cognitively demanding activities at the right moment in their development, they may fail to 'wire their brain' in an appropriate manner for their future life. Another important argument for cautiousness around media use by children is the amount of age-inappropriate content on the Internet or on television channels. In the scientific literature, there is indeed a dearth of studies focusing on the negative impacts that may result from media use, such as heightened aggressive behaviour; health risks; an early interest in sexuality leading to teen pregnancies, STDs and a stereotyped view of men and women; increased materialistic lifestyle; learning difficulties in school, and so on (see, e.g., American Psychological Association, 2007; Byron, 2008; Pagani et al., 2010; Papadopoulos, 2010). Based on the premise that media may not be so benign for children, parents also are advised to monitor their children's media use cautiously (see, e.g., the websites of commonsensemedia.org [USA], mediasmarts.ca [Canada], schau-hin. info [Germany], or mediaopvoeding.nl [the Netherlands]). Parents are encouraged to prevent their children from seeing inappropriate content at too young an age or visiting websites not meant for young users, and to discuss Internet safety issues, advertising, violence, and sexuality as shown on TV, in cinema and games, and on the Internet. Moreover, parents are told that it is wise to use media in collaboration with their children – that is, to watch TV programmes, play games with their children, and surf the web together.

However, as shown in the previous chapters, guiding young children's media use is not as easy as it once was when there was only a television at home. The technological revolution has brought about the Internet, Wi-Fi, smartphones, tablets, and all kinds of other interconnected and easily usable devices. As a result, even very young children, like toddlers and infants, are already capable of handling media devices like touchscreens on their own, which is unprecedented in history. Moreover, media use is no longer confined to the living room. Because of Wi-Fi-connected and portable devices, media can be consumed in every room of the house, and even beyond. Whereas some but not all older generations of children may have watched DVDs in the car when going on vacation, the majority of today's children are playing games on a smartphone during short trips and when shopping, or are communicating with their friends via social media while cycling to school. Finally, not only have the number of electronic screens within the house multiplied – and it is possible to use media devices anywhere in the world where there are batteries and Wi-Fi – the number of media content opportunities has increased exponentially too, especially for younger users. For example, as of June 2016, there are about 2 million app options for download in Apple's app store, of which over 80 000 are categorized as 'educational' (Rodriguez, 2016). Moreover, in addition to traditional television broadcasts on dozens of channels, children nowadays can also watch all kinds of clips, series and films on sites like YouTube or via illegal platforms like Popcorn or Pirate Bay, play thousands of varieties of off- and online videogames, and interact with others and express themselves on dozens of social networking sites (SNSs), like Facebook, Twitter, Instagram, Tumblr, Snapchat, WhatsApp, and so on. Within such incredibly high-density media-saturated environments, parents try to guide their children as best they can, but many parents are worried that they do not succeed. According to several recent Dutch studies among parents with children up to 12 years and adolescents and young people up to 25 years, media-related concerns are the highest in the parents' minds when it comes to daily difficult issues in raising children (Nikken and Markx, 2014; Sleeboom and Hermanns, 2014; Nikken and de Haan, 2015).

Media use in the family is increasingly becoming an individualized experience, which may last for hours, both for children and for parents. As such, parents may have trouble in knowing what exactly their children are up to on their small screens, what virtual connections are being made with the outside world, how or when to say enough is enough, how to pick interesting, funny or educational media content for their children and how to avoid inappropriate content. In addition, as seen in the previous chapters, parents themselves can be glued to electronic screens too, just like their children.

Furthermore, the media industry is highly driven by commercial interests. Producers of both media content and technology are anxiously striving for the attention of an audience, aiming for high market shares and revenues. Globally, billions of dollars are involved in advertising, marketing and product placement for the mere production of appealing media content and technology. Therefore, for many parents and children, it is hard to resist the strong urge to keep up with the latest media trends, such as *PokémonGo* in the summer of 2016. Families are constantly enticed to acquire the latest smartphone with new revolutionary technological possibilities and relatively cheap data volumes. This commercial aspect of media is, of course, inevitable and not in itself to be condemned. However, for many parents it does raise new concerns, such as at what age should a child have his or her own smartphone or tablet, whether one should acquire a new smart TV when a big sports event like the Olympics is approaching, and what it means to agree to the Terms of Service when creating an account for an SNS like Facebook, or Google.

If all media outlets were indeed risky for all children, parents could simply ban their children from all media, but that is not the case. Media cannot be ignored, and they may have many positive outcomes for children, ranging from merely passing the time or entertainment, to education, home- and schoolwork, self-expression, self-exploration, and sharing experiences, opinions and emotions with others. Every parent knows that children are highly motivated to use all kinds of media devices and types of content already from an early age. Media appeal to children's specific needs and desires. Children make deliberate choices, pay attention to content that matches their interests and cognitive capacities, and neglect media content that does not appeal to them at a specific developmental stage (see, e.g., Valkenburg and Vroone, 2004; Barr et al., 2008). Moreover, media preferences also differ with gender. In general, boys are more interested in content with adventure and action or in violence- and competition-based types of media, whereas girls are more often attracted by social interaction media or romantic types of content. Although the typical differences remain until adolescence, the extent of these gender differences may vary during the development of the child. Action-based media, for example, are predominantly attractive to boys in the six-to-ten-years age bracket, whereas social media are most interesting for girls when they are around 12–16 years old. Humour, on the other hand is gender-neutral and favoured by boys and girls alike. Children, apparently have a need for these types of media and use them as a tool for growing up and getting to know the world they are living in.

As parents experience how attracted their children can be to media on a daily basis, it may be hard for them to set limits or restrict that media use. Actually, 'excessive' screen time is seen by many parents as the main issue in the guidance of their children's media use (Nikken and Markxs, 2014; Sleeboom and Hermanns, 2014). However, although parents may have serious concerns about their child's media use, they usually find it difficult to believe that their child could be at risk. Parents rather believe that their child is having fun or educating themselves when using media. Moreover, media also provide important moments of rest at hectic points of the day, and parents themselves use media regularly. Parents may be reluctant to recognize the risks of media for a number of reasons. First, most negative effects of media use do not show immediately, so parents may underestimate the risks. Second, when parents do acknowledge risks, they rather believe that other children will be at risk rather than their own, an effect known as the third-person effect. Third, as noted by the Media Policy Project in the UK (LSE, 2016), parents receive recommendations about children's screen use from a variety of sources, but they are not in a position to reconcile every piece of advice and make an informed assessment. Two Dutch explorative studies (Duimel and Meijering, 2013; Nikken et al., 2015) corroborate the LSE finding that the majority of parental advice on child and media issues is skewed towards media risks, concentrates on 'older', sometimes already outdated media devices, focuses on broad groups of children instead of being age-specific, is usually aimed at 'white, middle-class' families and is not specific about different cultural or social economic backgrounds, and most of all often lacks a sound and consistent evidence base. Most advice for parents is well intentioned but of low quality. The media industry, on the other hand, often claims that its products are educational and 'good' for children of specific ages or in specific circumstances, even though it does not back up these claims. The result of this unbalanced and ungrounded palette of information about children and media is that many parents often do not know how to judge whether TV shows, games, apps or websites really are beneficial or harmful to their children, and therefore give them the benefit of the doubt.

In order to really assist parents today in their parental mediation enterprise, several steps and actions are necessary. For example, parents should no longer be advised about the maximum length of electronic screen use, such as the AAP's advice of no media for children under two years and no more than two hours per day for older children. First, such recommendations are outdated and impractical. Media devices today are used in all kinds and variations all day and cannot be discarded so easily any more. Children can no longer be kept away from electronic screens, which are ubiquitous. Second, most parents have difficulty in estimating the length of their children's media use, because most use nowadays does not happen in front of them. Third, content matters more than length of media use. Spending two hours watching *SpongeBob* cartoons is incomparable to spending two hours with educational apps, or Skyping with grandparents. It is better to advise parents about a media diet that is balanced with other important activities such as sleep, physical activity (e.g., going outside, playing with others, participating in sports), domestic errands, and having social contacts with others in real life. When parents notice that their child sleeps well and long enough, is doing okay at school and has interesting contacts with other children, they should not worry that much about their child's media use.

Furthermore, advice for parents should acknowledge that families may vary significantly in their media use and in their perceptions of the value of media for the child's development and family life. According to LSE (2016), low-income families often – and sometimes disproportionately – invest in digital technologies at home because they are hoping for positive socio-economic outcomes for their children in the long-term. In these families, however, the parents' aspirations related to digital technologies often contrast with reality. Digital technologies, for example, are purchased cheaply and may suffer technical malfunctions, but the parents and children lack the resources to troubleshoot if things go wrong. Usually, more highly educated families are more media literate and can therefore make better use of media for personal gain. Children in low-income or less educated families choose to spend their time with entertainment media rather than using media for educational purposes and home and schoolwork (Pijpers, 2015). Support for parents should thus acknowledge that lower educated families in particular may benefit from advice that is centred on stimulating media literacy, and on the beneficial outcomes that specific media content may have for their children. Specific programmes and methods should be developed to reach out to families that are most in need of parenting support, such as low-income or single-parent families and parents with a lower level of education.

Another aspect that parenting support with regard to child and media issues should pay more attention to is the child's development and the child's accompanying needs and interests in media. Advice for parents with young children, such as infants or toddlers, should address different topics than materials that are intended for families with older children or adolescents. The former should, for example, rather concentrate on the value of electronic games for the child's executive functioning, vocabulary and language development, as well as on the relationship of media use and brain development. Support for families with older children may accentuate typical gender differences, as well as the worth of social media or gaming for the development of children's social and cognitive skills. Advisory materials for families with adolescents could inform parents about media and identity development; normative topics like sexuality, drugs and alcohol; and the social value of horror and suspense, as these issues are typical for youngsters in this phase of development. Parenting support should also be aware of the fact that children with a mental or physical disability may have specific needs regarding assistance in their media use. In general, the risks of media use may be greater among these children when they are not guided sufficiently, and the opportunities may not be fully realized either. Children with an autism spectrum disorder (ASD), for example, may benefit from the rules and regulations that accompany many games, but also may need extra assistance to avoid losing themselves in the endlessness of online game environments.

A final important aspect is the immediate need to update and link existing advice and resources for parents to the appropriate evidence from scientific research. To be able to balance the risks, harmfulness, and opportunities of media for their children, families are in need of grounded support tailored to their circumstances. An example of such an approach is the Dutch Toolbox Mediaopvoeding (Parental Media Mediation Toolbox: www. nji.nl/toolboxmediaopvoeding), which was realized by the Netherlands

Youth Institute and financed by the Dutch Ministry of Health, Welfare and Sport. This toolbox offers background information on children and media for six different age groups ranging from zero to 18 years, is based on peer-reviewed scientific research, is balanced in terms of the risks and opportunities of media, and also deals specifically with children with a mental disability. The toolbox is aimed at professionals who work with children and/or families, but also contains materials that are meant for parents themselves.

REFERENCES

American Academy of Pediatrics (AAP), Committee on Public Education (2001), 'Children, adolescents, and television', *Pediatrics*, **107** (2), 423–6.

American Academy of Pediatrics (AAP), Committee on Public Education (2011), 'Media use by children younger than 2 years', *Pediatrics*, **128** (5), 1040–45.

American Psychological Association (2007), *Report of the APA Task Force on the Sexualization of Girls*, accessed 17 August 2016 at http://www.apa.org/pi/women/programs/girls/report.aspx.

Australian Government (2014), *Move and Play Every Day: National Physical Activity Recommendations for Children 0–5 Years*, Canberra: Department of Health, Commonwealth of Australia.

Barr, R., E. Zack, P. Muentener and A. García (2008), 'Infants' attention and responsiveness to television increases with prior exposure and parental interaction', *Infancy*, **13** (1), 3–56.

Byron, T. (2008), *Safer Children in a Digital World*, UK Government, Department for Children, Schools and Family/Department for Media, Culture and Sport, accessed 22 April 2017 at http://webarchive.nationalarchives.gov.uk/20120106161038/https://www.education.gov.uk/publications/standard/publicationDetail/Page1/DCSF-00334-2008.

Delfos, M. (2013), 'The virtual environment from a developmental perspective', in B. Heys, M. Matthes and P. Sullivan (eds), *Improving the Quality of Childhood in Europe 2013*, East Sussex, UK: The European Council for Steiner Waldorf Education, pp. 102–57.

Duimel, M. and I. Meijering (2013), *Professionals en ondersteuning bij mediaopvoeding* [Professionals and Support for Parental Mediation on Media Use], Utrecht, Netherlands: Netherlands Youth Institute.

Kindergesundheid-info.de (2016), *Kinder durch die Welt der Medien begleiten* [Guiding Children in the Realm of Media], Bundeszentrale für gesundheitliche Aufklärung, accessed 18 August 2016 at http://www.kindergesundheit-info.de/themen/medien/mediennutzung/medienerziehung/.

London School of Economics (LSE) (2016), 'Media Policy Project. Event note. Workshop families and "screen time": Challenges of media self-regulation', 10 May, accessed 17 August 2016 at http://blogs.lse.ac.uk/mediapolicyproject/files/2016/07/MPP-Event-Note-Families-and-screen-time-workshop-FINAL.pdf.

Nikken, P. and J. de Haan (2015), 'Guiding young children's Internet use at home: Problems that parents experience in their parental mediation and the need for parenting support', *Cyberpsychology: Journal of Psychosocial Research on Cyberspace*, **9** (1), Article 1, doi: 10.5817/CP2015-1-3.

Nikken, P. and I. Markx (2014), *Opvoeden met media: Een verkennend onderzoek naar 'lastige' opvoedsituaties en het gebruik van opvoedingsondersteuning bij ouders met kinderen tot en met 12 jaar* [Parenting with Media: An Explorative Study into 'Difficult' Parenting Situations and the Use of Parenting Support Among Parents of Children up to 12 Years], Utrecht, Netherlands: Netherlands Youth Institute.

Nikken, P., M. van Bommel and J. Berns (2015), *Quickscan mediaopvoeding: Een analyse van informatiemateriaal over media en opvoeding voor de toolbox mediaopvoeding* [Quickscan Media Education: An Analysis of Media and Education Information Material for the Media Education Toolbox], Utrecht, Netherlands: Netherlands Youth Institute.

Pagani, L.S., C. Fitzpatrick, T.A. Barnett and E. Dubow (2010), 'Prospective associations between early childhood television exposure and academic, psychosocial, and physical well-being by middle childhood', *Archives of Pediatric Adolescent Medicine*, **164** (5), 425–31.

Papadopoulos, L. (2010), *Sexualization of Young People: Review*, London: Home Office.

Pijpers, R. (ed.) (2015), *Monitor jeugd en media 2015* [Youth and Media Monitor], Zoetermeer, Netherlands: Kennisnet/Mediawijzer.net.

Rodriguez, K. (2016), 'Putting families first: Digital strategies for early literacy: Part 1', *New America.org*, accessed 18 August 2016 at https://www.newamerica.org/education-policy/edcentral/families-digital-strategies-literacy-one/.

Sleeboom, I. and J. Hermanns (2014), *Behoefte aan opvoedingsondersteuning en de rol van internet daarin: Ouders van pubers en jongvolwassenen aan het woord* [The Need for Parenting Support and the Role of the Internet Therein: Parents of Adolescents and Young Adults Report], Woerden, Netherlands: H & S Consult.

Valkenburg, P. and M. Vroone (2004), 'Developmental changes in infants' and toddlers' attention to television entertainment', *Communication Research*, **31** (3), 288–311.

14. Afterword

Jackie Marsh

This book offers important insights into the role of media in family life. The 'Media, Family Interaction and Children's Well-Being' project involved the collection of 665 hours of video data from 26 Finnish families, with a focal child in each family being either a five-year-old or a 12-year-old. This unique dataset has offered the researchers a range of opportunities to consider how media are impacting upon family relationships and practices. The purpose of this Afterword is to reflect on the themes addressed in the book and consider them in the light of global scholarship in this field. The aim is not to consider each chapter separately, but to draw together the overarching concepts and pose a number of questions about how the issues raised by the authors might inform future research in this field.

The study was focused on family uses of digital technology. This is an important topic for a number of reasons. Despite the growing prevalence of media use in families across the world (Rideout, 2014; Chaudron et al., 2015; Hjorth and Khoo, 2016; Lim, 2016a), albeit subject to uneven patterns of access and use of technology across the global North and South (UNICEF, 2012), there are relatively few studies that offer empirical evidence of the way in which family members interact around technology. The ubiquitous nature of digital media means that they offer an 'affective ambience' (Hjorth et al., 2016) for everyday family life and thus have an important role in shaping identities and social relationships. Given the pervasive nature of media in home contexts, deeper understandings of how the everyday practices of children and parents are informed by digital technologies need to be developed. The 'Media, Family Interaction and Children's Well-Being' project, therefore, makes a timely contribution to this field of study.

One of the key advances this book makes to knowledge in the area is that it enhances our understanding of how the use of media by individuals has an impact on the collective experiences of the family. There has been much negative media discourse about the potential for technology to create social isolation, with some scholars also offering a rather dystopian vision of human interaction in the twenty-first century (e.g., Bauman, 2003; Turkle, 2011), but this study develops a more even-handed understanding of how technologies can both disrupt and enhance intimacy within the family context. For example, in introducing the idea that families can be 'together individually', the project team identify that family members may pursue individual activities using digital media whilst being physically co-present and that the individual, digitally mediated activities do *not* preclude meaningful exchanges between family members. These moments serve to 'thicken' (Benkler, 2006, p. 357) family ties, not loosen them. This concept could be viewed alongside Hjorth et al.'s (2016) notion of 'intimate co-presence'; those times when individuals feel close to someone who is not present through the use of technology and/or social media, for example as they follow a child's updates on services such as Facebook or Instagram. Viewing family relationships through these different lenses provides insights into how technologies can extend social relationships and offers opportunities for fostering emotional ties across time and space.

As suggested, digital technologies both enhance *and* disrupt family life. Some of the chapters in this book provide finely grained analyses of such disruption. Researchers demonstrate how the use of a 'sticky media device', such as a smartphone, can interrupt social discourse between parent and child. The project team suggests that at times, children cannot work out what it is that parents do through the use of such devices and argue that this leads to 'bystander ignorance', which may mean children do not understand fully the nature of communication through such technologies and thus fail to learn from these episodes. The study demonstrates how children recognize and manage their parents' distraction due to 'sticky media devices', but also indicates that such resourceful management may potentially come at a cost to the child and his or her relationship with the parent. Whilst some may argue that non-digital media have also played a role in the past in diverting parents' attention away from their children (as they read books or magazines, for example), the mobility of smartphones and other such devices means that they may be always on and always present, and it is such characteristics that indicate that they are potentially much 'stickier' and thus potentially more troublesome in terms of maintaining quality parent–child interactions. McDaniel and Coyne (2016) refer to interruptions in social discourse due to digital media as 'technoference', and the technoference between children and parents' relationships in this respect may be detrimental to family life, as suggested by researchers in this study.

This project also offers insights into the parental mediation of children's uses of technology. Parental mediation has a long-established history as a research area, with various models being developed that offer a means of understanding the phenomenon (see Chaudron et al., 2017). Parents oversee and shape children's media use, and the way in which they do this differs from family to family, dependent upon parents' ethnotheories. Ethnotheories are systems of beliefs within families (Kenner et al., 2008) that are informed by the cultural contexts in which they live, and various studies have identified how these ethnotheories inform how parents mediate children's use of technologies (Plowman et al., 2008; Marsh et al., 2015; Chaudron et al., 2017). In the 'Media, Family Interaction and Children's Well-Being' project, various ethnotheories were clearly at work as parents mediated children's use of digital technologies, but the researchers also posit the interesting notion that parental mediation is a co-constructed phenomenon, with children playing an active role in shaping how parents mediate use. As Van den Bulck et al. (2016) suggest, the 'child-effect' in the socialization of media use has been under-researched to date and the study reported in this book offers valuable insights into this phenomenon.

Such a perspective is predicated on the understanding that children have a great deal to contribute to family life and that they have a range of digital skills and expertise to share. Indeed, some reports point to the 'media-savvy' child, suggesting that some might be more competent in this area than their parents (Gardside, 2014). However, Savic et al. (2016) remind us that technological expertise is not necessarily located within parenthood *or* childhood, but in fact can be viewed as a shared proficiency, with the adult leading learning some of the time and children at other times. They suggest that the concept of 'cooperative mentorship' might offer a more useful lens for examining this dynamic and identifying how the mediation process takes place within specific families. In considering the relationship between parents and children with regard to mediating the use of digital technologies, it may be the case, as Henderson (2016, p. 18, original emphasis) suggests, that 'family *is* mediation'. She explains this proposition thus: 'Through daily interactions, routines and most importantly *relationships*, family enacts and reproduces its values, which include ideas and practices around media engagement and use. It is through relationships that approaches of mediation are devised, implemented, contested and embraced' (ibid.)

Whilst Henderson's work is focused on Caribbean families' experiences with media, the same practices and processes could be observed in the reports on the Finnish families in this study. The relationship between various family members was key to the socialization of media use. This reinforces the message conveyed in other cross-national studies of children's media use in family contexts – there are more similarities than differences across countries (Chaudron et al., 2015). Across all families, media use fits into the pre-existing modes of interaction and daily practices

(Clark, 2013; Yoon, 2016) and many of these ways of engaging are similar across national and cultural groups. Nevertheless, local contexts do impact upon family practices and in the study reported upon in this book, the Finnish context is taken into account, with it being noted that in many Finnish families, co-use of media is prevalent, perhaps more so than is the case in other countries. This offers a strong platform for the diversification of media practices in future years, as co-viewing practices in relation to television, for example, may transfer to the use of other technologies such as tablets.

It is the case that parenting in a digital age is becoming a more complex role than ever. All families that have access to mobile media and cloud-based services are entering into a phase in which 'transcendent parenting' (Lim, 2016b) is the becoming the norm, where parents oversee, and engage with, their children's activities across physical and virtual, online and offline spaces. The 'Media, Family Interaction and Children's Well-Being' project has provided a range of insights that can inform a study of transcendent parenting practices in future studies. I will focus here on just three. First, the study has offered methodological insights into the nature of observations in the home environment. Placing fixed cameras in homes leads to performative practices in which particular types of normative family relations are rehearsed, as discussed by the team, but it can also provide rich and varied multimodal data that cannot be gathered through surveys or interviews. Second, the study has made clear that any study of media use in families should consider children's insights and experiences as well as parents'. Indeed, the study has gone further to indicate that it is only by studying both children's and parents' practices separately *and* together that meaningful insights can be gained into family use of media. Third, the study has outlined how the study of media use in family life has to be undertaken with recognition of both the risks and opportunities technologies pose. Focusing on one or the other will lead only to partial and partisan insights that fail to engage with the complexities of families' everyday lifeworlds. In this study, the researchers were careful to document, and then interpret, data that point to both the limiting and the affirmative potential of technologies to inform family interactions, thus enabling an insightful and reflective account of everyday digital lives in the home.

Given the paucity of studies of family engagement in the use of media in the home, this study provides useful information about an under-researched topic. There is an urgent need to consider in greater depth the nature of 'digital kinships' (Hjorth et al., 2016). The 'Media, Family Interaction and Children's Well-Being' project also embeds a number of important implications about future research needs in this area. There are issues that have been identified in this study that deserve further consideration. For example, if families are 'together individually' some of the time, what is the tipping point at which they might become 'individually together', that is, so immersed in individual uses of technology when physically co-present that any meaningful social interaction between co-present family members is precluded? And, importantly, does this matter if these instances form only one part of ongoing family life, in which family members have numerous other opportunities to interact? Further, if 'sticky media devices' serve to distance parents from children at times and render a child unable to discern the purposes of particular technological activities, what is the impact on children, both in terms of their own digital literacy skills and their emotional resilience? Finally, how can researchers identify the impact of children's own contributions to socialization practices within families in which media use is domesticated and normalized? What might such insights tell us about the way in which age, gender, the child's position in the family (e.g., first, middle, last, or only child) and other vectors of identity impact on children's technological agency within the family? In this way, the book provides fascinating insights into media use within these families and leaves the reader with a range of questions about the nature of children's and parents' engagement with technologies, which is at it should be. We can therefore look forward to the years ahead in which further understandings of family interactions in the digital age may be developed, with the 'Media, Family Interaction and Children's Well-Being' project offering an important contribution to such work.

REFERENCES

Bauman, Z. (2003), *Liquid Love: On the Frailty of Human Bonds*, Cambridge, UK: Polity Press.

Benkler, Y. (2006), *The Wealth of Networks: How Social Production Transforms Markets and Freedom*, New Haven, CT: Yale University Press.

Chaudron, S., M.E. Beutel and M. Černikova et al. (2015), *Young Children (0–8) and Digital Technology: A Qualitative Exploratory Study across Seven Countries*, Joint Research Centre, European Commission, accessed 2 September 2016 at http://publications.jrc.ec.europa.eu/repository/handle/JRC93239.

Chaudron, S., J. Marsh and V.D. Navarette et al. (2017), 'Rules of engagement: Family rules on young children's access to and use of technologies', in S. Danby, M. Fleer, C. Davidson and M. Hatzigianni (eds), *Digital Childhoods*, Singapore: Springer.

Clark, L.S. (2013), *The Parent App: Understanding Families in the Digital Age*, Oxford: Oxford University Press.

Garside, J. (2014), 'Ofcom: Six-year-olds understand digital technology better than adults', *The Guardian*, accessed 7 August 2014 at https://www.theguardian.com/technology/2014/aug/07/ofcom-children-digital-technology-better-than-adults.

Henderson, A. (2016), 'Family as mediation – a Caribbean perspective', *MEDIA@ LSE Working Paper Series*, accessed 23 April 2017 at http://www.lse.ac.uk/media@lse/research/mediaWorkingPapers/pdf/WP38-FINAL.pdf.

Hjorth, L. and O. Khoo (eds) (2016), *Handbook of New Media in Asia*, New York: Routledge.

Hjorth, L., H. Horst and S. Pink et al. (2016), 'Digital kinships: Intergenerational locative media in Tokyo, Shanghai and Melbourne', in L. Hjorth and O. Khoo (eds), *Handbook of New Media in Asia*, New York: Routledge, pp. 251–62.

Kenner, C., M. Ruby, J. Jessel and E. Gregory (2008), 'Intergenerational learning events around the computer: A site for linguistic and cultural exchange', *Language and Education*, **22** (4), 298–319.

Lim, S.S. (ed.) (2016a), *Mobile Communication and the Family*, Dordrecht: Springer.

Lim, S.S. (2016b), 'Through the tablet glass: Transcendent parenting in an era of mobile media and cloud computing', *Journal of Children and Media*, **10** (1), published online ahead of print 18 January, doi: 10.1080/17482798.2015.1121896.

Marsh, J., P. Hannon, M. Lewis and L. Ritchie (2015), 'Young children's initiation into family literacy practices in the digital age', *Journal of Early Childhood Research*, published online ahead of print, June 18, doi: 10.1177/1476718X15582095.

McDaniel, B.T. and S.M. Coyne (2016), '"Technoference": The interference of technology in couple relationships and implications for women's personal and relational well-being', *Psychology of Popular Media Culture*, **5** (1), 85–98.

Plowman, L., J. McPake and C. Stephen (2008), 'Just picking it up? Young children learning with technology at home', *Cambridge Journal of Education*, **38** (3), 303–19.

Rideout, V. (2014), *Learning at Home: Families' Educational Media Use in America*, The Joan Ganz Cooney Center, accessed 23 April 2017 at http://static1.1.sqspcdn.com/static/f/1083077/24261539/1390575104883/jgcc_learningathome.pdf?token=yx6TRlQMa1xFGA8y7TZbA%2FLX108%3D.

Savic, M., A. McCosker and P. Geldens (2016), 'Cooperative mentorship: Negotiating social media use within the family', *M/C Journal*, **19** (2), accessed 23 April 2017 at http://www.journal.media-culture.org.au/index.php/mcjournal/article/view/1078.

Turkle, S. (2011), *Alone Together,* Cambridge, MA: MIT Press.

UNICEF Innocenti Research Centre (2012), *Child Safety Online: Global Challenges and Strategies. Technical Report*, accessed 23 April 2017 at http://www.unicef-irc.org/publications/pdf/ict_techreport3_eng.pdf.

Van den Bulck, J., K. Custers and S. Neilssen (2016), 'The child-effect in the new media environment: Challenges and opportunities for communication research', *Journal of Children and Media*, **10** (1), published online ahead of print 18 January, doi: 10.1080/17482798.2015.1121897.

Yoon, K. (2016), 'The cultural appropriation of smartphones in Korean transnational families', in S.S. Lim (ed.), *Mobile Communication and the Family*, Dordrecht: Springer, pp. 93–108.

Appendix 1: Data collection and management

The project aimed to obtain detailed information about (1) how family members, especially children, use digital media; (2) how media use and family interaction intertwine in everyday family life; and (3) what kind of options and challenges media bring to family life.

We chose two age groups as our target children: five-year-olds, who are still beginners in media use and depend on their parents to access digital media, and 12-year-olds, who are at the border of childhood and adolescence and are rather independent media users. The objective of using the two age groups was to compare the role of media in family interaction between these two groups.

We decided to video-record family life for one afternoon and evening from the time that the child came home from daycare[1] or school until the time he or she went to bed. In order to acquire a comprehensive picture of family life and media use, we used four video cameras that were focused on the dinner table, the main television set, the place where family members watched television (usually the living room sofa), and the computer that the target child used.

The first phase of data collection was to deliver questionnaires to the parents of five- and 12-year-old children to obtain general information concerning the media equipment of the families, and to recruit families for a more detailed data collection. We chose families from high- and low-income neighbourhoods living in a medium-sized town in Finland, and delivered the questionnaires through schools and daycare centres in these areas. The questionnaire consisted of questions concerning information about the target child, the family's structure and income, the education and occupation of the parents, the size of the housing, and the media equipment possessed. At the end of the questionnaire, the parents were asked whether they would like to participate in data collection that included interviews and video recordings of home life (those that chose to participate are henceforth referred to as 'video families').

A total of 580 questionnaires were delivered, half of them to the parents of five-year-olds in 13 daycare centres, and half to the parents of 12-year-olds in seven schools. A total of 110 questionnaires were returned by the families of five-year-olds (38 per cent), and 149 were returned by the families of 12-year-olds (51 per cent). The parents in high-income neighbourhoods were more likely to return the questionnaire; the portion of returned questionnaires in high-income areas was 42 per cent for the five-year-olds and 71 per cent for the 12-year-olds, whereas in low-income areas the percentages were 34 per cent for the five-year-olds and 37 per cent for the 12-year-olds.

Our aim was to obtain a representative sample of Finnish families according to family structure, income and media equipment. We recruited 12 families with a five-year-old and 12 families with a 12-year-old. The number of children in the video families was one to five, and the age varied from two months to 17 years, so we gained a wide view of family life. The family structure was in line with the Finnish average (Tilastokeskus, 2012); five of our target children had single parents, while the remainder lived with two parents. Based on satisfaction with income level and the size of housing, the sample of the video families was somewhat biased in favour of higher income compared to average Finnish families (possibly due to the higher response rate of the questionnaire in high-income areas). Before starting the data collection with the video families, we executed test recordings and interviews with two families with five- and 12-year-old children. These data were added to the main data corpus.

The data collection started with our research assistant visiting each video family and conducting a pre-interview in which she asked about the family's everyday routines and media use. This was done to decide the most suitable day for the video recording and the best locations for the video cameras. On the recording day, the research assistant installed the video cameras in fixed locations and turned them on. The parents turned the cameras off in the evening after the target child had gone to bed. The next day, the research assistant came to collect the video cameras and conduct the post-recording interviews with one parent and/or the 12-year-old target child. The interview contained questions about the previous day and the media use and well-being of the target child. Four questionnaires concerning the target child's sleeping habits, strengths and difficulties (Strengths and Difficulties Questionnaires – SDQs), and media use were filled during the interview. The same interview questions and questionnaires were used with the parents and 12-year-old target children. The 12-year-olds were also interviewed about their Internet use. These interviews were recorded with two cameras, one targeting the child using the Internet, and the other recording the computer screen. The children were asked to show and tell how they usually used the Internet, and tell about their experiences of the Internet, such as cyberbullying. These interviews were not analysed in this book.

The video data were copied onto several hard drives. The total amount of video data was about 665 hours, with each recording lasting from three to 11 hours. The research assistant compiled ethnographic descriptions of the video data, creating stories of the main events of the video families' afternoon and evening. The events were documented in ten-minute intervals, and an Excel chart of the time codes for each recording was created to help the researchers to find the events they were interested in. The researchers created video clips of the events that they analysed closely, and these clips were transcribed according to the traditions of conversation analysis (the transcript symbols are explained in Appendix 2). The interviews were transcribed and copied onto the researchers' hard drives.

NOTE

1. In Finland, the children start school at the age of seven.

REFERENCE

Tilastokeskus (2012), *Suomen tilastollinen vuosikirja 2012* [Statistical Yearbook of Finland], Helsinki: Tilastokeskus.

Appendix 2: Transcription symbols

(.)	micropause, less than 0.2 seconds
(0.5)	pause, length in seconds
wo[rd	
[word	overlapping talk of different speakers
°word°	spoken in quieter voice than surrounding talk
WORD	spoken louder than surrounding talk
wo::rd	elongating the prior sound
↑word	rising intonation
↓word	falling intonation
wo̲rd	emphasis
>word<	faster than surrounding talk
<word>	slower than surrounding talk
wo-	cut-off of a word or a sound
word=	immediate latching onto of successive talk
()	transcriber has not heard the sound or speech is indistinct
(( ))	transcriber's comments of actions, facial expressions etc. while talking
.hhh	inbreath, every h indicates 0.1 second
hhh	out-breath, every h indicates 0.1 second
word.	falling/stopping intonation
word,	continuing intonation
word?	rising intonation
#word#	squeaky voice
@word@	other change in voice quality such as imitating other people's talk
→	pace of the dialogue grows faster

Index